Egypt of the Saite pharaohs, 664–525 BC

Manchester University Press

Egypt of the Saite pharaohs, 664–525 BC

Roger Forshaw

Manchester University Press

The right of Roger Forshaw to be identified as the author of this work has been asserted by him in accordance with the Copyright, Designs and Patents Act 1988.

Published by Manchester University Press
Altrincham Street, Manchester M1 7JA
www.manchesteruniversitypress.co.uk

British Library Cataloguing-in-Publication Data
A catalogue record for this book is available from the British Library

ISBN 978 1 5261 4014 2 hardback
ISBN 978 1 5261 5578 8 paperback

First published 2019

The publisher has no responsibility for the persistence or accuracy of URLs for any external or third-party internet websites referred to in this book, and does not guarantee that any content on such websites is, or will remain, accurate or appropriate.

Typeset
by Toppan Best-set Premedia Limited

It is said that the reign of Amasis (Ahmose II) was a time of unexampled material prosperity for Egypt; the river gave its riches to the earth and the earth to the people.

Herodotus (II, 177)

Contents

List of figures

Foreword

Most histories of ancient Egypt focus on the perceived 'high-points' of the civilisation, rarely giving much credence to anything that happened after the death of King Ramesses II around 1200 BC. The artificial impression of progressive steps of development towards the 'climax' of the New Kingdom assumes an inevitable decline thereafter. Of course, history is never so simple.

Egypt's 26th Dynasty has suffered particularly poor publicity amongst non-specialists because of a lack of coherent archaeological finds or readily identifiable royal sculptures, but also due to the preponderance of rather non-Egyptian-sounding names like 'Psamtek' and 'Apries'.

The recent initial misidentification of a colossus of Psamtek I as his much more illustrious predecessor Ramesses II is a case in point. Few might have expected that such a giant statue, found in fragments at Heliopolis in 2017 – apparently a newly commissioned sculpture rather than a usurped one – would have belonged to a king of the Saite Period. Yet the well-known *Histories* of Herodotus describe several such statues at the capital, Sais, and their cult is attested by the titles of a number of individuals.

The Saite Period is, as Roger Forshaw emphasises, one of resurgent power in terms of relatively strong internal unity and expansionist ambition. It was also one of acute historical awareness, drawing on over two millennia of established Pharaonic history, no doubt inspired by a consciousness of the ruling Dynasties' Libyan roots. This combination of features makes the Saite Period of particular interest to historians of both Egypt and comparable peoples.

Roger Forshaw provides an extensive survey of Egypt at this time, drawing together disparate material little known outside a handful of specialists. The author is to be congratulated for presenting this in a form that is both accessible and honest about the drawbacks of our source material – something students of ancient history, especially that of Egypt, perhaps need to consider.

Dr Campbell Price
Curator of Egypt and Sudan, Manchester Museum
The University of Manchester, August 2018

Preface

I have always been fascinated by ancient history, but it was not until I took early retirement from my career as a dental surgeon that I was able to pursue this subject in some depth. A chance encounter with a magazine on ancient Egypt kindled my attraction for this particular culture, and I soon became an avid reader and student of all things related to Egyptology. I was able to combine this new interest with a study of ancient dentistry when undertaking a Master's Degree in Biomedical Egyptology at the University of Manchester in 2006. My further studies in Egyptology culminated in attaining a PhD in 2013 on *The Role of the Lector in Ancient Egyptian Society*, a work which is now published.

My specific interest in the Saites arose from my early online studies at Exeter University with Dr Robert Morkot when I not only became intrigued by the Saite Dynasty but realised that the 26th Dynasty seemed less well known and under-published compared with many of the other periods in Egyptian Pharaonic history. The Saite Period was a high-achieving one historically, and is often neglected in the literature dedicated to ancient Egypt. I became committed in attempting to understand, research and put into print an account of this enthralling early time, an undertaking that has taken me a number of years.

The reader who has an interest in ancient Egypt may be unaware of the dynamic nature of this period, of the astuteness of the Saite rulers and their considerable achievements in the political, economic, administrative and cultural spheres. The story of Saite Egypt is a fast-moving epic, a time of no mean achievement. Within a period of under ten years, Psamtek I, the first ruler of the Saite Dynasty, reunited a politically divided country after almost four hundred years of disunity and bouts of foreign domination. The Saites then re-established central government, reformed the economy and promoted trade, and the country grew wealthier. Egypt achieved a pre-eminent role in the Mediterranean world and was able to preserve its independence as a sovereign state for over 140 years against powerful foreign adversaries.

I am truly indebted to Dr Campbell Price, curator of Egypt and Sudan at the Manchester Museum, for his many helpful comments and scholarship during the preparation of this book, a topic with which he is also fascinated. I am pleased that he kindly agreed to write a foreword to this volume. My grateful thanks to Associate Professor Penny Wilson from the University of Durham for her very many observations, useful suggestions and insight into this period. I would like to thank the anonymous reviewers of the book for their very many helpful comments. Also, my thanks to those who kindly supplied images for use in the book – Aidan Dodson, Sarah Griffiths, Glenn Janes, Peter Phillips, Campbell Price, Dietrich Raue, Penny Wilson and the Egypt Exploration Society. Lastly, to Meredith Carroll and all at Manchester University Press for their assistance in finally helping to bring this project to fruition.

Roger Forshaw

Abbreviations

ANET	J. B. Pritchard (ed.), (1969), *Ancient Near Eastern Texts Relating to the Old Testament* (3rd edn. Princeton, NJ: Princeton University Press)
ASAE	*Annales du Service des Antiquités de l'Égypte, Cairo*
BA	*Biblical Archaeologist*
BASOR	*Bulletin of the American Schools of Oriental Research*
BdE	*Bibliotheque d'Étude*
BIFAO	*Bulletin de l'Institut Français d'Archéologie Orientale*
BMSAES	*British Museum Studies in Ancient Egypt and Sudan*
BSFÉ	*Bulletin de la Société Française d'Égyptologie*
CdÉ	*Chronique d'Égypte*
CdK	*Cahairs de Karnak*
CHRON	A. K. Grayson (1975), *Assyrian and Babylonian Chronicles* (Texts from Cuneiform Sources; Locust Valley, NY: J. J. Augustin)
CIS I	*Corpus Inscriptionum Semitarum, Pars Prima*. Paris: Republicae, 1882–1962
CRAIBL	*Comptes Rendus de l'Académie des Inscriptions et Belles-lettres* (Paris)
CRIPEL	*Cahiers de Recherches de l'Institut de Papyrologie et d'Égyptologie de Lille*
EA	*Egyptian Archaeology*
Geneva	*Bulletin de la Société d'Égyptologie Genève*
GM	*Göttinger Miszellen*
IFAO	L'Institut français d'archéologie orientale du Caire
JA	*Jewish Antiquities*
JANES	*Journal of Ancient Near Eastern Studies of Columbia University*
JAOS	*Journal of the American Oriental Society*
JARCE	*Journal of the American Research Center in Egypt*
JEA	*Journal of Egyptian Archaeology*

JEgH	*Journal of Egyptian History*
JNES	*Journal of Near Eastern Studies*
JSSEA	*Journal of the Society for the Study of Egyptian Antiquities*
KRI	K. A. Kitchen (1968–90), *Ramesside Inscriptions* (8 vols) (Oxford: B. H. Blackwell)
LÄ	W. Helck, E. Otto and W. Westendorf, eds (1972–92), *Lexikon der Ägyptologie*, 7 vols (Wiesbaden: Otto Harrassowitz)
LR	H. Gauthier (1907–17), *Le Livre des Rois d'Égypte*, 5 vols (Cairo: Institut français d'archéologie orientale)
MÄS	Münchener ägyptolische Studien, Munich – Berlin
MDAIK	*Mitteilungen des Deutschen Archäologischen Instituts, Abteilung Kairo*
MIFAO	*Mémoires publiés par les membres de l'Istitut Français d'Archéologie Orientale*
OLP	*Orientalia Lovaniensia Periodica*
Or	*Orientalia*
PM	B. Porter,, L. B. Moss and J. Málek (1927–), *Topographical Bibliography of Ancient Egyptian Hieroglyphic Texts, Reliefs and Paintings* (1st edn 7 vols, 2nd ongoing) (Oxford: Griffith Institute)
PSBA	*Proceedings of the Society of Biblical Archaeology*
RITA	K. A. Kitchen (2008), *Ramesside Inscriptions Translated and Annotated: Translations*, vol. 5, *Translations*. (Oxford: Blackwell; Chichester: Wiley-Blackwell)
RdÉ	*Revue d'ÉgyptolAogie*
RecTrav, RT	*Recueil de Travaux Relatifs à la Philologie et à l'Archéologie Égyptiennes et Assyriennes*
SAA	State Archives of Assyria
SAK	*Studien zur Altägyptischen Kultur*
SAOC	*Studies in Ancient Oriental Civilisation*
VT	*Vetus Testamentum*
ZA	*Zeitschrift für Assyriologie und Vorderasiatische Archäologie*
ZÄS	*Zeitschrift für ägyptische Sprache und Altertumskunde*

Conventions used in the transliterations and translations

[] encloses damaged or missing sections in the original that are shown as restored
( ) encloses sections that are supplied for clarity and omissions

Chronologies

Dynasty 24	**727–715 BC**
Bakenrenef (Bocchoris)	720–715
Dynasty 25	**747–656 BC**
Kashta	747
Piye	747–716
Shabitqo	716–702
Shabaqo	702–690
Taharqo	690–664
Tanutamun	664–656
Dynasty 26	**664–525 BC**
[Nekau I]	672–664]
Psamtek I	664–610
Nekau II	610–595
Psamtek II	595–589
Haaibra (Apries)	589–570
Ahmose II (Amasis)	570–526
Psamtek III	526–525
Neo-Assyrian Period	**912–612 BC**
Tiglath-Pileser III	744–727
Shalmaneser V	727–721
Sargon II	721–705
Sennacherib	705–681
Esarhaddon	681–669
Ashurbanipal	669–627
Ashur-etil-ilani	c. 631–627
Sin-shumu-lishir	626
Sin-shar-ishkun	c. 627–612 (Fall of Nineveh)

I

Political turmoil and 'Libyan' settlers: setting the scene

Histories of eras before the Saite Dynasty (26th Dynasty) in ancient Egypt have been largely based on Egyptian evidence, in spite of its inherent distortions and biases, as this has been the only major source available. With the Saite Period there is for the first time a much broader range of archaeological and written evidence from outside the borders of the country as well as the traditional Egyptian sources. The Assyrian prisms, Babylonian and Persian sources and the accounts of the Classical authors allow cross-referencing and contribute to our understanding of this era. Particularly notable are the narratives of Herodotus which are still an important source on Saite Egypt and have been especially dominant in establishing a history of this period in modern accounts. Although caution is required when evaluating data from Herodotus's *Histories*,[1] there is much to be gleaned from a judicious study of his works. In addition, the dates for the 26th Dynasty are well established, tied as they are to the firm chronologies of Greece, Babylonia and Persia.

The Saite reunification of Egypt in the mid-seventh century BC appears to have brought an end to the Third Intermediate Period and the occupation of Egypt firstly by the Kushites and then later by the Assyrians. This so-called Intermediate era was a time of diminished centralised power, political fragmentation and the appearance of rulers of non-Egyptian extraction. It resulted in significant changes in society and culture and represents a distinct phase in the history of ancient Egypt. The Third Intermediate Period continued the gradual loss of political unity already apparent at the end of the New Kingdom and concluded with the restoration of centralised authority, and the reunification of Egypt by Psamtek I, usually accepted as the first ruler of the 26th Dynasty.

I Political turmoil

Monarchy and administration

The Third Intermediate Period is typically considered to commence with the death of Ramesses XI at the end of the 20th Dynasty.[2] The power of Egypt and the authority of the later Ramesside rulers had been diminishing for a number of years. During the height of the New Kingdom, foreign trade, tribute and plunder had made Egypt wealthy and powerful, but the late Ramesside kings suffered a number of crises, and the history of the 20th Dynasty is one of apparent decline. Many of the factors that hastened the demise of the New Kingdom are well recognised, others less so, but a number are relevant to the revival of the power of Egypt during the Saite Period.

Ramesses III, the last significant ruler of the New Kingdom, died in the mid-twelfth century BC and was succeeded during the next century by a further eight rulers who bore Ramesses as one of their names. Little is known about some of these rulers; a number were elderly and reigned for only a short period of time, and on occasions appear to have been weak and unprepared for leadership.[3] There was a diminution in royal authority and a decline in temple building programmes, and foreign activity was reduced. The lack of any significant military achievements and failure to campaign beyond the borders of Egypt would have reduced the military prestige of the monarch, an important attribute of the Pharaonic institution. The monarch increasingly relied on officials to control the provincial administration. Such a strategy resulted in a reduction in the personal influence and esteem of the king, which inevitably would have increased power in the hands of the regional administrations.

At Thebes, the authority of the priesthood of Amun and particularly the First Priest of Amun continued to increase as it had been doing throughout much of the New Kingdom. The Great Harris Papyrus dated to the reign of Ramesses III enumerates the huge donations of land-holdings that were now being made to the larger temples in Egypt, particularly the temple of Amun at Thebes.[4] The god Amun was now considered to rule like a king of Egypt and, through oracles, to intervene directly in affairs of state, increasingly assuming the king's role in appointing officials. The king's role was now reduced to that of a representative of Amun and this ideology finds expression in a hymn to Amun (ll. 39–40):[5]

> The King of Upper and Lower Egypt, Amun-Re, King of the Gods,
> Lord of heaven and earth,
> Of the water and the mountains,
> Who created the land through his transformation.
> He is greater and more sublime
> Than all the gods of primordial times.

Thebes was now a theocracy and the priests were the representatives of the god. Government consisted of a regular Festival of the Divine Audience at Karnak where the god's statue communicated through oracles, with a particular motion of the barque being interpreted as acceptance or rejection of a proposal or ruling. A similar state of affairs may have occurred in Lower Egypt as implied in the story of *Wenamun* (mentioned below) when Smendes and his wife, Tentamun, are referred to as 'the pillars Amun has set up for the north of his land'. Smendes is not given the title of king in this passage and may at that time have been high priest at Tanis and governor, before then later becoming ruler.[6]

Administratively, the late New Kingdom was characterised by the political significance of hereditary office and the ability of some powerful families to control state and temple offices through intermarriage and inheritance. Throughout this period the office of High Priest at Thebes became increasingly more independent, with the monarch having only nominal control of Upper Egypt.[7] In the reign of Ramesses IX, Ramesses is depicted in the form of a statue in a large relief on a temple wall opposite the sacred lake at Karnak, rewarding the High Priest Amenhotep with gifts. Amenhotep is portrayed with a stature almost equal in size to that of the king, indicating equality of status in iconographic terms (Figure 1.1).[8] A far cry from the all-powerful 'god-king' of previous eras, when it would have been unprecedented to depict a priest at the same scale as the king, particularly in a large scene and in such a visible location.

Failing economy and loss of empire

The economy weakened during the last years of the New Kingdom and the beginning of the Third Intermediate Period. The tribute and plunder that had arrived in Egypt at the height of the New Kingdom were now a thing of the past, and foreign trade had been diminishing since the reign of Ramesses III. The revenues from the Levant and the African interior were very much reduced.

This unfavourable economic climate resulted in internal strife. In Year 29 of Ramesses III there were strikes by the craftsmen who worked on the royal and elite tombs at Thebes, in protest at their rations being in arrears, a state of affairs that would recur throughout the remainder of the 20th Dynasty.[9] Rising inflation, particularly related to the supply and cost of grain, was evident during this period but its causes and effects are not fully understood. Tomb and temple thefts became more common towards the end of the Dynasty with the Tomb Robbery Papyri,[10] a major source of information on this era, revealing the extent of corruption and economic distress in late Ramesside Egypt. In addition, there were persistent problems with groups of 'Libyan' intruders and famine affecting Thebes.[11]

Associated with this reduced economic activity was a decline in Egypt's prestige abroad which is well illustrated in the *Report of Wenamun*,[12] an account

1.1 Large relief of the High Priest Amenhotep being rewarded by Ramesses IX on the outside of the temple of Amun-Re at Karnak, opposite the sacred lake. The inscription dates to Year 10 of Ramesses IX and is unusual in that Amenhotep is depicted in the same scale as the monarch.

of a voyage to Byblos by an agent of the temple of Amun at Thebes in order to purchase timber for the building of a new barque, a journey in which Wenamun is beset by many difficulties. This engaging tale, although incomplete, is skilfully related and is a vivid and descriptive narrative of Egypt during the late New Kingdom and early Third Intermediate Period. Opinions of scholars are divided as to whether it is a genuine historical document or a literary fiction of remarkable realism.[13] Whatever its category, the tribulations of Wenamun reflect the decline in Egypt's international standing during the last years of the New Kingdom and the beginning of the 21st Dynasty.

This deterioration in Egypt's international power culminated in the loss of its last territories in western Asia during the late Ramesside Period. However, it was major political events in the south of Egypt that are usually recognised as one of the key factors in the collapse of the New Kingdom model. An episode occurred known as the 'Suppression of the High Priest, Amenhotep',[14] an event which is linked to the appearance of Panehesy, Viceroy of Kush, in Thebes at the head of a Kushite army. The chronology and details of this incident are not certain, with Egyptologists offering different interpretations of these events. One suggestion is that Panehesy came to Thebes at the request of Ramesses XI to restore law and order, and in so doing came into conflict with Amenhotep and subsequently removed him from his post of high priest. An alternative interpretation, although now less well accepted, is that Amenhotep had been ousted by a rival, and Panehesy arrived in Thebes to restore him to office.

Panehesy remained in Thebes for a number of years but eventually, after being ordered to withdraw from Thebes by the Pharaoh, he rebelled. He attacked the High Priest of Amun who fled north, and was subsequently pursued by Panehesy's army as far as the city of Teudjoi in Middle Egypt. During Panhesy's absence from Thebes, order among his troops who had been left to guard the city broke down, and they became involved in a series of robberies in the Valley of the Kings and the temples at Thebes. In Year 19 of the reign of Ramesses XI, Panehesy was eventually forced out of Egypt and withdrew to Nubia[15] where he remained in conflict with the Pharaoh.[16] One serious consequence of this civil war was the final loss of the occupied Nubian territories after nearly five hundred years of Egyptian rule. This had crucial implications, as the forfeiture of Nubian gold and the cessation or substantial reduction in the lucrative trade of the products of sub-Saharan Africa would have caused a significant decline in state revenue.

Egypt divided – the Third Intermediate Period
Following Panehesy's withdrawal to Lower Nubia, Ramesses XI established a new beginning by using in his inscriptions a phrase *wehem mesut* 'the Repeating of Births' or 'Renaissance', a term that had previously been used by the kings at the beginning of the 12th and 19th Dynasties to signify that the country had been 'reborn' after a time of unrest.[17] Ramesses assigned two powerful officials to oversee this new era. The army leader, General Herihor, was appointed Governor of Upper Egypt and Viceroy of Kush, although this latter title was more nominal than effective, as Panehesy remained in Lower Nubia as an independent ruler. Herihor soon added the high priesthood of Amun to his titles and now civil, military and religious authority was combined in the hands of one individual. Herihor's power extended from Elephantine to el-Hibeh, whilst his northern counterpart, Smendes, another general, was based at Tanis where he controlled Lower Egypt.[18]

Therefore, from Year 19 of the reign of Ramesses XI, Egypt was divided, and centralised power was lost. The country was now split into two provinces, each controlled by an official seemingly owing allegiance to Ramesses but wielding considerable power. With the death of Ramesses in *c.* 1069 BC, the 20th Dynasty came to an end and Smendes was declared king, the first ruler of the 21st Dynasty, now based at Tanis in the Delta. In Thebes the military or priestly regime continued in parallel with the monarchy under a series of powerful individuals who on occasions assumed Pharaonic titles. Although the authority of the Tanite kings was formally recognised, the southern commanders effectively controlled Middle and Upper Egypt, and this division of the country continued throughout the Third Intermediate Period.

For the Third Intermediate Period in general, a detailed historical framework is difficult to identify and is the subject of continuing debate, particularly in relation to some of the provincial rulers who were later to declare themselves independent.[19] Although Thebes has yielded numerous records helping to establish the course of events there, evidence from the Delta and Middle Egypt, where many of the significant developments from this period occurred, is lacking. Consequently, a balanced overview of events during this period is difficult to achieve, but an important factor is the movement of the 'Libyan' or western tribes into Egypt.

II 'Libyans' in Egypt

Conspicuous during the late New Kingdom, the Third Intermediate Period and subsequently an important factor in the rise of the Saite state was the movement and settlement of peoples from the west into Egypt. The 'Libyan' character of this era and its significance has been recognised only gradually but the steady rise of the 'Libyan peoples' to positions of major political power within the country had important long-lasting effects for Egypt. The consequence of their migrations and invasions would eventually result in many of the monarchs of the first millennium BC being 'Libyan' in origin, including the rulers of the Saite Period. The 'Libyan' component of Dynasties 21 to 26 is not to be underrated.

The word 'Libyan' is typically used to describe the inhabitants to the west of the Nile Valley and Delta regions, but this is a fairly modern term and one that suggests specific geographical, political and socio-cultural associations, which are not readily applicable to an ancient population group.[20] In ancient Egypt, the term encompassed several different groups of peoples who were primarily organised along tribal lines. The earliest group to appear in the Egyptian record is the Tjehenu; a hieroglyph representing the word Tjehenu appears on the Libyan Palette from the Protodynastic Period. Tjehenu was originally used for the northern inhabitants of the western desert in the Early Dynastic period, while by the 6th Dynasty a new group, the Tjemehu, is recognised, perhaps associated with groups as far south as the Third Cataract.[21] Harkhuf in his expedition to Nubia tried to restore peace between the Nubian ruler of Yam and the leader of the Tjemehu.[22] Although the terms Tjehenu and Tjemehu were formerly distinct, they came to be used interchangeably, and by the New Kingdom no longer had any real geographic value.[23]

The inhabitants of the lands to the west of Egypt feature throughout the Pharaonic Period, but much of the information we have depends on the Egyptian sources, as native sources are extremely limited.[24] Although there are frequent images and mentions of 'Libyans' in the Egyptian textual record, these are often official documents which usually relate to their suppression, frequently categorising the 'Libyans' as merely bearers of tribute.[25] Such references are often formulaic and generalised and so are lacking in any real historical information. Actual accounts that supply specific information relating to the 'Libyans' are rare, and it is not until the military campaigns of Merenptah and Ramesses III, directed against the 'Libyans' and Sea Peoples, that such details become available. The other traditional enemies of Egypt, the Nubians and Syrians, receive far more attention in the Egyptian inscriptions and reliefs owing to their greater economic and strategic importance. Later in the fifth century BC, 'Libya' and its peoples became better understood when the Greek author Herodotus documented an account of them in Book IV of his *Histories*.

Egyptian iconographic and textual sources indicate that the 'Libyans' were primarily nomadic hunters and herdsmen. They left no textual record, and the nature of the terrain they occupied, its vast size, and the fact that constantly moving tribes of nomadic pastoralists tend to leave few traces behind on their journeying, has resulted in little in the way of surviving archaeological evidence.[26] However, excavations at Bates's Island in the bay of Mersa Matruh, to the east of Egypt, has unearthed some evidence, as finds indicate that this island may have been a centre of trade in the Bronze Age between the local inhabitants and the Cretans or Cypriots. It has also been suggested that the Cretans and Cypriots were casting bronze weapons on the island, which were then bartered with 'Libyans' on the mainland. Numbers of these weapons and objects of gold and silver as well as chariots were captured by the Egyptians during the wars of Merenptah and Ramesses III. The booty suggests a high level of material culture and the 'Libyans' would probably have acquired these through trade, perhaps with western Asia.[27] It would seem likely there were other trading centres similar to Bates's Island.

Textual sources suggest new and different names for 'Libyan' groups and that some of the groups lived in permanent settlements: the 'town' (*dmi*) of the ruler of the Libu is located in 'his land'[28] and, again, in the Year 2 campaign of Ramesses III, the Meshwesh fled to 'their towns' (*dmiw*).[29] However, in using the term *dmiw* it is possible that the Egyptians may have been projecting on to the 'Libyans' their own cultural expectations. The mention of the burning of 'Libyan' towns in various inscriptions such as 'my heat has burned up their villages'[30] and 'every survivor from his hand (fled) to their towns'[31] may be more the standard Egyptian literary method of expressing defeat of their enemies, rather than pointing to the existence of known towns. In addition, there is as yet no archaeological evidence for specific non-Egyptian settlements west of Egypt during this period.[32]

'Libyan'/Egyptian interactions

'Libya' had always been recognised as one of the traditional enemies of Egypt, with some of the earliest records being the Battlefield and Libyan Ceremonial Palettes of the Protodynastic Period. Occasional contact with the 'Libyans' is then documented up to the New Kingdom, after which interaction becomes more frequent. A scene on the 5th Dynasty mortuary temple of King Sahure depicts a captured Tjehenu chieftain with his family bearing 'tribute' (*inw*). Scenes in the later pyramid complexes of other Old Kingdom rulers such as Niuserre, Pepy I and Pepy II record numerous captured 'Libyan' cattle, although these may be stereotypical and copied depictions. The Middle Kingdom story of *Sinuhe* makes reference to the return from the land of the Tjemehu of an expedition bringing captives of the Tjehenu and cattle, although again, being a literary work, it is uncertain whether this represents historical reality. There is increasing reference to the Tjehenu in the 18th Dynasty, with Theban tomb scenes showing them as bringers of 'tribute'. 'Libyans' are depicted as being present at Akhenaten's court, as members of his military escort and their presence is shown in a number of the Amarna tombs.[33]

There appears to have been little in the way of trade between the two peoples before the late 18th Dynasty as there were few raw materials or 'Libyan' urban centres to attract Egyptian interest. In the later New Kingdom, the textual and pictorial record indicates goods, such as cattle products ('fresh fat of bulls of Meshwesh') and ostrich eggs coming from 'Libya', and 'Libyan' mercenaries were increasingly being recruited into the Egyptian army.[34]

As well as trading contacts there had always been a degree of infiltration and settlement of western tribes into the westernmost Delta regions of Egypt over the millennia. The border was porous and crossed by pastoral populations some of whom would then cross Lower Egypt towards the Levant in what can be interpreted as a pastoral continuum stretching from 'Libya' to Palestine.[35] In addition, sub-Saharan cattle herders would travel via the oases to the pastures of the north coast. Until the 18th Dynasty there seems little evidence of such peoples being considered a threat. This changed with attempts by 'Libyan' groups to migrate into Egypt in larger numbers and now, as well as the Tjehenu and the Tjemehu, new ethnic groups such as the Libu and the Meshwesh (later abbreviated to 'Ma') are recognised. These groups are believed to have originated, in part, from Cyrenaica and territories to the west of the Tjehenu. Again, they were herders of cattle, sheep and goats, and were primarily nomadic pastoralists.[36]

Certain differences can be recognized between the different Libyan groups in relation to dress, hair style and general appearance. The Egyptian representation of the 'Libyan' type seems to involve a distinctive type of hair dressing, a sharply defined, relatively long thin beard, a long cloak or robe, open in front and tied at one shoulder and, in the case of chiefs, ostrich feathers in their hair. The Libu typically display a short kilt, and the Meshwesh a distinctively shaped phallus sheath.[37]

Conflict

In the 19th and 20th Dynasties a series of major conflicts developed between the Egyptians and the 'Libyans'. During the reign of Sety I increasing numbers of 'Libyans' attempted to settle in Egypt, and Sety embarked on military action to confront what was perceived to be a developing crisis. In the encounter that ensued, Sety appeared to have been largely successful and defeated the intruders. However, the well-known war scenes at Karnak depicting this action reveal only general details and do not include a specific geographical location. That this clash was not merely a skirmish is indirectly indicated by its large-scale inclusion on the exterior wall of the hypostyle hall at Karnak, comparable with other major campaigns of Sety's reign.[38] This was the first serious conflict that was recorded on the western border of Egypt since the Middle Kingdom some six centuries earlier.

Continuing Egyptian concern with the growing 'Libyan' threat caused Ramesses II to construct a series of military fortifications westwards along the Mediterranean coast, the furthest of these being the massive, largely self-sufficient fortress town of Zawiyet Umm el-Rakham, some 300 km to the west of the Delta. Probably designed to deter and warn off any major passage of 'Libyans' into Egypt, the installation may also have been involved in foreign trade with the eastern Mediterranean.[39]

More significant movements occurred a generation later when, according to the Libyan War Inscription of Merenptah, a five-year campaign against the 'Libyans' was launched. This was as a result of the migration eastwards into Egypt of a coalition of western tribes lead by the Libu accompanied by their Sea Peoples allies.[40] The so-called Sea Peoples were the Sherden, Shekelesh and Ekwash, originating in the Aegean and western Anatolian region; the Teresh, of unknown origin; and the Lukki, from Lycia, also in Asia Minor.[41]

These groups may have migrated to 'Libya' as a result of some form of disruption in their homelands.

Despite their cultural differences these separate population groups appeared to work together effectively and they eventually reached the western border of Egypt, bringing with them their families and their cattle. This movement and attempted settlement in Egypt seems to have been due to a major ecological disaster in their native country, such as a prolonged drought or famine, perhaps coupled with economic competition following the arrival of the Sea Peoples. The Libyan War Inscription of Merenptah at Karnak describes a famine existing in the Meshwesh or Tjehenu homelands and they were said to be 'fighting in order to fill their bellies daily. They have come to the land of Egypt just to seek the necessities of their mouths.'[42]

The numbers of 'Libyans' involved in this passage appear to have been substantial, with an average of estimates from different sources suggesting that about thirty thousand individuals attempted to enter Egypt.[43] However, there may well have been, as always, a hyperbolic element associated with the recording of high numbers of 'Libyans', and such figures are unreliable. The aim of these groups was to settle in the Delta and Fayum regions, but they were resisted by the Egyptians, and the armed struggle that ensued resulted in the eventual defeat of these tribes' people. The Egyptian accounts come partly from the Libyan War Stela set up at Athribis[44] which records that the 'Libyans' abandoned their camps in the Delta, and also from the conclusion of the Victory Hymn of Merenptah which states that Merenptah drove them back. This Egyptian victory prevented further incursions into the country, and Egypt was then at peace:[45]

> The cattle of the field are left [free] to roam
> no herdsman having to cross the Nile in flood.
> There is no shout or call by night:
> 'Stop! See, who comes with foreign speech!'
> With singing, people come and go.
> and no piercing lament of people in mourning.
> The towns are settled once again.

For nearly two decades following the death of Merenptah, Egypt entered into an unsettled period characterised by weak government, struggles for the succession to the throne and a series of short-lived rulers. Eventually, Ramesses III ascended the throne but not before the 'Libyan' tribes had used the opportunity to penetrate the western Delta again, reaching as far south as the central Nile branch. At first this peaceful immigration seems to have been accepted, but during Years 5 and 11 of his reign two more significant encounters occurred with the 'Libyans'. The Year 5 inscriptions indicate that it was primarily an alliance of the Libu, Soped and Meshwesh who were attempting to penetrate the Nile Valley. In contrast, the sources for the Year 11 invasion list the Meshwesh as having taken over the leadership of the various tribes confronting Egypt.[46]

Initially, Ramesses endeavoured to find a diplomatic solution to the 'Libyan' incursions by trying to influence the succession of their leadership. He attempted to appoint an overall chief with whom he could negotiate, but his bid to impose a single ruler over the tribal groups proved a failure and war resulted:[47] 'His majesty brought a little one from the land of the Tjemehu, a child supported by his strong arms, and appointed for them to be a chief to regulate their land. It had not been heard of before, since Egyptian kings had come into existence.'

Various estimates, based on the inscriptional evidence, have again been proposed for the numbers of peoples involved in this migration. One suggestion is that as many as nineteen thousand attempted to enter Egypt during the Year 11 campaign of Ramesses III.[48] Again, caution has to be exercised in interpreting such figures.

Unlike the earlier incursions during the reign of Merenptah, the inscriptions for the Years 5 and 11 confrontations do not mention that famine was the reason for their movements, but they do record the large numbers of livestock accompanying the migrants.[49] However, if the 'Libyans' were forced to Egypt through famine, they may no longer have possessed much in the way of livestock. Possibly the migrations were driven by external pressure from incoming new arrivals in their own country or maybe there was a desire to settle in Egypt, which was perceived as a more desirable locality to inhabit.

Again, the 'Libyans' were defeated and the Egyptian victories are recorded in Ramesses's mortuary temple at Medinet Habu and in the Great Harris Papyrus. Despite Ramesses's claim to have conquered them, a steady influx of 'Libyans' continued to arrive and settle in the country throughout the remainder of the 20th Dynasty and beyond.[50] In Upper and Middle Egypt there were disruptions due to bands of marauding 'Libyans', and Ramesses III built new enclosure walls to protect temples in Middle Egypt. Towards the end of the 20th Dynasty work on the royal tomb in the Valley of the Kings was repeatedly interrupted by attacks on the workers' settlement; these aggressors were sometimes specified as western tribesmen but could also have been bands of marauders from the western desert and oases regions. 'The chiefs of the Medjoy police came down saying: "The enemy has come down". The workforce stood (by), to keep watch, stayed (off work) for the time.'[51] The growing state of insecurity brought about by these bands of roving intruders, and the powerlessness of the state to cope with the problem, would undoubtedly have been a destabilising influence, and another factor in the internal decline of the country.

The settlement of 'Libyan' captives

Thousands of captives from the wars of Ramesses III were forcibly relocated to military settlements (*nḫtw*) both in the Eastern Delta and in Middle Egypt, as attested in the Great Harris Papyrus and the Rhetorical Stela from Deir el-Medina referred to below.[52] There is little evidence for 'Libyan' sites in Upper Egypt, but Herakleopolis in Middle Egypt is mentioned in the Wilbour Papyrus as being a 'Libyan' community during the reign of Ramesses V.[53] There may have been other settlements in the more predominantly Egyptian environment of Upper Egypt, but this is not as clear in the archaeological record due to more rapid Egyptianisation of the 'Libyans' which may also have included changes to their names.[54]

The 'Libyans' were taught the Egyptian language in these settlements, and efforts were made to assimilate them into Egyptian culture, as attested in the Rhetorical Stela from chapel C at Deir el-Medina:[55]

> He has captured the land of the (Tjemehu), Libu and Meshwesh. He made them cross the Nile streams, brought to Egypt and made (to settle) into camps ($nhtw$) by the victorious king so that they might hear the speech of the Egyptian people before following their king. He made their speech disappear, changing their tongues; and they went upon the road which (they) had not descended.

Some of the captured 'Libyan' soldiers who were billeted in the military settlements joined the Egyptian army. There they would have had the opportunity of rising through the ranks and thus improving their status in society along with that of their families and dependants. The 'Libyans' had a long tradition of service in the Egyptian army, and as early as the reign of Akhenaten they are documented as being military guards. Former soldiers were often rewarded for their services by being granted allocations of land, and high-ranking military personnel could rise to prominent positions in the bureaucracy.[56] Such an example is the army commander Herihor who, although his background is rather obscure, is thought to have had 'Libyan' origins and was able to rise to a position of great power.[57] Around the end of the 20th Dynasty he was appointed High Priest of Amun and went on to claim royal status, putting his name in a cartouche within the confines of the Khonsu temple at Karnak, although using the title 'High Priest of Amun' as his prenomen.[58]

Acculturation or retention of ethnic identity?

Settlement and integration are topics referred to in the Great Harris Papyrus, but how effective was this acculturation? Both the speed and scale of the numbers that arrived and were settled, either as captives or peaceful immigrants, together with the density of their settlements in the Delta would have allowed them to maintain a greater degree of ethnic integrity. Their leadership remained essentially intact and their tribal structure would have endured in these isolated camps. The 'Libyans' and their descendants maintained their traditional social organisation, including their lineage chiefs. In addition, the 'Libyan' settlers who were not captives and not forced to learn the Egyptian language lived predominately amongst large numbers of their own people and may have been little affected by their Egyptian environment.[59]

There are a number of indicators that the 'Libyans' did preserve aspects of their ethnic individuality. Non-Egyptian-sounding 'Libyan' personal names were retained, as can be seen amongst high-ranking officers in the army, where names such as Sheshonq, Osorkon and Takeloth are recorded, names that endured for centuries. The change from 'Libyan' to Egyptian names was slow and uneven, and some 'Libyan' names are still recognised as late as the Ptolemaic Period.[60] Similarly, 'Libyan' local elders of small groups and 'Libyan' chiefdom titles were retained, as were the feather symbols of identity seen on the heads of the 'Libyan' chiefs of the Libu and Meshwesh.

Such retention of titles is demonstrated by an inscription on the Philadelphia-Cairo statue and stela[61] of Osorkon III of the 22nd Dynasty, where Osorkon petitions Amun that his children will achieve high office: '[You will] fashion my issue, the seed that comes forth from my limbs, [to become] great [rulers] of Egypt, princes, high priests of Amun, great chiefs of the Ma, and [great chiefs] of the foreigners' (ll. 7–8). And: 'You will establish my children upon their [offices] [... that] I gave to them, without a brother being resentful of his brother' (ll. 11–12).

These inscriptions illustrate the kinship notion of brotherhood and importance of 'Libyan' titles of tribal authority as late as the 22nd Dynasty. The term 'brotherhood' is a common term in the 'Libyan' record. Extensive genealogies based on patrilineal lineage inscribed on private stelae and statues become more common in this era, demonstrating an individual's attachment to a particular tribal lineage. These long genealogies, which are rare earlier in Egyptian history, enable extensive family trees to be constructed.[62]

Similarly, a limestone stela set up by Pediese, High Priest in Memphis under Sheshonq III, indicates exclusively his 'Libyan' lineage title 'great chief of Ma', and he is depicted wearing the distinctive Meshwesh feather in his hair.[63] Pediese is stressing his tribal position, and the important Egyptian religious title is, instead, transferred to his son, Peftjauawybast. This use of 'Libyan' tribal titles and allegiance is not only evident in the 22nd Dynasty but a stela relating to the transfer of land dated to Year 21 of the 23rd Dynasty ruler King Iuput II indicates the title and local power of the tribal chief: [64] 'Regnal Year 21 (of) King Iuput (II); a donation to Harpocrates, resident in Mendes, through the agency of (*m-dr.t*) the Great Chief of the Ma and leader, Smendes, son of the Great Chief (of) the Ma and leader, Hornakht'. Here Smendes, in his role as great chief of Ma and leader, is donating land to a god in Mendes, perhaps for a cult offering. This act of appropriation might suggest tribal ownership of the territory and implies that the lands were now outside royal or temple control.

The donation of land is also a demonstration of the local power of the tribal chief.

The shared lineage status of the 'great chief of the Ma' would mean that holders of this title were politically equal, potentially resulting in segmentation of lineages. This can be noted, for example, for the 22nd Dynasty which arose as a collateral branch of the 21st Dynasty, and also for the whole series of local dynasties or princedoms that flourished in the Delta for the century preceding the rise of Sais.[65]

Other than these ethnic designations in the textual and pictorial record, known 'Libyan' names or titles are borne only by a few individuals, so it is difficult to identify 'Libyans' in the archaeological record.[66] By the 22nd Dynasty the 'Libyans' do not appear to be seen as foreigners in Egyptian texts or in Manetho's Dynastic classification, not as the Hyksos of the Second Intermediate Period or the later Persian rulers were perceived to be.[67] Additionally, the royal iconography adopted by the later 'Libyan' rulers shows little hint of a foreign influence; they followed more of a traditional Egyptian model. Importantly, these population groups had an impact on Egyptian society, as 'Libyan' influence can be identified in fundamental aspects of the period such as political structure, concept of kingship, language and writing, as well as in burial practices.[68]

Self-governing principalities

By the end of the 20th Dynasty, the 'Libyans' were well established in Egypt, particularly in the Delta regions. The extent of their influx into Egypt, the formation of settlements and the retention of their 'Libyan' lifestyle would have been conspicuous. Some 'Libyans' achieved high-ranking positions within the military. During the 21st Dynasty various chiefs and high-ranking 'Libyans' ('great ones/chiefs' (wrw), 'elders' (^{c}3w), 'foremost ones' (h3wtyw)) gradually began to dominate and control the areas they had settled into. Within these territories tribal structures were maintained, and a number of these regions ultimately became self-governing principalities.[69] This occurred not only in the Delta but also along the Nile Valley at sites such as Memphis and Herakleopolis, although the exact mechanism by which these chieftains rose to power is uncertain.

The fragmentation of the country was accentuated by the continued decentralisation of government during the 21st Dynasty. A notable landmark occurred c. 945 BC, when the throne at Tanis passed to a powerful family of 'Libyan' descent, whose first ruler was Sheshonq I (c. 945–924 BC) and who now ruled as the 22nd Dynasty. Sheshonq came from a family that had settled at Bubastis, and whose members through marriage had links with the High Priests at Memphis and the previous royal family at Tanis. Sheshonq was the nephew of the earlier Tanite king, Osorkon the elder.[70]

During the later rule of Sheshonq III (*c.* 825–773 BC) and subsequently, a number of rulers of self-autonomous territories, particularly in the Delta, began to assign themselves royal titles and declare themselves king, although how they were perceived beyond their own territories is uncertain. These rulers were based at various centres and have been attributed by some scholars to the 23rd Dynasty. Although various reconstructions of this confusing period have been posited, no overall chronology is universally accepted as textual detail is lacking.[71] The continuing process of decentralisation further diminished the power of the 22nd Dynasty.

The territories of the western Delta were known as the 'great chiefdoms of the Ma', and these autonomous rulers appeared to co-exist independently. Military titles are quite frequently attested amongst the leaders, and there is textual evidence that they constructed fortified enclosures in the Delta territories, although military activity between these chiefdoms is not well documented.[72] For the first-time 'Libyan' chiefs are recognised on donation stelae as replacing the king in presenting an endowment of land, the basis of Egyptian royal power.[73]

Foundation of the Kingdom of the West and the early Saite rulers

One of the territories, the principality based on the city of Sais, became known as the Kingdom of the West. The first attested ruler who declared himself king was Tefnakht, but it may be possible to trace the previous rulers of this territory back earlier to Pimay, a ruler of the 22nd Dynasty. Pimay, a son of Sheshonq III of the 23rd Dynasty, while still a prince dedicated a small statue-group that was found at Sais, perhaps in his role there as governor.[74]

Perhaps a decade later a chief of the Ma, Osorkon C, became ruler at Sais. Osorkon then steadily extended his rule northwards from Sais to incorporate Buto and south-westwards to include Imu (Kom el-Hisn). The extent of the territory he controlled is attested by an inscription on an amulet,[75] 'the Great Chief of Ma, Army Leader, God's Servant of Neith, God's Servant of Buto (and of) the Lady of Imu, Osorkon'. Similarly, two shabtis[76] with the inscription 'the Great Chief of the Ma, Osorkon' attest to this individual.[77] The pattern of these titles is analogous to those borne by Tefnakht, and he has been proposed as an ancestor or even an immediate predecessor of Tefnakht.[78] The combination of princely, military and priestly functions is commonly observed in principal 'Libyan' chiefs at that time. His status as Great Chief of the Ma and the name Osorkon could perhaps suggest a link back to the Tanite rulers.[79]

The earliest dated records of Tefnakht are two donation stelae, probably from Buto, which list his titles and the geographical area that he controlled. The first stela[80] is dated to Year 36, *c.* 732 BC, of an unnamed ruler, who, because of the high year-dates, could only relate to either Sheshonq III or V of the 22nd Dynasty, with Sheshonq V usually considered to be the likely candidate. This first stela describes a donation of land by the 'Great Chief of the Ma, the Army-Leader, Tefnakht', as well as in a separate scene the title of 'Great Chief of the Libu'. A statuette,[81] donated to Amun by Tefnakht, indicates that he was the son of a certain Gemenefsetkapu, son of Basa and a priest of Amun. Therefore, the evidence would suggest that his predecessors were probably not chiefs of the Meshwesh or Libu but were of Egyptian priestly origin.

The second stela[82] is dated to Year 38 and gives Tefnakht more extensive titles, 'Great Chief [of the Ma], Army-leader, Great Chief of the Libu, Prophet of Neith (at Sais), of Buto and of Lady of Imu (Hathor) ... Mek-prince of Pehut and of Kahtan, Ruler of the Nomes of the West, Te[fnakht]'. The titles prince of Pehut and Kahtan, perhaps relating to Libyan areas along the Mediterranean coast or even towards the oases, together with Tefnakht's final title, the ruler of the western nomes, encapsulate the extent of the territory that Tefnakht now administered, an area which involved the western half of the Delta from the Mediterranean to Memphis. It would seem that between Years 36 and 38 of Sheshonq V, Tefnakht was actively expanding his control of the Delta.

Further evidence to substantiate the extent of the territories administered by Tefnakht is detailed on the Victory Stela[83] of the Kushite ruler Piye, dated to Year 21. The direct factual style of the text on this stela provides a unique picture of political subdivision in Egypt by the late eighth century BC, and makes it a very important historical document, one of the foremost of the first millennium BC. The inscriptions describe a Kushite invasion of Egypt in *c.* 737–729 BC and define similar geographical boundaries for the Kingdom of the West.[84] The Victory Stela recounts how Tefnakht, previously having gained the fealty of the princes in the Eastern Delta, advanced into Middle Egypt to subdue the local princes. He besieged Peftjauawybast, King of Herakleopolis, and continued on to Hermopolis where the local ruler, Nimlot, who formerly had given allegiance to Piye, now defected and supported Tefnakht. With Thebes now potentially threatened, Piye ordered his local Egyptian-based forces to recover Hermopolis, and he also sent a further army from Nubia north to the Bahr Yusuf to confront the coalition led by Tefnakht.

The Kushite forces failed in their initial attempt to defeat the Egyptians, resulting in Piye taking personal command of the campaign. In a series of further military engagements and following a siege at Memphis, Piye overcame the combined Egyptian forces of Tefnakht. Subsequent to this defeat all the rulers of this coalition surrendered to Piye in person. The lunette scene of the Victory Stela shows Piye as Pharaoh standing in front of the god Amun and the goddess Mut, and before Piye are four kings, their names written in cartouches, making their submission to him. One of these, Nimlot of Hermopolis, who surrendered through the intervention of the royal wives (ll. 33–44), has a prominent position on the lunette, depicted standing and leading his horse. The other three rulers – the 23rd Dynasty ruler of Leontopolis, Iuput II; the 22nd Dynasty ruler of Bubastis, Osorkon IV; and Peftjauawybast of Herakleopolis – are all prostrated before Piye. It would appear that Nimlot had now been restored to favour with him as he is shown standing and the only one allowed to enter the palace as he was ritually pure and didn't eat fish: 'The three stood there while the one entered the palace' (ll. 152–53).[85] However, his status is somewhat diminished as the queen occupies the male position at the head of the register, whilst Nimlot adopts the standard position and gesture of a queen with raised sistrum.[86]

Behind Piye, five other rulers, who were not recorded as kings, also prostrate themselves: Great Chief of the Ma, Djedamuniufankh of Mendes; Great Chief of the Ma, Akanosh of Sebennytos; the Mayor Pimay of Busiris; the Mayor Patjenef of Pi-Soped; and Prince Petisis of Athribis (Figure 1.2).[87] In contrast Tefnakht remained in the Kingdom of the West and retained a degree of dignity in defeat, as Piye sent envoys, with a lector and a military officer, to Sais to receive his submission, an arrangement which was accomplished without the two kings meeting. This submission may have been more of a mutual agreement, in which Tefnakht accepted the superiority of Piye's forces and promised, by means of an oath, to cease waging war against him. However, Tefnakht had been forced to retreat to the western Delta, he had lost his newly acquired territories and he had to agree to present tribute to the Kushite king. But his submission was unlike that of the other Delta rulers in that there is no explicit recognition of the supremacy of the Kushite king over his territory. Piye appears to have accepted this submission and allowed Tefnakht to remain in power. He may have wished to remove Tefnakht but was faced with the difficulty of trying to conquer the western Delta during the inundation season. In his earlier siege of Memphis, the water was already rising, and a short time later the Delta would have been a vast swamp.[88]

1.2 Lunette of the Piye Victory Stela. The stela was discovered at the temple of Amun, Gebel Barkal in 1862, bears a 159-line inscription and is in good condition. Grey granite. H. 1.84 m; W. 1.8 m; D. 0.43 cm (Egyptian Museum, Cairo).

Piye returned to Kush in his twentieth regnal year but seemingly left no new administration in place to govern Egypt. However, the powerful local authority in Thebes controlled by the God's Wife of Amun, daughter or sister of the Kushite leader, and her administration appeared to be an efficient system, with perhaps no need to replace it. The various Egyptian rulers retained their seats of power, perhaps obligated to Piye by oaths of loyalty.[89] Tefnakht retained control in the Delta with his sizeable kingdom intact, whereas all the other leaders had ignominiously surrendered to Piye. By this time the power of the rulers of the 22nd and 23rd Dynasties, which had been diminishing for a number of years, was reduced to their being little more than chiefs, so, with seemingly no rivals in the Delta, Tefnakht seized the opportunity and assumed royal titles, declaring himself king as Shepsesre Tefnakht in *c.* 728 BC.[90]

Although probably the most powerful of the Delta rulers, Tefnakht diplomatically chose not to challenge the other Delta leaders and expand his kingdom eastwards, nor did he attempt to campaign southwards in pursuit of territorial control, perhaps not wishing to antagonise the Kushites. Little further is known about his reign and the only other information is the presence of the name Shepsesre Tefnakht on two later donation stelae, namely the 'Athens Stela'[91] which is dated to Year 8 and the undated 'Michaelides Stela'.[92] Tefnakht is considered to have ruled until *c.* 720 BC.

Two unnamed sons of Tefnakht are mentioned on the 'Victory Stela', one of whom was killed in combat and the other captured by the Kushites near the Faiyum. However, it was Bakenrenef (Bocchoris) who became the next King of Sais, the only ruler that Manetho attributed to the 24th Dynasty. The connection between Tefnakht and Bakenrenef is uncertain but a father/son relationship is often assumed. Later traditions of Diodorus (45, 1) and Plutarch (*De Iside et Osiride* 8) relate to 'Tnephachtos the father of Bocchoris the wise', but this could indicate a 'Tefnakht II', possibly a later ruler of Sais, although scholars disagree on the identity of this individual.[93]

Few details of the reign of Bakenrenef are known although he is well attested in later Classical literature as a legal reformer or law giver.[94] In Manetho's history (III, fr. 65) 'Bocchoris' (Bakenrenef) is recorded as receiving a prophecy of foreign conquest from an oracle, handed through the medium of a sacred lamb. The highest attested date of his reign is Year 6 which is derived from a votive stela located at the Serapeum at Saqqara. A small limestone fragment, considered to have been from a building block, inscribed with a cartouche of Bakenrenef has been found at Tanis, although it could have originated elsewhere.[95] This could indicate the acquisition of the city by Bakenrenef, and the expansion of Saite control across the Delta, following the disappearance of Osorkon IV, the last ruler of the 22nd Dynasty. Additionally, no ruler is recorded at Tanis on the 'Victory Stela' of Piye, which would support this suggestion.[96]

Three artefacts, all of faience, from major centres in Italy, have also been ascribed to Bakenrenef. Two situlae excavated from Motya and Tarquinia bear his cartouche, but these are often considered to be Phoenician versions rather than Egyptian originals.[97] A Bakenrenef scarab was found amongst the grave-goods in a child's burial (G 325) at the early Greek colony of Pithekoussai, also in Italy.[98] The scarab was found alongside fifteen other imported Greek, Syrian and Phoenician trade goods, demonstrating the extensive trade networks in operation during that period. It is possible that goods were being traded by Egypt with the cities of the western Mediterranean, possibly using Phoenician merchants.[99] Attempts have been made to use the Bakenrenef finds to help establish the chronology of this period.[100] Lack of reliable information associated with these artefacts, and the fact that the royal name on a scarab is often that of an earlier ruler, make such efforts unsound.

According to Manetho, Bakenrenef was captured and burned alive by Shabitqo, the successor to Piye (see revised chronology, p. xvi) who was consolidating Kushite control of the Delta regions at that time.[101] Following Bakenrenef's death in *c.* 715 BC it is not certain who was in control of the Kingdom of the West until the reign of Nekau I, father of Psamtek I. There is little evidence for this period and here we have to rely on Manetho for further information. He records three rulers before Nekau, beginning with 'Ammeris the Nubian', the first ruler of the 26th Dynasty, and ascribes him a reign of between twelve and eighteen years. It would seem quite possible that, following the demise of Bakenrenef, a Kushite governor was appointed by Shabitqo, and Ammeris may well have been this official. However, the existence of this ruler is not accepted by a number of Egyptologists.[102]

Manetho then lists a certain 'Stephinates' as ruler and assigns him a reign of seven years. There are no surviving monuments or texts that can be ascribed to such a ruler, whose Egyptian name is unknown. 'Stephinates' has been suggested as equating to 'Tefnakht II' who is referred to above. Again, according to Manetho, the next ruler and immediate predecessor of Nekau I is Nechepsos, who has often been identified as Nekauba, as attested on a fragment of a menat amulet.[103]

To confuse this situation further, Ryholt[104] has proposed that the Berlin fragment (Papyrus Berlin P. 13640) relating to the narrative *Naneferkasokar and the Babylonians* attests to a name 'Nekau son of Tefnakht' (*N*^{c}*-k3w s3 T3y.f-nḫt.t*) which he suggests refers to King Nekau I as being the son of a King Tefnakht II. Ryholt[105] also identifies other indigenous Egyptian attestations of Nechepsos in Demotic texts and posits that Nechepsos should refer to Nekau II. He suggests that Nechepsos is placed in an incorrect position in Manetho's king-list. Perdu[106] also accepts Manetho and conducted a comparative study into the iconographic and stylistic features of the Athens and Michaelides stelae in an attempt to produce evidence for the existence of 'Tefnakht II'. Kahn[107] does not support Perdu's arguments and considers the Manethonian tradition to be full of flaws and finds the iconographic and stylistic evidence far from conclusive.

Therefore, the sequence of kings for the 24th Dynasty, prior to Nekau I ascending the throne and the beginning of the Saite Period, is still uncertain, with some disagreement amongst scholars. Further conclusive evidence is required to firmly establish the rulers at Sais for this period and, although there does appear to have been a ruling line at Sais, in common with other locations, the lack of stone-built and extant material makes it difficult to reconstruct this era.

There is little further evidence to suggest how Sais eventually became a powerful state other than the potential Bakenrenef trade link mentioned above. It is possible that western trade links were developed, utilising the riverways of the western Delta, which would then have reduced Saite reliance on the traditional eastern routes to the Levant. Such a scenario would have lessened dependence on these eastern trading intermediaries, improved profitability on foreign trade and been a factor in the development of the Saite state.

Notes

1   For a translation of Herodotus see Herodotus 1996. For commentaries see Lloyd 1975, 1976, 1988; Asheri, Lloyd and Cocella 2007; Baragwanath and de Bakker 2010.
2   For a discussion on the late Ramesside Period and Third Intermediate Period see Kitchen 1996; Taylor 2000; Dodson 2001; Cline and O'Connor 2012; Jansen-Winkeln 2017.
3   Kitchen 1982 and 1996: 243–54; Cline and O'Connor 2012.
4   Grandet 1994.
5   The hymn is from the funerary decree of Amun for Princess Neskhons (P. Cairo 58032), daughter of King Smendes and wife of Pinedjem II, founder of the 21st Dynasty. The decree opens with this extended hymn which has been termed by Vernus the official 'credo' of the theocratic state, see Ritner 2009a: 145–58.
6   Taylor 2000: 331–33; Van de Mieroop 2011: 265–66.
7   Polz 1998: 283–88; Van Dijk 2000: 307; Eyre 2012: 106, 125.
8   Lefebvre 1929: fig. 29b; Myśliwiec 2000: 18.
9   The most celebrated demonstrations are those of Year 29 of Ramesses III which are recorded in the Turin Strike Papyrus (P. Turin 1880). Other reports of unrest include O. Turin 57072, 2–13, which details monthly shortfalls in rations recorded by a member of the gang of workmen, and O. Varille 39 r 10–15 which mentions protests carried out at night. See McDowell 1999: 22–23, 237 and 265 for a bibliography relating to these sources. Also see Eyre 1980.
10 See Peet (1930) for the classic treatment of the major papyri detailing the robberies, an account that includes hieroglyphic transcriptions and extensive commentaries. See also McDowell 1990 and Goelet 1996.
11 For details see P. BM 10052 (Peet 1930: 135–69) and P. Mayer A (Peet 1920).

12 For the text, translations and discussions of *The Report* or *Voyage of Wenamun* (P. Moscow 120) see Gardiner 1932: 61–76; Lichtheim 1976: 224–30; Ritner 2009a: 87–99.

13 Ritner 2009a: 87.

14 The classic study of this incident, also known as the 'War of the High Priest', is Wente 1966. For alternative views and discussion of the events relating to Panehesy's time in Egypt see Jansen-Winkeln 1992; Kitchen 1996: 247ff; Török 1997: 104–7; Morkot 2000: 98–101; Thijs 2003.

15 Nubia and Kush are terms often used interchangeably although the Kushite kingdom lies in the southern part of the land known today as Nubia. It was at the end of the Middle Kingdom that Lower Nubia became dominated by an indigenous Kushite culture centred on the Dongola Reach.

16 Morkot 2000: 98–100; Thijs 2003; Gregory 2014: 157–58.

17 Van Dijk 2000: 309.

18 Kitchen 1996: 248–51; Morkot 2000: 100–2; Thijs 2003 and 2014.

19 See for example Hornung et al. 2006.

20 Moreno Garcia 2014: 611.

21 For a discussion of the Tjehenu and Tjemehu as well as other tribal terms see Spalinger 1979c; O'Connor 1990: 30; Manessa 2003: 82–85 and bibliography; Sagrillo 2013: 4071.

22 Lichtheim 1975: 25; O'Connor 1986: 29.

23 O'Connor and Quirke 2003: 5; Kitchen 2012: 7.

24 For a review of the Egyptian evidence see Hölscher 1937; Osing 1980; O'Connor 1990; Snape 2003. Also see White 1994a for an overview of the archaeological evidence for pre-Greek Libyans.

25 Leahy 2000: 291.

26 See Reiger et al. 2012. For a review of the archaeological surveys carried out in this region see Snape 2003: 96. For examples of painted and rock art, from the south-west of Libya, depicting Libyan peoples of this period see Ritner 2009b: 48–52.

27 Hulin 1987: 125; White 1994b; Morkot 2000: 92.

28 *KRI* IV 14.16–15.1.

29 *KRI* V 61.14; for a discussion of aspects of Libyan culture and their geographical origins see O'Connor 1990.

30 *KRI* V 17.12.

31 *KRI* V 62.14.

32 O'Connor 1990: 63–66; Ritner 2009c: 329.

33 Leahy 1985; O'Connor 1990.

34 Kitchen 1990: 16; Snape 2003: 94.

35 Moreno Garcia 2014: 614.

36 O'Connor 1990: 95; Snape 2003: 98.

37 O'Connor 1983: 277 and 1990: 47.

38 Kitchen 1990: 16–17; Morkot 2000: 92.

39 Snape 2003: 100–4.

40 *KRI* IV 3.6; 4.2–4; 8.5; 9.2; for studies of the Libyan war inscription of Merenptah at Karnak see Spalinger 1982; Manassa 2003.

41 For a treatment of the Sea Peoples see Sandars 1985; Gitin et al. 1998; Oren 2000.

42 *KRI* IV 4.14–15; Ritner 2009b: 47–48.

43   O'Connor 1990: 44.

44   Cairo JdE 50568.

45   *KRI* IV 18.9–15; Wente 2003: 360; Ritner 2009b: 47–48.

46   Kitchen 2012: 7–11.

47   *KRI* V 22.12–23.4; Ritner 2009c: 331.

48   O'Connor 1990: 40–45.

49   O'Connor 1990: 92.

50   Snape 2012: 419–22.

51   O. Deir el-Medina 35 – see *RITA* 521:1; Kitchen 1990: 22; Dodson 2012: 8.

52   Snape 2012: 418–19.

53   Gardiner 1948: 80–81.

54   Leahy 1985: 55.

55   For a discussion of prisoners of war in Egypt see Leahy 1985: 56 and Snape 2012: 418–19. Translation of the Rhetorical Stela is from *KRI* V 91; *RITA* V.

56   O'Connor 1990: 88–89; Manessa 2003: 89.

57   Kitchen 1996: 540–41.

58   For a discussion of Herihor as king see Kitchen 1990: 23; Broekman 2012a: 198; Thijs 2005; Gregory 2014: 138–45.

59   Leahy 1985; Ritner 2009c.

60   Leahy 1980: 62 and 1984b.

61   Statue Philadelphia E. 16199 + stela Cairo JdE 37489. For translation and discussions see Jacqet-Gordon 1960; Kitchen 1996: 317; Ritner 2009a: 283–88.

62   Leahy 1985: 55; Ritner 2009c: 333–39; Broekman 2010.

63   First Serapeum Stela of Pediese (Louvre S IM. 3749). For discussions see Malinine et al. 1968: 19–20, pl. 7 [No. 21]; Ritner 2009a: 388–90; Ritner 2009c: 336; Broekman 2010: 90.

64   Donation Stela of Smendes, son of Hornakht (Geneva Inv. No. 23473). See Chappaz 1982; Ritner 2009a: 432–34 and 2009c: 337.

65   Kitchen 1996: 345; Ritner 2009c; Yoyotte 2012.

66   Leahy 1985: 54.

67   Leahy 1985: 56.

68   Leahy 1985: 58–62; Broekman 2010.

69   Jansen-Winkeln 1994; Yoyotte 2012.

70   Taylor 2000: 335; Dodson 2012: 83ff.

71   The classic study is Kitchen 1996, but cf. Jansen-Winkeln 2006; Aston 2009; Dodson 2012 for subsequent discussions and alternative reconstructions.

72   Leahy 1985; O'Connor 1990.

73   Yoyotte 1963 and 2012: 38–39.

74   Daressy 1894: 48.

75   A faience amulet that is referred to as the 'Talisman of Osorkon' (Louvre E 10943). See Yoyotte 1960a: 13–22, figs 1–4; Ritner 2009a: 435–36.

76   Shabti University College London Nos 475 and 476. See Petrie 1935: pls 11, 18, 45; Ritner 2009a: 436.

77   Kitchen 1996; 350–51; Ritner 2009a: 435–36.

78   Dodson 2012: 136.

79   Morkot 2000: 181.

80   Farouk donation stela. Kitchen 1996: 104, 139; Ritner 2009a: 436–37; Jansen-Winkeln 2007b: 272–73 (28.14); Yoyotte 2012: 47–52.

81 Florence 1777. Del Francia 2000: 76–82; Kahn 2006b: 45–46; Jansen-Winkeln 2007b: 270–71 (28.11).

82 The stela was discovered in the home of a local guard at Ibtu near Tell Faraïn (Buto): Kitchen 1996: 138–39; Ritner 2009a: 437–38; Jansen-Winkeln 2007b: 273 (28.15); Yoyotte 2012: 48–49, pl. I.1.

83 The massive granite Victory Stela of Piye (Cairo JdE 48862 + 47086–47089) was discovered in the temple of Amun at Gebel Barkal and is now in the Egyptian Museum at Cairo. See Lichtheim 1980: 66–84; Ritner 2009a: 465–92; Broekman 2009: 96–100; Gozzoli 2006: 54–67. For further discussions regarding the campaign see Spalinger 1979a; Kitchen 1996: 363–66; Morkot 2000: 179–96; Kahn 2006b.

84 Broekman 2009: 93.

85 Broekman 2009: 99–100.

86 Ritner 2009a: 467.

87 Kemp 2006: 343–45.

88 Spalinger 1979a: 288–92; Kahn 2006b.

89 Dodson 2012: 153.

90 Kitchen 1996: 371–72; Kahn 2006b: 60; Yoyotte 2012: 56–59.

91 Spiegelberg 1903; el-Sayed 1975: 37–53, pl. 7.

92 Yoyotte 1971: 37–40.

93 'Tefnakht II' has also been recognised as *Stephinates* of Manetho, see discussions in Petrie 1905: 318–19; Priese 1972: 19–21; Baer 1973: 23–24; Kitchen 1996: 145–47, 395; Perdu 2002a. However, this suggestion has not been accepted by other Egyptologists such as Morkot 2000: 198–99; Dodson 2012: 153–54; see in particular the discussion in Kahn 2009.

94 See Diodorus I, 79 and I, 94.5. Opinions vary as to whether the tradition of Bakenrenef as a law giver should be accepted; see Redford 2004: 80–82 for discussion and references.

95 GD39, Yoyotte 1971: 44–45, fig. 3.

96 Morkot 2000: 207; Ritner 2009a: 443; but contra Kitchen 1996: 377.

97 Smith 1998: 236, fig. 399 and 276 n. 21; Ridgeway 1999: 145.

98 Coldstream 1968: 316–17, 327.

99 Redford 1985: 6 n. 16.

100 Gill and Vickers 1996, contra Ridgeway 1999.

101 Leahy (1984c) suggests that Bakenrenef was a figurehead of resistance to the Kushites, and his rejection of the authority of Piye was a revolt against his overlord and therefore his execution would not be unlikely. The destruction by fire of the enemies of Egypt is a recurring theme in the theological literature of the New Kingdom and some Ramesside texts. However, Kitchen (1996: 377 n. 763) states that there is no evidence to support this tradition, and such an event, particularly if unaccompanied by burial of the remains, would have caused considerable discontent and animosity towards the Kushites.

102 Ammeris is often considered to be a corruption of the name of other rulers such as Kashta or Piye; see Kitchen 1996: 145; Morkot 2000: 232, 320 n. 14.

103 Weidemann 1886: 64; Gauthier 1914: 414; Kitchen 1996: 145–47.

104 2011a.

105 2011b.

106 2002a.

107 2009.

2

Kushite and Assyrian invaders

The end of the eighth century and the first half of the seventh century BC witnessed the Kushite conquest of Egypt, and subsequent clashes between the Egyptian-Kushite forces and those of the Assyrian Empire. These conflicts eventually resulted in the expulsion of the Kushites from Egypt, the rise to power of the Kingdom of the West centred at Sais and the departure of the Assyrians.

Nubia (Kush)

The Kushite invaders who went on to rule Egypt originated from the land recognised today as Nubia and are known to Egyptology as the 25th Dynasty. The dynasty and its pharaohs are also referred to as 'Napatan' from the city of Napata, which was located near the Fourth Cataract of the Nile, one of the Kushite kingdom's principal cities.

There was always a close relationship between Egypt and its southern neighbour, Nubia. In the Early Dynastic and Old Kingdom periods, Egypt ruthlessly exploited Nubia in pursuit of mining and trading profits. During the Middle Kingdom, in response to increasing Nubian hostility, Egypt built a series of fortresses along the Nile to protect its trade in the economic resources of Lower Nubia and the revenues obtained from trade with countries further south. With Egypt's decline at the end of the Middle Kingdom, an indigenous culture based at the Dongola Reach, the kingdom of Kerma or Kush, came to dominate Nubia.

The coming of the New Kingdom saw Egypt once again looking to Nubia. In a series of extensive military campaigns, Egypt not only subdued the Kingdom of Kerma but also campaigned into Nubia further south than it had ever been before. Egypt built temple-centred towns in the conquered territories and Nubia was administered as a separate region for some five hundred years. Egypt governed Nubia through the establishment of the post of 'Overseer of the Southern Countries' usually referred to as the 'King's son of Kush' (*s3-nsw n K3š*). In addition, indigenous chiefs were incorporated into the local administration.[1] During this period, the settled population became increasingly Egyptianised, a feature more noticeable in Lower Nubia where assimilative acculturation appears to have been more rapid. In the more distant Upper Nubia, local rulers maintained a degree of autonomy by retaining elements of native Nubian culture within the Egyptian imperial system.[2]

At the end of the New Kingdom Egyptian control of Nubia was lost, and the nature of the political transition that then occurred in the country is unclear, as there may have been some form of continuity of occupation rather than full withdrawal.[3] During the subsequent Third Intermediate Period, Nubia entered what in the past has often been termed a 'Dark Age', so-called because of the lack of historical records and the dearth of recovered archaeological material.[4] In the mid-eighth century BC the Kushite Kingdom of Napata rose to power, extending its influence not only to the north but also far to the south in central Sudan. The Kushite kings were later to emerge as important figures in the ancient Near East, following their conquest and rule of Egypt. These rulers displayed a strong emulation of Egyptian traditions, adopting the ideology and symbols of Pharaonic kingship, which, on being transferred to their native lands, supported the creation of a distinctive new Napatan culture.[5]

The principal evidence for the emergence of the Napatan state consists of a limited number of inscriptions from the temple at Gebel Barkal and archaeological evidence from the nearby cemetery of el-Kurru. Here George Reisner[6] discovered the main tombs of the 25th Dynasty kings with the exception of that of Taharqo.[7] In addition to these tombs there are some earlier graves assumed, but not certain, to be the ancestors of the Napatan kings. The archaeological material excavated from the earlier graves is too fragmentary to form any meaningful historical reconstruction.[8] Studies of Third Intermediate Period and Late Period pottery have aided in understanding the chronology of this era.[9] Although the 25th Dynasty finds help to provide a semblance of a historical framework for the royal genealogies, development of the Napatan state during the three-hundred-year period from the end of the New Kingdom until the rise of these Kushite rulers is still uncertain.

A number of theories have been proposed to elucidate the origins of these kings and the influences behind their Egyptianisation.[10] It is possible that the Kushite elite survived the end of Egyptian colonial rule and together with the descendants of the original Egyptian colonists took control, eventually creating the Kushite or Napatan state.[11] Another proposal is that an influx of peoples from the south, perhaps near Meroe, led to a Nubian revival, replacing the old colonial system with the formation of a new Nubian polity.[12] Finally, by adapting an earlier model, it is suggested that the suppression of a series of rebellions by Prince Osorkon, as High Priest of Amun at Thebes (*c.* 839 BC), resulted in a number of priestly families fleeing to Nubia, where they revived the cult of Amun and helped to forge a new Egyptianised state.[13]

Recent excavations and analyses of human remains by isotopic and biological techniques, together with the study of artefacts from cemeteries and pyramids at Tombos near the Third Cataract, have disproved the suggestions that Egyptian or southern Nubian immigrants were an important part of the development of the Napatan state. Rather the cultural, geographic and biological data indicate that the original New Kingdom Egyptian settlers and local Nubians interacted to establish a multicultural and biologically heterogenous community that continued to flourish, long after the end of the New Kingdom.[14] This group, and others like it such as that at Amara West,[15] with an amalgam of Egyptian and Nubian elements, may well have been the basis of the political revival that established a new Kushite kingdom in the region, a state that embraced the earlier Pharaonic ideology.[16]

How individual groups of people from different centres such as Tombos coalesced into the Napatan state under one ruler is unknown. Traditions of kingship were already long-established in the region, probably with a strong religious foundation and may have existed for many generations. It is also likely that civil war and alliances had a part to play in the process, and the allusion to unrest and turbulent times in inscriptions, such as that of Queen Katimala at Semna[17] and the prayer of Alara,[18] could be an indication of opposition to former Napatan rulers.[19] Because of their geographical location the earlier rulers from el-Kurru may have played a key role in the trade of gold and exotic African goods as well as controlling the trade networks to central Africa. Such trading activity could well have been a stimulus for the growth of the Napatan polity, gradually transforming a chiefdom or chiefdoms into a complex state. Trading contacts with Egypt may well have continued after the New Kingdom, as attested by the presence of imported wares in the el-Kurru tombs.[20]

The Napatan kings did not merely imitate Egyptian culture and theology but revitalised it. They selectively emulated aspects of Pharaonic ideology and adapted them to suit Nubian sensibilities. They built small steep-sided pyramids imitating elite New Kingdom tombs, while maintaining the use of Nubian funeral beds. Innovations, like the cap crown and ram-imagery associated with Amun, indicate Kushite influences on Egyptian theology, while amulets of Egyptian deities were also worn.[21]

Kashta is considered to be the first of the Napatan rulers, having the earliest grave in the Kurru cemetery in which was inscribed the name of a king. There are some later inscriptions that refer to an earlier ruler, Alara, often regarded as the founder of the Napatan state, although little is known about his reign.[22] When Kashta ascended the throne in the middle of the eighth century BC the process of Napatan consolidation of Nubia would probably have been largely complete. By then the Kushites must have wielded considerable military power, reinforced by a strong economic base and political control of the Napatan kingdom.[23] Kashta is known to have reoccupied the Nile Valley northwards in Nubia, and then established Kushite rule in Abu (Elephantine), as attested by a stela that he dedicated in the temple of the local god, Khnum.[24] Unfortunately, no year-date or narrative text for this stela survives.[25] It is possible that he then advanced further northwards, establishing a presence in Upper Egypt, perhaps even taking control of Thebes, although there is no direct evidence to support this. However, the incumbent God's Wife of Amun, Shepenwepet I, daughter of Osorkon III, adopted a daughter of Kashta as her eventual heiress with the name Amenirdis I, an event that probably occurred during the reign of Kashta,[26] although it is possible that Amenirdis was installed during the later reign of Piye.[27]

Kashta's successor Piye built upon the military prowess of the Kushite kingdom when in Year 20 Piye invaded Egypt, reaching Memphis. The events of the campaign are recorded on the Victory Stela of Piye (see p. 16). Another earlier sandstone stela of Piye[28] recounting the events of Years 3 and 4 includes a dialogue between Amun and Piye in which Amun tells Piye he is to be ruler of Egypt, echoing an earlier Pharaonic form of legitimisation: 'I said of you in your mother's womb that you were to be ruler of Egypt. I knew you in the semen, while you were in the egg, that you were to be lord' (cols 2–6). Piye replies: 'Amun in Thebes has granted me to be ruler of Egypt. He to whom I say, "Make appearance (as king)!" He shall make his appearance' (cols 19–20).

The suggestion has been put forward that this sandstone stela and fragments from a third granite stela of Piye hint at a Year 3 or 4 date for Piye's northern campaign into Egypt, indicating that Piye had control of Egypt earlier in his reign. Such a proposal has not been universally accepted and would have implications for the chronology of the period, bringing forward Piye's campaign by some fifteen years; it seems unlikely that the date of the stela would be so far removed from the events related.[29] It is possible that there may have been more than one campaign to conquer Egypt and control of the country was not finally achieved until Year 20.

Piye eventually defeated a coalition of Egyptian rulers and laid claim to the whole of Egypt, thus inaugurating the 25th Dynasty (see pp. 16–18). Although Piye had occupied Upper and Middle Egypt it was not until the reign of his successor Shabitqo (see below for the recent revision of the Kushite order of succession) that the conquest of Lower Egypt was completed. Few details are known of the campaign by Shabitqo into Lower Egypt to achieve this objective, but it was probably undertaken around 711–709 BC, and by Year 2 of his reign he was in control of Memphis.[30]

Assyria and early contacts with Nubia

The earliest contacts between Nubia and Assyria can be dated even earlier than these Egyptian campaigns. An Assyrian administrative record, Nimrud Wine List No. 9 (c. 732 BC), includes references to Nubians present at the court of the Assyrian king, Tiglath-Pileser (744–727 BC).[31] The Nubians were recognised as experts in the breeding and management of horses, and it is known that the Assyrians began importing horses from Nubia at about this time. There are many references to the 'large' horses from Egypt and Nubia in the Assyrian records and these horses were particularly prized by Assyrian charioteers.[32] Chariotry and cavalry were essential to success in military battles of the first millennium BC, none more so than for Assyria, which undertook numerous military campaigns in pursuit of its imperial aims.

Artistic connections between Assyria and Nubia have been recognised for this period. Incised ivory inlays of an Assyrian style have been found in the tombs of the early 25th Dynasty rulers, perhaps suggesting the visits or exchange of craftsmen. Caryatids manufactured from ivory and dated to the reign of Sargon II have been discovered at Nimrud, these having a strong resemblance to silver caryatids on a mirror handle found in the tomb of Shabaqo.[33]

The Assyrian Empire[34] was the dominant force in the Near East at that time and possessed considerable military forces. Between the eighth and sixth centuries BC it had considerably expanded the territories under its control. The Assyrian rulers Tiglath-Pileser III and Sargon II (721–705 BC) led their armies on campaigns almost yearly, extending their dominance over the entire Near East. The multi-ethnic empire they created was a uniformly structured political entity, centrally controlled with well-defined and well-guarded borders, but, like many ancient empires, was beset by constant rebellions.

Under the influence of these two powerful rulers, Assyria became even more militaristic, with the Assyrian war machine being the most efficient force in the ancient world up until then. The secret to its success was the large professionally trained standing army, use of iron weapons, advanced engineering skills, effective tactics and complete ruthlessness in the waging of warfare (Figure 2.1). The large efficient military forces that Assyria was able to put into the field enabled Assyria to extend its territories into Babylonia, western Iran, Anatolia and the Levant, as well as controlling the major trade routes.

Assyria relied on international trade to sustain its economy and had a particular interest in the western Mediterranean, the lucrative maritime trade of Philistia and the main Phoenician cities of Byblos, Arvad, Sidon and Tyre. These cities

2.1 Assyrian helmet. Discovered by Flinders Petrie during excavations of the temples on the west bank at Thebes. Reliefs from Assyrian palaces depict soldiers of the Neo-Assyrian Empire wearing this type of pointed helmet. *c.* 690–664 BC. Copper alloy. H. 21 cm; Max. Diam. 9.7 cm (Manchester Museum, Manchester).

enjoyed considerable success in commerce, as they were strategically located where major trade routes from Mesopotamia, Egypt, Arabia and the Mediterranean converged.[35] Though subject to Assyria, the Philistine cities such as Ashkelon, Ashdod and Gaza managed to retain some degree of independence by paying a high tribute to it. This area acted as a buffer zone between Assyria and Egypt, and the evidence would suggest that the loyalties of the various cities to the two powers continually changed, depending on the fluctuating political situation at the time, with the cities sometimes even swearing allegiance to both sides.[36]

Sources

The various Assyrian and Egyptian texts that provide the sources of information for relations between the two countries differ in numbers and content. The uneven distribution and dominance of the Assyrian texts over the Egyptian sources makes it difficult to avoid an Assyrocentric approach, but they clearly provide the greatest resource for this period. The texts vary in approach in that the Assyrian rulers describe and underline their military success, emphasise their protection of Assyrian interests and depict themselves as an instrument of the gods. By contrast the Egyptian and Kushite sources highlight the divinity of the pharaoh and role of the ruler in imposing order and preventing chaos, the maintenance of *Maat*.[37]

The main Assyrian sources are the royal inscriptions, correspondence and various administrative documents. The royal inscriptions consist of the so-called annals, which record principal events of a king's reign, and the summary or display inscriptions which relate group events according to their geographical location or political significance.[38] For the reigns of the Assyrian rulers Sargon and Sennacherib the texts are arranged chronologically but are not for the later reign of Esarhaddon. Here the principal documents are seven historical prisms together with the *Babylonian Chronicle*, a document which is complete for the years of Esarhaddon's reign. Further sources are the so-called *Esarhaddon Chronicle* which records brief statements concerning the ruler, and the *Questions to the Sungod*, Shamash, in which Esarhaddon questions the deity concerning his campaign to Egypt and from whom Esarhaddon constantly sought advice during his reign.[39] A number of stelae set up by the Assyrians are also informative, such as that at Nahr el-Kalb (Dog River in the Lebanon) and those in the provincial cities of Zenjirli and Kar-Shalmaneser which recount the details of the later 671 BC campaign against Egypt-Kush.[40]

In comparison to the Assyrian evidence, surviving Egyptian and Kushite sources are few in number. Information is principally derived from inscriptions on royal monuments such as those at Karnak and Memphis, and monuments at Napata, el-Kurru and Gebel Barkal in Nubia.[41] This sparse material is supplemented by inscriptions such as Theban statue biographies, an example of which is that of Djedkhonsefankh. The text on his block statue illustrates one of the methods by which the ruling kings brought the Theban region back under royal control during the 22nd Dynasty – that of creating marriage alliances with local families.[42]

However, these sources tend to focus primarily on internal Egyptian and Kushite affairs such as enthronements, coronation journeys and religious activities, while events outside Egypt are hardly ever mentioned. This approach coupled with the traditional Egyptian manner of highlighting success and glossing over failure, results in the Egyptian sources being limited in value for understanding international affairs, and particularly relations with Assyria.[43]

Tang-i Var and chronology

Soon after the consolidation of Kushite control of Lower Egypt, Egyptian commercial interests in western Asia were intensified. Goods from the Phoenician cities and timber from Lebanon were traded with products from Kush. Initially, friendly relations existed between Assyria and Egypt-Kush, with the trade in horses continuing. In addition, evidence from clay seals found at Kuyunjik, the Northern Palace, at Nineveh indicates that Sargon II, the Assyrian ruler, and Shabitqo exchanged diplomatic correspondence.[44]

In 711 BC, the coastal city of Ashdod in Philistia began orchestrating a regional rebellion against Assyria in an attempt to cease paying further tribute. Ashdod, although not an Assyrian province, was a tribute-paying vassal city and so under the ultimate control of the Assyrian king. The Assyrians moved in to crush the revolt and annexed Ashdod. Iamani, the ruler of Ashdod and leader of the rebellion, fled to the *land of Meluhha* (Nubia/Kush) where he may then have resided for a number of years.[45] A rock inscription and relief dated to 706 BC during the reign of Sargon II, discovered in the Tang-i Var pass, indicates that it was the Nubian ruler Shabitqo who decided to extradite Yamani back to Assyria (Figure 2.2). Perhaps the intention was not to antagonise the

2.2 The rock inscription of Sargon II at the Tang-i Var pass near the village of Tang-i Var, in the district of Sanandaj, Kurdistan, Iran. Dated to 706 BC.

Assyrians but rather promote friendly relationships with them by this gesture. At that time the Kushites seemed not to be involved in political manoeuvring in the Levant.[46]

The Tang-i Var inscription is both a useful historical document to understand better Egyptian/Kushite and Assyrian relations and crucial for the chronology and succession of the 25th Dynasty. Previous to the republication of this inscription in 1999 by Grant Frame and later discussion by Dan'el Kahn in 2001, the accepted chronology of the 25th Dynasty was based on Manetho. The succession consisted of the Nubian ruler Piye (*c.* 747–716 BC) followed by Shabaqo (*c.* 716–702 BC) and then Shabitqo (*c.* 702–690 BC). The capture of Ashdod by the Assyrians and Iamani's flight took place in 712/711 BC. As Sargon died in 705 BC[47] and the inscription is dated to 705 BC, it then follows that the reign of Shabitqo covered the period from 712 to 705 BC.[48]

From this chronology, a problem arises in that for the decade preceding 713/712 BC the Assyrian and Biblical records contain several allusions to Egyptian rulers, but none of them can be interpreted as a Kushite king ruling over Egypt. Therefore, when Iamani sought help from Egypt, Shabaqo's invasion of Lower Egypt had not occurred and Shabaqo's Year 1 must be in or after 713 BC.[49] One solution tentatively put forward to this problem has been to posit a co-regency between Shabaqo and Shabitqo,[50] but most scholars have rejected this due to the lack of evidence to support such a hypothesis.[51] Certainly, the monuments from this period provide no trace of double dating and joint rule or any reason for suggesting a co-regency.[52] It has been noted that, in the Tang-i Var inscription, Shabitqo is termed ruler of *Meluhhu* (Nubia/Kush) and not Egypt, and Shabitqo is termed ruler and not king. Therefore, another suggestion is that Shabaqo, the ruling Kushite king in Egypt, involved Shabitqo, then a prince, in dealings with Assyria.[53]

More recently a number of scholars have undertaken a significant study of the available evidence and suggested a reversal of the order Shabaqo–Shabitqo in the succession of 25th Dynasty kings, as a more satisfactory solution to this problem.[54] An examination of the Kushite Nile Records (NLR) inscribed on the quay wall at Karnak shows that the upper edge of Shabaqo's NLR No. 30, Year 2 is superimposed upon the left-hand side of the lower edge of Shabitqo's NLR No. 33, Year 3 inscription which indicates that Shabitqo must have preceded Shabaqo.[55] Another factor is that only in the pyramids of Piye (Ku 17) and Shabitqo (Ku 18) are the burial chambers open-cut structures with a corbelled roof, whereas tunnelled substructures are found in the pyramids of Shabaqo (Ku 15), Taharqo (Nu 1) and Tanwetamani (Ku 16), as well as with all subsequent royal pyramids in el-Kurru and Nuri. The fully tunnelled structure of Shabaqo and subsequent rulers suggests an architectural development in these later tombs.[56]

Among the titles and epithets on the statue of Horemkhet,[57] High Priest of Amun and son of Shabaqo, are 'King's son of Shabaqo, justified, who loves him, Sole Confidant of King Taharqo, justified, Director of the palace of the king of Upper and Lower Egypt, Tanwetamani, may he live for ever'. However, there is no reference to Horemkhet serving under Shabitqo which is puzzling as the statue inscription renders a chronological sequence of kings who reigned during Horemkhet's life, each of their names being accompanied by a reference to the relationship that existed between the relevant king and Horemkhet. The evidence suggests, therefore, that Shabitqo was probably dead before Horemkhet was born.[58]

Also, there is the question of the evolution of the shabtis of the Kushite kings. Those belonging to Shabitqo are small (about 10 cm), have a very brief inscription and are similar to those of Piye. The shabtis of Shabaqo are larger (about 15–20 cm) with more developed inscriptions, including a quotation from the Book of the Dead, which is also present on those of Taharqo, Tanwetamani and Senkamanisken.[59]

The evidence therefore suggests a Shabitqo–Shabaqo succession, and with this hypothesis there is then no need to postulate a coregency, or for Shabitqo to be considered a deputy of Shabaqo. This revised sequence is also compatible with the Assyrian sources. This scenario is now accepted by many Egyptologists[60] and used in this publication (see Chronology, p. xvi above).

The Kushites and Assyrians clash

In the years following the Ashdod rebellion of 711 BC there appears to have been little direct intervention by the Assyrians in the west, probably due to Assyria's increasing preoccupation with problems elsewhere in its vast Empire. In 705 BC Sargon was killed on campaign at Tabal in central Anatolia, and his demise ignited a massive revolt in the Assyrian Empire.[61] Eventually, his son, Sennacherib (704–681 BC), established himself on the throne as the successor of Sargon, but not before the western states took the opportunity to assert their independence from their overlord. This was a persistent problem for Assyria, as is the case with many large empires where neighbouring tribes or kingdoms tend to stir up unrest in the remoter areas of the domain, particularly when the eyes of the empire are occupied with problems elsewhere in the territories.[62]

Around 702 BC Hezekiah, the ruler of Judah, began to expand his kingdom into Philistia and also attempted to gain independence from Assyria. A number of western city states including Ashkelon, Ekron and Sidon decided to cease paying tribute to Assyria and formed a coalition with Judah against Assyria. On receiving reports of this the Assyrian army marched against them, threatening Judah and ultimately Jerusalem itself.

Following pleas for help, Egypt-Kush joined this alliance against Assyria, and in 701 BC an Egyptian-Kushite army advanced into Palestine.[63] The coalition forces clashed with the Assyrian army, led by Sennacherib, at Eltekeh, thought to be located in the region of Ashdod in southern Palestine.[64] According to Assyrian sources the coalition was defeated but the outcome of the battle is not clear. No tangible details of the defeat are given, no numbers of prisoners are mentioned and no booty is listed, as would have been the case had the Assyrians achieved a victory. Indeed, the later adoption of New Kingdom-style 'imperial' titles by the Kushite ruler, Shabitqo, might suggest that he regarded himself as the victor.[65] The Egyptian-Kushite army withdrew and was not pursued by the Assyrians, again, as would have been expected had they suffered a total defeat. The Assyrian claim to have captured in the battle numbers of Egyptian charioteers and princes as well as Kushite charioteers would suggest only a partial success achieved by the Assyrians. This differentiation between Egypt and Kush is a constant feature in the Assyrian records, where the ethnic identity of the Kushites is stressed in comparison with that of the Egyptians. However, this distinction seems to be a propaganda motif influenced by political considerations as it appears only half a century later in the inscriptions of Esarhaddon and Ashurbanipal.[66]

Following the confrontation at Eltekeh the Assyrians continued their march southwards, capturing several other cities along the way but without seizing and devastating Jerusalem. There has been much debate relating to these events and a number of suggestions have been posited as to why Jerusalem was spared when cities nearby such as Lachish and Libnah were conquered with great brutality, particularly when there was seemingly little to stop the Assyrians from subjugating Jerusalem[67] (Figure 2.3). A popular theory among both biblical scholars and Egyptologists has been that some form of epidemic ravaged the Assyrian army, resulting in its early return to Nineveh.[68] The concept is based on biblical accounts that an angel of Yaweh annihilated many of the Assyrian troops while they were in their camp besieging Jerusalem.[69]

A number of difficulties[70] exist with this proposition: the Assyrians had all but won the campaign against the rebellious cities, with Jerusalem being the last major city still to be taken. Also, the Assyrian forces were likely to have split into different units besieging the various cities as mentioned in II Kings (18.17, 19.8), and so such an epidemic may not have spread throughout all the Assyrian forces. Once the health of the army had returned or new forces been obtained, why did Sennacherib never return to Jerusalem, although it is recognised that he was involved with unrest in Babylon and Elam over the next decade, and so undertook no further campaigns to the west?

One solution to the problem could be that there were two separate Egyptian-Kushite armies, with II Kings (19.9) stating that the Assyrians were about to destroy

2.3 Detail from the Lachish reliefs which originally decorated the South-West Palace of Sennacherib in Nineveh. The scene shows the city of Lachish being attacked by the Assyrians in 701 BC. Some of the city's inhabitants are fleeing Lachish, holding their personal belongings and a number of captured Lachish soldiers are being impaled outside the city walls (British Museum, London).

Jerusalem when Sennacherib learnt about a Kushite-led army advancing towards them. It has been suggested that this was a second Kushite expeditionary force, which according to the biblical account was led by a certain 'Tirhakah' which is a variation of Taharqo, the Kushite prince who was later to be pharaoh. The conclusion that there were two armies is based on the wording of Sennacherib's annals in which there is no mention of Kushite royalty when referring to the battle of Eltekeh; rather they name the adversary as 'the kings of Egypt' which has been assumed to be the monarchs of the Delta.[71] Combining this with the Bible's reference to Taharqo at the head of the advancing forces, possibly troops from Kush who took longer to reach Jerusalem, has led to the conclusion that this army is different from the one at Eltekeh led by the Delta rulers.[72]

Perhaps this second army led by Taharqo advanced on Jerusalem, and the Assyrians who were besieging the city then fled. The Assyrians may have had only a modest contingent at Jerusalem as the Assyrian strategy was one of deploying forces in a number of areas simultaneously, besieging several cities at the same time. Also, the inhabitants of Jerusalem had not only strengthened the city's defences but had been able to limit the Assyrian access to water by previously diverting water from the Gihon Spring outside the city walls through a 520-metre conduit into the Pool of Siloam within the city.[73] The nearest adequate supply of water available for use by the Assyrians would then have been quite some distance away in the surrounding hills.

Therefore, with the Assyrian forces depleted after the battle of Eltekeh and the sieges of cities such as Lachish and Libnah as well as other cities in Judah, Philistia and Phoenicia, combined with a lack of water supplies for an extended siege, the Assyrian forces may simply have withdrawn from Jerusalem. Possibly some form of agreement was reached in which Jerusalem paid some form of penalty to Assyria for its assurance not to return. There is no mention of any engagement between the Assyrians and the Egyptian-Kushite forces, and the annals record that the Assyrian army returned to Nineveh. Nothing is then known of any further encounter between Assyria and Egypt-Kush until the reign of Taharqo.[74]

In the years following the Assyrian withdrawal, Egypt-Kush appears to have enjoyed political and commercial influence in the Levant and Judah, authority which is consistent with having emerged from the conflict with the Assyrians not as a vanquished state. This is attested by an inscription on the seventh pylon at Karnak[75] which indicates Kushite commercial interest in the Levant, evidence further supported by inscriptions on a number of stelae in Nubia. One of these stelae (Kawa III) from the temple of Amun at Gematon (Kawa) founded by Taharqo, lists the endowments that Taharqo donated to the temple between his second and eighth years. These donations include acacia, cedar and juniper wood, timber which grows in the Lebanon. Inscriptions on a similar stela (Kawa VI) dated to Years 8–10 of Taharqo's reign record that the doors of the temple of Amun were constructed of true cedar from the Lebanon, and the bolts of Asiatic bronze (*ḥmt Sṯ.t*). In addition, there is reference to the tribesmen of Asia (presumably from the Levantine region) being brought to Kawa to work as gardeners at the temple.[76] This Kushite procurement of products from Lebanon was in disregard of a decree of 734 BC by the earlier Assyrian ruler Tiglath-Pileser III which had forbidden the inhabitants of Sidon to sell any timber from Lebanon, either to the Egyptians or to their Philistine allies.[77] Similarly, Shalmaneser V (727–721 BC), the successor to Tiglath-Pileser, may also have undertaken operations against Tyre to prevent Egyptian maritime trade in these products.[78]

At this time in the Kingdom of the West it is uncertain if Sais was ruled directly by the Kushites or whether a local ruler controlled the region. Tefnakht and Bakenrenef, the 24th Dynasty rulers, were now dead, and Nekau is known to have been ruler at Sais in the later years of Taharqo's rule. As discussed earlier (see p. 19) it is not clear for this intermediate period whether some members of the princely family were in control, possibly as Kushite vassals, or whether a Kushite governor ruled the territory.

Meanwhile, Assyria was again involved in military activities, on this occasion with Babylon to the south of its empire. This preoccupation again swayed the Levantine rulers to enter into another anti-Assyrian alliance with Egypt. Egypt actively supported these rulers against the Assyrians, probably in an attempt to regain further control of trade in the Mediterranean and particularly access to products such as Phoenician timber and fir tree resin.[79]

With the death of Sennacherib in 681 BC, his son, Esarhaddon (681–669 BC), became ruler of Assyria, and on ascending the throne Esarhaddon oversaw a more aggressive policy towards southern Philistia, a territory that his father Sennacherib seemed to have lost control of towards the end of his reign. Within a year he campaigned westward to reaffirm Assyrian control over the Levant and to attempt to eliminate Kushite influence there. He plundered the city of Arza which was at the south-western limit of the Assyrian Empire, near the border with Egypt, often referred to as the 'Brook of Egypt',[80] the traditional Egyptian border in the eastern Sinai. However, at this time he did not venture into Egyptian territory.[81]

In the years 677–676 BC Esarhaddon quelled a rebellion in Sidon with exceptional brutality and strengthened Assyrian control over Tyre. Esarhaddon probably viewed Taharqo as the source of unrest among his vassals in Palestine and Phoenicia as Taharqo may have been providing them with aid as he was later to do for Ashkelon (see below).[82] The Assyrians realised that to consolidate their rule over the Levant they would have to deal firmly with the Egyptian-Kushite problem, by driving them away from their zone of influence and their repeated interference in the Levant. A brief statement in the *Babylonian Chronicle*[83] records an expedition to Egypt in March 673 BC in which the Assyrians clashed with Taharqo just over the border in Egyptian territory, an engagement in which the Assyrians were defeated:[84] 'The seventh year: on the fifth day of the month Adar, the army of Assyria was defeated in a bloody battle in Egypt'.

The *Esarhaddon Chronicle*, not unsurprisingly for an Assyrian source, preserves a different tradition from its Babylonian counterpart and rather than recording this failed campaign, reports instead on an insignificant campaign in southern Babylonia, which occurred about the same time:[85] 'The seventh year: On the eighth day of the month Adar the army of Assyria [marched] to Sha-amile'. There may be a reference to this Assyrian defeat in the later Egyptian literary work the *Pedubastis Cycle* dated to the Graeco-Roman Period.[86] Here Pemu of Heliopolis caused a foe *3slstny* (not only an Assyrian name but thought to be a late form of Esarhaddon) 'chief of the land [...], to retreat eastwards', after the latter had tried to seize Egypt from the rule of King Pedubast.

Following his victory over Esarhaddon, Taharqo continued his policy of supporting the cities of the Levant in their rebellion against Assyria. An oracle request by Esarhaddon to the Sun-god, Shamash, refers to Egyptian troops being stationed in the city of Ashkelon:[87]

[I ask you Samas, great lord], whether Eserhad[don, king of] Assyria [should plan and] go [with] men, horses, and [an army as great as he wishes], to the city of Ashkelon (whether), as long as [he stays] and sets up camp in the dis[trict of Ashkelon, the troops of ...], or Egyptian troops, [or ... troops will come t] o wage war [against Esarhaddon, king of Assyria, and (whether) they will fight] against each other.

Opposition to Assyria was now once again growing in the Levantine region, a situation perhaps buoyed by Egypt's defeat of Assyria, and thus Egypt's perceived superiority. A fragmentary inscription carved on a stela (Mnm. C) set up by Esarhaddon at the estuary of Nahr el-Kalb names Ashkelon, Tyre and 'twenty-two' kings in the coalition against Assyria.[88] Although the high number of twenty-two may have been an exaggeration, nevertheless, tribute was not being paid and there was widespread opposition to Assyria in the west of its empire, a situation that ultimately provoked Esarhaddon to take action.

First Assyrian invasion of Egypt in 671 BC

In 671 BC, during his tenth year, Esarhaddon again set off from Assyria to invade Egypt and this time he was successful in defeating the Egyptian-Kushite army. The various sources record little of the build-up to war or details of the march of the Assyrian army to Egypt, but there are a number of versions of how this victory was achieved. The Assyrian sources[89] state that battles raged daily over a period of fifteen days, whereas the *Babylonian Chronicle*[90] indicates that there were three separate battles within a period of fifteen days, all in the region of Memphis. The city of Memphis was eventually taken with considerable bloodshed, Taharqo was wounded but escaped, probably to Thebes, while many members of his family including his eldest son were captured alive (Figure 2.4):[91]

> From the town of Ishhupri as far as Memphis, his royal residence, a distance of fifteen days (march), I fought daily, without interruption, very bloody battles against Tirhakah (Taharqo), king of Egypt and Nubia, the one accursed by all the great gods. Five times I hit him with the point of (my) arrows (inflicting) wounds (from which he should not recover), and (then) I laid siege to Memphis, his royal residence, and conquered it in half a day by means of mines, breaches and assault ladders; I destroyed (it), tore down (its walls) and burnt it down. His queen, the women of the palace, Ushanahuru, his 'heir apparent', his other children, his possessions, horses, large and small cattle beyond counting, I carried away as booty to Assyria.

Rather than relating many details of the military engagements, the various sources tend to emphasise the numbers and types of objects brought back to Nineveh as booty, which included military equipment, statues of the gods and numbers of prisoners. The reiteration of descriptions of the plunder in all the texts suggests that the Assyrians were astonished with the extent and quantities

2.4 The Victory Stela of Esarhaddon (also known as the Zenjirli Stela) commemorating the return of Esarhaddon after his army's battle and victory over Taharqo in Lower Egypt in 671 BC. Discovered in Zincirli Höyük, Turkey. Dolerite. H. 3.46 m; W. 1.35 m (Pergamon Museum, Berlin).

they had appropriated.[92] That members of the Kushite royal family were captured perhaps indicates the unexpected nature of the defeat for the Kushites, although the king and his retinue were resident at Memphis. With Taharqo's earlier victory in 673 BC the Kushites had probably assumed that they were capable of standing up to and defeating the Assyrians once again.

Meanwhile the local kinglets in the Delta yielded to Assyria, becoming vassals, and Egypt was incorporated into the Assyrian Empire. Esarhaddon now set about forcing his will on Egypt and seemed intent on trying to eradicate the Kushite influence. The Zenjirili Stela specifically includes details such as the removal of the 'root of Kush from Egypt', before listing the new administrators that were appointed to oversee the Delta cities. Esarhaddon removed only the Kushites from their positions, emphasising that they were interlopers from the south, and probably considered them as responsible for the problems in the Levantine region that Assyria had been encountering.[93] Similarly, as the records relating to the earlier battle of Eltekeh demonstrate, the Assyrians again made the distinction between the Egyptians and the Kushites. Esarhaddon deported both Egyptians and Kushites to Nineveh, including not only high-ranking members of court and craftsmen but other occupations such as bakers, snake-charmers and singers. These latter rather specialist groups would probably have been particularly chosen by Esarhaddon to demonstrate his victory at court.

Of the new officials that Esarhaddon appointed in many of the Delta cities, some were Assyrian, but he also confirmed a number of local kinglets in their previous positions. These local rulers and the cities they controlled are listed in the Assyrian records,[94] with all the rulers being referred to by the Assyrian term *sharru*, king, which does not distinguish them from their Egyptian titles. The Egyptian equivalents of many of the names and towns can be understood but some remain uncertain. The main rulers included Nekau of Memphis and Sais, Sharruludari of Tjel, Pishanhuru of Nathu, Pekrur of Pi-Soped, Bakennefi of Athribis and Nahke of Herakleopolis Magna.[95] Although the cities were given Assyrian names, they retained much of their independence, particularly as the local administration was seemingly left intact.

According to the Assyrian records, within a month of the conquest Esarhaddon had appointed these vassal rulers and set up a new administration to rule over the Delta and Memphis. A month seems a very short period to implement such changes and so it is quite likely to have been an ideologically motivated date.[96] Another suggestion is that the speed of the appointments could indicate that these new nominees may have been princes or sons of princes who had been taken as hostages at the battle of Eltekeh, and lived at Nineveh for many years, possibly even marrying Assyrians. Previous Assyrian texts also document numbers of Egyptians living at Nineveh after 701 BC.[97] The Assyrian practice, similar to that known to have occurred in Egypt, of high-born hostages or guests living at court is well attested. The intention would have been that by the time they returned to their home country they would have adapted to Assyrian sensibilities, thus helping in future to ensure their dependable conduct with respect to Assyria.[98] This could be a reason why there is no evidence of some of the highest-ranking Assyrian officials, such as the *turtanu* (senior military commanders) being resident in Egypt at this time, as it was hoped that the newly appointed Egyptians had been appropriately indoctrinated and were now sufficiently pro-Assyrian. Before Esarhaddon returned to Nineveh, he imposed a regular tribute on each city rather than the country as a whole, perhaps attempting to foster division and impede attempts at unification. He also decreed that offerings were to be made to the Assyrian gods in the Egyptian temples.

It has been suggested that the Assyrian invasion of Egypt in 671 BC and the subsequent later offensives were aimed at ridding the country of the Kushites, whom they considered as foreigners from the south, rather than intending to subjugate the Egyptians.[99] It is possible that the Assyrians did not have long-term plans to invade and incorporate Egypt into their empire, but rather intended to pacify Egypt in order that Assyria could access its commercial interests in the Levant without Egyptian-Kushite interference. This was an area that Assyria seemed to consider its own personal dominion and which gave it clear access to the Mediterranean. Assyria obtained substantial tribute from these territories and as a result would not tolerate any outside interference. Additionally, Memphis was at the extremity of its empire, some 3700 km from Nineveh, and so the logistics involved in conquering the country, moving and supplying a large army, and then maintaining a realistic presence in the country would have been immense, and a considerable drain on Assyrian resources.[100]

An unusual Kushite source relating to these events is a poetical invocation by Taharqo to Amun, a text which records Taharqo's defeat by the Assyrians and the capture of his son, Ushanhuru.[101] Taharqo grieves over the subsequent lost tribute from Syria-Palestine (*Ḫȝrw*) and requests Amun to help him to regain control over the lost territories: 'Let me do it with your tribute (*inw*) of Khor (Syria-Palestine) which has been turned aside from you' (column 16). Taharqo also requests that Amun should protect his family: 'O Amun my wives, let my children live. Keep death away from them for me. Save me from [… evil words(?)] of their mouths and turn them over (the evil words?) back on them' (cols 17, 18). The text is remarkable in that it not only demonstrates Taharqo's assessment of the Assyrian conquest but also reveals the extent of his piety towards Amun and his acknowledgement of his personal responsibility in the defeat and loss of territory.

The Assyrians now controlled the Delta and Middle Egypt as far as Teudjoi, but Taharqo in the south was still seen as a threat to Esarhaddon, as is attested in a letter sent to him by his adviser, Mar-Istar, barely six months after the 671 BC campaign. In the communication Mar-Istar stated that the main adversaries in the west were Taharqo, King of Kush, Ba'al, King of Tyre, and Mugallu of Tabul.[102] Nekau, ruler of Sais, and Sharruludari, ruler of Tjel, were not mentioned in the letter and so were probably not perceived as a problem, although Kahn[103] considers that these rulers and their vassals formed an active opposition against the Assyrians. In contrast Perdu[104] sees the ascendancy of Nekau as an opposition to the Kushites rather than the Assyrians.

Nekau had probably inherited the title of king from his father (of whom there appears no record) and ascended the throne at Sais in 672/671 BC. The territory he ruled over, the Kingdom of the West, included Memphis and comprised about a third of the Delta region. There are few surviving monuments relating to his reign, one exception being a glazed statuette of the god Horus[105] which gives his full cartouche. Princess Takheredentaihet[-weret], a daughter of Nekau, was given in a politically arranged marriage to the local ruler of Herakleopolis, Pediese.[106] Such a union would have helped form ties between the Saites and northern Middle Egypt.

There are indications that in the aftermath of the invasion the Assyrians had failed to pacify and control parts of the conquered territory, and so Assyrian domination of Egypt was short-lived. An oracle request to the Assyrian god, Shamash, enquires whether the Chief Eunuch Sa-Nabu-su should be sent to Egypt to undertake a mission, and, if so, whether he would be attacked by Nekau, Sharruludari of Si'nu (perhaps to be identified with Pelusium)[107] or the other Delta leaders.[108] Such doubts would suggest the precariousness of Assyrian control of Egypt.

The Kushites return

It was perhaps in this climate of uncertainty that Taharqo seized the opportunity to return to Memphis in an endeavour to re-establish his rule. This action provoked Esarhaddon in 669 BC to launch a second campaign to once again deal with the uprising in Egypt; however, Esarhaddon became ill en route and died in Palestine the same year. His successor, Ashurbanipal (669–627 BC), after a period of establishing his authority in Assyria, determined to resolve the persistent Egyptian-Kushite problem.

Although the reign of Ashurbanipal and his various campaigns are well documented, there are a number of difficulties with the Assyrian records at that time, in that they appear to lack a proper chronological arrangement as well as differing from each other in considerable detail. One problem in interpreting these records is that, by the end of the eighth century BC, it was common practice among the royal scribes who were composing these texts to appropriate reports from the early recensions and place them ahead of the newer material in the later recensions. The texts listed in chronological order are prisms E, B, D, K, F, D, A and the Harran tablets. Prism A is also represented by the celebrated Rassam Cylinder, dated to around 636 BC, which is the most complete record of Ashurbanipal's annals, and describes nine campaigns against various enemies. The Rassam Cylinder, which was compiled following Ashurbanipal's ninth campaign, is often used in historical reconstructions, but caution has to

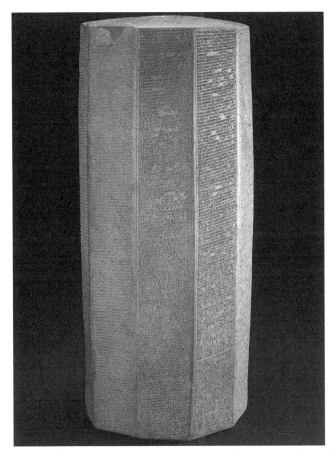

2.5 The Rassam Cylinder. Ten-sided cylinder inscribed in cuneiform with the annals of Ashurbanipal. It represents the most complete record of Ashurbanipal's annals. Inscribed in 1304 lines with the first to ninth campaigns of Ashurbanipal, and the construction of buildings in Nineveh. Discovered in the North Palace at Nineveh. Fired clay. H. 49 cm; W. 6.35 cm; Diam. 20.3 cm (British Museum, London).

be exercised in its interpretation as it is a blend of prisms E, B and the Harran tablets[109] (Figure 2.5).

Second Assyrian campaign against Egypt in 667 BC

Ashurbanipal set off for Egypt in 667–666 BC, and en route received the submission of cities along the Levantine coast which wisely demonstrated their loyalty to the overwhelming forces[110] of Ashurbanipal, rather than side with Taharqo whose credibility would have been weakened by his defeat at Memphis.

Ashurbanipal forced the Syria-Palestinian vassals, including Judah, Edom and Moab, to join him in his campaign. He also obtained ships from Phoenicia and Cyprus capable of sailing up the Nile, and now with this enlarged military force he invaded Egypt. The Assyrian coalition defeated the Egyptian-Kushite forces at Karbaniti, thought to be located near Per-Sopdu in the eastern Delta.[111] Following his victory Ashurbanipal re-established local government in the Delta, and then returned to Nineveh, taking with him a large number of prisoners and great quantities of booty.[112] Nekau was one of the kings who were reinstated and his mention in the Assyrian records before the other rulers might imply his perceived importance amongst the Delta leaders. This suggestion is supported by evidence that a number of the Delta rulers, such as Akunosh B of Sebennytos had begun to ally themselves with Nekau in opposition to the Kushites.[113]

Taharqo retreated to Thebes and was pursued by the Assyrian forces that Ashurbanipal had left behind in Egypt. A fragmented Egyptian stela found at Karnak describes an encounter between Taharqo's forces and an unnamed enemy, possibly the Assyrians. In this confrontation Taharqo was victorious[114] although there is no mention of this clash in the Assyrian records. The encounter may then have prompted a rebellion by the Delta dynasts, particularly Nekau, Sharruludari of Si'un and Pekrur of Pi-Soped in the eastern Delta, who had secretly communicated with Taharqo to form an alliance. It does appear strange that Nekau who usually opposed the Kushites was now conspiring with them against the Assyrians.[115] Perhaps the Kushites at this time were perceived to be the more favourable overlord, especially with the Assyrian reputation for brutality towards their vanquished foes. However, the messengers whom the Delta rulers had sent to Taharqo were intercepted by the Assyrians and detained, resulting in the Assyrian army returning northwards to suppress the revolt.

Rebellion quashed

The Assyrian texts indicate that the rebellion was dealt with severely, with many of the rulers of the Delta cities executed. Nekau and Sharruludari were arrested and taken to Nineveh whereas Pekrur escaped, but some time later appears to have returned to rule over his territory. After the uprising was quashed, local kinglets were again installed by the Assyrians as governors. Nekau was subsequently pardoned and reinstated as ruler of Sais and Memphis, and perhaps unexpectedly treated as a friend and ally. The Assyrian annals describe in detail how Nekau was given an improved treaty and was presented with many gifts including horses, chariots, golden rings and a golden chain as insignia of kingship. Psamtek, Nekau's son, who had spent some time at the Assyrian court, was given an Assyrian name, *Nabushezibanni* (O Nabu save me), perhaps suggesting some attempt at assimilation and friendliness on the part of the

Assyrians.[116] Psamtek was installed as ruler in Athribis and received the title of 'hereditary prince'. Esarhaddon stated that he treated him with more friendliness and favour than he had received from his own father.[117] It is considered that the previous ruler of Athribis, Bakennefi, had participated in the attempted rebellion and hence was removed from office.[118]

Although initially it might seem surprising that Nekau was pardoned and not executed, as the other Delta leaders had been, but in contrast rewarded, it is likely that Assyria was attempting to forge an alliance with Nekau and Psamtek. This friendliness may well have been because the Assyrians had repeatedly found Egypt difficult to govern and they had utilised considerable military resources in subduing it, located at the extreme limits of the empire. They probably would have regarded the repeated incursions of the Kushites and rebellion of the Delta rulers as an ever-present threat.[119] By allying themselves with Nekau and Psamtek rather than subduing them, the Assyrians were hoping for their support to stave off any future attempted Kushite takeover of Egypt and subsequent interference in the Levant. A strong ruler and ally in the Delta, at the western extremity of the Assyrian Empire, would not only be preferable to an enemy who would rebel at the earliest opportunity but would also be a bulwark against any possible incursions from the west. Nekau for his part may have considered that friendly relations with Assyria, now once again proved to be the stronger opponent, would have been more advantageous in helping to retain his own power base than relying on the Kushites. This concern would have been reinforced by the recent Delta rebellion against the Assyrians in which the uprising had been crushed with considerably brutality.

Following the suppression of the Delta cities, Taharqo may have retired to Napata as there is no further evidence of him before his death in 664–663 BC. He was succeeded by Tanwetamani, the son of Shabaqo, although there is some debate on Tanwetamani's parentage.[120] Tanwetamani's succession and the final events in the Kushite domination of Egypt are described in the 'Dream Stela', a monument discovered at Gebel Barkal and now in the Nubian Museum, Aswan.[121] The stela relates how Tanwetamani experienced a dream in which he saw two serpents, one on his right hand and one on his left. On waking, the king's dream was interpreted by his courtiers as: 'The South-land is yours, seize for yourself the North-land. The Two Ladies appear in glory on your brow, and the land is given to you in its length and its [width. There is no] other who will share it with you' (ll. 5–6). The serpents were identified as the double cobra-uraeus on the Kushite crown, a symbol of the united kingdoms of Egypt and Kush. This event occurred in Tanwetamani's first regnal year, and the interpretation of the dream corresponds with the existing political situation in Egypt at that time, in which Thebes was in Kushite hands and Lower Egypt was dominated by the Assyrians, but with local rulers nominally in control.[122]

Again the Kushites invade

The text on the 'Dream Stela' then describes how, as a result of this positive omen, Tanwetamani, who was probably in Napata at the time, mobilised his army and in 664 BC set off northwards, stopping at Elephantine and Thebes en route to worship the local gods. He captured Memphis after defeating a coalition of Assyrian troops and Delta rulers, among whom was Nekau. According to Herodotus (II, 152) Nekau was killed in the conflict and his son, Psamtek, escaped to Syria. In Classical sources Syria and Assyria were often confused and it seems likely that Psamtek would have fled to Nineveh, in Assyria.[123]

From Memphis, Tanwetamani continued northwards to confront the other Delta leaders, who according to the Dream Stela 'entered into their fortifications as [vermin slink] into their holes' (l. 25). Tanwetamani besieged these strongholds but no battles are documented, and then because of the inundation he returned to Memphis. It was here that the Delta rulers, headed by Pekrur, who is the only leader mentioned by name, came to surrender. Evidence from the inscriptions of Esarhaddon and Tanwetamani would suggest that Pekrur was one of the main political powers in the Delta at that time, now that Nekau was dead. Pekrur was centred at Pi-Soped, at the eastern extreme of the Delta, and he is constantly referred to as 'the chief of the East' (*p3 wr i3bt*).[124] Pekrur entreated Tanwetamani for clemency, a plea which was granted, and the rulers then returned to the Delta and sent gifts to the Kushite king in thanks.

The third Assyrian invasion in 663 BC

While these events were unfolding in the Delta, Ashurbanipal received a messenger from Egypt informing him of the loss of Memphis and the capitulation of the Delta leaders to Tanwetamani. Ashurbanipal quickly mobilised his forces and in 663 BC again set off for Egypt. It is thought that Psamtek accompanied the army, perhaps hoping he would be restored as an Assyrian vassal, although the Assyrian sources make no reference to him in the account of Ashurbanipal's journey to Egypt.[125]

With the arrival of the Assyrian army once again in Egypt, the various sources differ as to the extent of any clashes between the opposing forces, with the Harran tablets indicating that a battle occurred between the Assyrian troops and those of Tanwetamani. It is not certain where the encounter occurred, only that it took place north of Thebes. Prism A, which is largely derived from Prism B, simply states that Tanwetamani fled south to Kush without facing the Assyrian army. The Dream Stela makes no reference to an encounter with the Assyrian forces or to a retreat by the Kushites.[126] Meanwhile, in the Delta the rulers professed their loyalty to Ashurbanipal before the Assyrian army marched south to Thebes.

On reaching Thebes the Assyrians wrought great destruction on the city, pillaging it and deporting its inhabitants. This event was considered one of the great tragedies of the ancient world and was even mentioned by the Jewish prophet Nahum some fifty years later.[127] The Assyrian sources again provide a very detailed account of the booty that was taken back to Nineveh, plunder that included some of the greatest treasures from the temple of Amun, such as the doors of the temple and two obelisks of electrum as well as quantities of gold, silver, precious stones, clothing, linen, horses and even 'fantastic' animals. In contrast, the Dream Stela of Tanwetamani does not refer to a defeat or even a retreat by the Kushites from the Assyrian forces. After the plundering of Thebes there are then no further records of any Assyrian activity within Egypt and it is not certain when they finally left the country, and in what circumstances.

Despite the destruction of Thebes, Tanwetamani was still acknowledged as ruler in the city until his eighth regnal year (656 BC), as attested by inscriptions indicating that the Thebans continued to date by his reign. Inscriptions at Luxor temple records two priests being installed in Year 3 (662 BC) and the sale of some land involving a Chantress of Amun in Year 8; there are also references to Kushite officials remaining in Thebes.[128] Did Tanwetamani ever return to Egypt and try to take control once again? It seems not unlikely that a further attempt would have been made once the Assyrians had left, particularly as the Kushites had been claiming sovereignty and occupying Egypt for some eighty years. There is nothing in the Assyrian or Egyptian records to confirm this, but some later Greek sources indicate that a further attempt to recover the country may have occurred (see Chapter 3).

Notes

1 Török 1997: 98–101.
2 Smith 2013: 86.
3 Buzon et al. 2016: 286.
4 Morkot 2000: 129–35 and 2003a; Edwards 2004: 116–20; Buzon et al. 2016: 286.
5 Edwards 2004: 112; Smith 2013: 84.
6 Published by Dunham 1950 and re-assessed by Kendall 1999. For a discussion of the debates and controversies around the el-Kurru finds see Morkot 2000: 129–44.
7 Morkot 2003a: 151.
8 Edwards 2004: 118.
9 Aston 1996, 1999.
10 Morkot 2000: 129–44; Buzon et al. 2016: 287.
11 Török 1995.
12 Priese 1973; Trigger 1976: 140–44.
13 Kendall 1999.
14 Van Pelt 2013; Buzon et al. 2016.
15 Binder 2011; Spencer 2014.
16 Smith 2013.

17 This difficult-to-read inscription, carved on the existing fortress of Thutmose III at Semna, seems to record a rebellion relating to a Queen Katimala, a ruler of the early Napatan period. She, perhaps, reigned over an Egyptianised polity at the Second Cataract region early in the Third Intermediate Period. See Caminos 1994; Darnell 2006; Dodson 2012: 140–41. Contra a suggestion that Katimala was the daughter of Osochor and wife of Siamun then see Bennet 1999; Edwards 2004: 117.

18 Alara is usually regarded as the founder of the Kushite state and is mentioned in inscriptions of several later Napatan kings. See Morkot 2000: 156 for an inscription of King Natasen, who ruled around the middle of the fourth century BC, which refers to a plot against Alara.

19 Morkot 2000: 149–57.

20 Török 1997: 144.

21 Leahy 1992; Buzon et al. 2016: 296.

22 Török 1997: 109ff; Morkot 2000: 156–57.

23 Morkot 2000: 161.

24 JdE 41013; Leclant 1963: 74–78.

25 Morkot 2014: 5.

26 Priese 1972: 16–18; Kitchen 1996: 151; Török 1997: 149–50; Morkot 2000: 161; Ayad 2009: 16.

27 The first attestation of Amenirdis is alongside that of King Nimlot of Hermopolis, who is one of the kings who submitted to Piye, and listed on his Victory Stela (Dodson 2012: 144).

28 The sandstone stela of Piye was discovered broken and toppled from its base in the colonnaded court of the Temple of Amun at Gebel Barkal (Gebel Barkal Stela No. 26 of Year 3) and is now in Khartoum Museum (No. 1851). See Reisner 1931: 89–100; Priese 1972: 24–28; Gozzoli 2006: 51–53; Ritner 2009a: 461–64.

29 Priese (1972: 25–26) proposes that the sandstone stela (Gebel Barkal Stela No. 26 of Year 3) should be dated to Year 3, whilst Morkot (2000: 172–73) considers the possibility of the third stela (Gebel Barkal 29 + 30 of Years 3–4 [Cairo 47085 + Berlin 1068]) also being dated to Years 3 and 4. Contra Gozzoli 2006: 53; Dodson 2012: 146 n. 50.

30 Redford 1985; Kitchen 1996: 378–79; Morkot 2000: 207–8; Edwards 2004: 120.

31 Regnal dates for the Assyrian kings are taken from Brinkman 1977. For the Nimrud Wine Lists see Kinnier Wilson 1972.

32 See Dalley (1985) and Heidorn (1997) for discussions on the presence of Nubians and Nubian horses in Assyria during the reigns of several of the Assyrian kings. The main evidence comes from a group of administrative cuneiform tablets labelled the 'Horse Lists' (Dalley and Postgate 1984: Nos 99–118).

33 See comments by Smith (1998: 232) on the treatment of muscles in Assyrian reliefs, found on the side of a granite naos from Esna. For further examples of Nubian/Assyrian artefacts see Dalley 1985: 45 nn. 88–91.

34 For studies on the Assyrian Empire see Kuhrt 1995: vol. 2, 473–546; Van de Mieroop 2004: 232–52; Parpola 2004; Zamazalová 2011.

35 Aubin 2002: 44.

36 Tadmor 1966: 87.

37 Zamazalová 2011: 300.

38 Tadmor 1994: 18, 22; Zamazalová 2011: 300.

39 Spalinger 1974a: 296–97.

40 Morkot 2000: 264–65, 323 n. 19.

41 Some notable studies that discuss this evidence are Kitchen 1996, Török 1997, Morkot 2000 and Yoyotte 2012.

42 Statue inscription of Djedkhonsefankh from the temple of Luxor, CGC 559. See Lichtheim 1980: 13–18; Kuhrt 1995: vol. 2, 625; Kitchen 1996: 119, 289, 308.

43 Zamazalová 2011: 298–99.

44 See Morkot 2000: 208 and n. 12 for BM 84527, 84884 and Hall 1913: 290, Nos 2775, 2776, but note the revised Kushite chronology described on pp. 32–33.

45 *ANET* 285; this incident is described in Sargon's Great Summary Inscription, see Fuchs 1994: 219 and Lawson Younger 2000: 296.

46 Morkot 2000: 203; Zamazalová 2011: 321–22; Broekman 2015.

47 Tadmor 1958: 92–96.

48 Broekman 2015: 18.

49 Redford 1999; Broekman 2015: 24–25.

50 Redford 1999.

51 Kahn 2006c; Bányai 2013; Payraudeau 2014; Broekman 2015, 2017.

52 Kahn 2001: 6.

53 Kitchen 2009: 163.

54 Bányai 2013; Payraudeau 2014; Broekman 2015, 2017.

55 Broekman 2017: 13.

56 Dunham 1950; Bányai 2013: 76; Payraudeau 2014: 121; Broekman 2015: 21–22.

57 CG 42204 published by Legrain 1914: 12–13.

58 Broekman 2015: 23–24.

59 Payraudeau 2014: 121.

60 Including Aidan Dodson, Koen Donker van Heel, Karl Jansen-Winkeln, Claus Jurman, Olaf Kaper, René van Walsem, Gerard Broekman, Michael Bányai, Fredéric Payraudeau (see Broekman 2017: 13 n. 4).

61 Kahn 2004: 109.

62 Spalinger 1974a: 302; Kuhrt 1995: vol. 2, 495–97.

63 Tadmor 1966: 95–97; Morkot 2000: 212.

64 *ANET* 287–88; Kitchen 1996: 385 n. 815.

65 Tadmor 1966: 97; Kahn 2004: 109; Melville 2006: 346.

66 Spalinger 1974a: 322–24; Kahn 2001: 5.

67 See among others Hoffmeier 2003; Aubin (2002) devotes an entire book to this topic and incudes an extensive bibliography.

68 For example, see: Adams 1977: 264; Lloyd 1988: 104; Kitchen 1983: 245, 251; Kuhrt 1995: vol. 2, 477–78; Orlinsky 1972: 190; Japhet 1993: 990–91.

69 II Kings 19.35; Isaiah 37.36; II Chronicles 32.21; Aubin 2002: 119.

70 Aubin 2002: 120–24.

71 Aubin 2002: 140.

72 Spalinger 1978a: 36; Na'aman 1979: 65–66; Yurco 1980: 225–28; Kitchen 1983: 250.

73 Radiometric dating, palaeography and the historical record relating to the Siloam tunnel all converge about 700 BC (Frumkin et al. 2003).

74 For discussions of the reign of Taharqo see Spalinger 1978a: 22–33; Kitchen 1996: 387–91; Morkot 2000: 229–58; Kahn 2004; Dodson 2012: 162–65; Pope 2014.

75 Vernus 1975: 31.

76 For the Kawa Stela III (Ny Carlsberg Glyptotek Æ.I.N. 1707) see Macadam 1949:
    4–14, pls 5–6, also see Ritner 2009a: 527–35 for text, translation and discussion.
    For Kawa Stela VI (Khartoum SNM 2678 = Merowe Museum 53) see Macadam
    1949: 32–40, pls 11–12 and Ritner 2009a: 545–52.

77 Nimrud letter XII [ND. 2715], Saggs 1955: 127–30.

78 Redford 1992: 345 n. 122.

79 Morkot 2000: 262.

80 The 'Brook of Egypt' has been identified with modern Nahal Besor, a wadi in the
    Negev desert (Radner 2008: 306–7). But see an earlier interpretation by Hooker
    (1993) who recognised Nahal Besor as the traditional border of Egypt, but suggested
    on the basis of Assyrian texts that there was a shift in identification to the Wadi
    el-'Arish in the late eighth and early seventh centuries AD.

81 *ANET* 290; Spalinger 1974a: 299; Tadmor 1999: 58ff; Kahn 2006a: 252.

82 Tadmor 1966: 97–98; Kitchen 1996: 391.

83 *ANET* 302; Grayson 1975: 84, Chron. 1.16.

84 Tadmor 1966: 99.

85 Grayson 1975: 126, Chron. 14.20. Sha-amile has been identified as a city in southern
    Babylonia.

86 Bresciani 1964: 12; Kitchen 1996: 458–59; Gozzoli 2006: 264–71.

87 AGS 70; Starr 1990: 97 n. 82.

88 Borger 1956: 101–2.

89 The Assyrian records are those documented on Cylinder C (*ANET* 292), the Nahr
    el-Kalb stela (*ANET* 293), a victory stela from the city of Zenjirli (*ANET* 293) and
    a weathered stela from the city of Till Barsip.

90 Grayson 1975: 85–86, Chron. 1.23–8.

91 Zenjirli (Victory) Stela, *ANET* 293.

92 Spalinger 1974a: 303–4.

93 *ANET* 293; Spalinger 1974a: 308.

94 *ANET* 295.

95 For discussions of the political geography of Nubian Egypt see Fecht 1958: 112–19;
    Kitchen 1996: 395–98; Verreth 1999: 234; Morkot 2000: 273–75; Pope 2014: 256–74.

96 Kahn 2004: 123 n. 39.

97 Radner 2012.

98 Zawadski 1995; Radner 2012.

99 Spalinger 1974a.

100 Eph'al (1983: 88–106) examines warfare and military control in the ancient Near
    Eastern empires looking at the main forms of warfare, logistics with the possibility
    of strategically placed arsenals, and imperial communication.

101 Vernus 1975; Spalinger 1978a; Kahn 2004.

102 Parpola 1993: 287 n. 351.

103 2006a: 256.

104 2004: 104–6, 109–11.

105 Petrie 1917: pls 54, 25, 5.1.

106 Kitchen 1996: 235–36 n. 173.

107 See Kitchen 1996: 393 n. 877 and 395–97; Morkot 2000: 273–74.

108 SAA IV 88, Starr 1990: 102.

109 For discussions of these texts see amongst others Spalinger 1974b, Onash 1994
    and Borger 1996.

110 It is difficult to assess the size of ancient armies, and approximations of several hundred thousand for the seventh century BC seem high considering estimated population levels at that time. A figure approaching fifty thousand is suggested by Van de Mieroop (2004: 217), while Dupuy and Dupuy (1993: 10–11) as well as Aubin (2002: 50) suggest a figure sometimes approaching one hundred thousand men.

111 For the various suggested locations of Karbaniti see Verreth 1999: 238–39 and Van de Mieroop 2004: 23.

112 *ANET* 294.

113 Perdu 2004: 105.

114 Redford 1994; Revez 2004.

115 Morkot 2000: 279.

116 Spalinger 1974a: 325.

117 *ANET* 295.

118 The Assyrian records state that Bakennefi was ruler of Athribis, but include no further details. Ryholt (2004: 489) suggests that Inaros was the son of Bakennefi in the *Pedubastis Cycle*, a Demotic literary text concerning the fortunes of a military leader and hero named Inaros. Also see comments by Kitchen 1996: 393 n. 878; Spalinger 1974a: 318; Gozzoli 2006: 264–71.

119 Spalinger 1974b: 323.

120 Leahy 1984a: 43–45; Morkot 2000: 291–92.

121 Ex-Cairo JdE 48863 bears similarities to the Victory Stela of Piye. For the text, translation and discussion see Grimal 1981: vii–xv, 3–20, pls I–IV; Eide et al. 1994: 193–209 and Ritner 2009a: 566–73.

122 Kahn 2006a: 262.

123 Asheri et al. 2007: 353.

124 Ryholt 2004: 487–88.

125 *ANET* 295.

126 Spalinger 1974b: 324–25; Burstein 1984; Kahn 2006a: 264–65.

127 Nahum 3.8–10.

128 See Legrain 1906: 226–27; Kitchen 1996: 399 nn. 924–26; Morkot 2000: 297; Vittmann 2001a.

3

Psamtek 'the Great': reunification of Egypt

Psamtek I inherited the throne of the Kingdom of the West in 664 BC[1] following the death of his father, Nekau, by which time the Kingdom had become the most powerful state in the Delta. The territory he ruled extended from the Mediterranean coast south to Memphis and included sovereignty over the important cities of Athribis and Heliopolis. There is some uncertainty over the events of the early years of Psamtek's reign as much of the available information is based on Classical sources and derived from an oral tradition, transcribed centuries after the events. There are only isolated stelae that can be dated to this period, such as a hieratic stela set up at Memphis[2] relating to the sale of a tomb and dating to Year 8 of Psamtek.[3] However, such an example provides little relevant information that is able to assist with a reconstruction of this period.

The family of Psamtek

Individually, as is the case with the majority of other ancient Egyptian rulers, very little is known about Psamtek (Figure 3.1). He is known to have married Mehytenweskhet C, the daughter of the High Priest of Heliopolis, Harsiese S, and she is confirmed as being the King's Great Wife. Three children are attested for Psamtek: his only known son, Nekau, who was to succeed him as ruler, and two daughters, Nitiqret, who was to become God's Wife of Amun, and Mery-etneith B.[4]

Mehytenweskhet C may have accompanied her daughter Nitiqret to Thebes for her adoption as God's Wife of Amun. Although she is not mentioned on the Adoption Stela of Nitiqret (see below), she is referred to in the text of Ibi relating to her investiture as God's Wife in 639 BC. She is also named on Nitiqret's sarcophagus, and originally she was assumed to have been buried in a western extension to the tomb chapel of her daughter at Medinet Habu.[5]

3.1 Plaque with Horus name of Psamtek I. Discovered at Thonis-Heracleion.
Bronze. H. 11 cm; W. 7 cm (Maritime Museum, Alexandria).

There are inscriptions referring to her in the tomb chapel, and on a pillar in the 18th-Dynasty temple, the so-called Small Temple, at the same site.[6] However, it is possible that the chapel inscriptions may be merely a memorial as no burial equipment has been found there. Recently it has been questioned whether or not the God's Wives of the 23rd to 26th Dynasties were buried under the chapels of Medinet Habu. Based on a consideration of architecture, decoration programme and inscriptions in the chapels, the suggestion is that these buildings are merely memorial places for the God's Wives.[7]

Additionally, if Mehytenweskhet C is the mother of Nekau, the future King of Egypt, her departure from the court at Sais to travel to Thebes leaving behind Psamtek, her husband and the King of Egypt, as well as the crown prince appears rather puzzling. It would therefore seem that more importance was attached to her role as the mother of the future God's Wife of Amun than to her responsibilities at the court at Sais.[8] Possibly Mehytenweskhet's journey to Thebes may have originally been intended to be of short duration but she may have died there at a relatively young age. She may not even have been the biological mother of Nekau, but there again she does carry the title 'Great Royal Wife' and no other wife is attested for Psamtek.

Obstacles to reunification

Although the exact events following the expulsion of the Kushites from Egypt and the departure of the main Assyrian army are uncertain, a power vacuum developed in Egypt, a vacuum that Psamtek was able to exploit. It would seem that early in his reign he began the process of consolidating power within his domain and embarked on a phase of expansion eastwards into the neighbouring Delta states. At this juncture there is no way of knowing if Psamtek's territorial ambitions were limited to the north of Egypt or whether his ultimate aim was the reunification of the whole country. However, the unity of the two lands and the concept of divine kingship were ancient ideals and Psamtek would probably have aspired to live up to these notions.

Psamtek would have been confronted by a number of problems in his attempts at territorial expansion. At the beginning of his reign he was still an Assyrian vassal ruler and so would have to have been respectful of his overlord, even though the Assyrians were becoming increasingly involved with problems elsewhere in their empire. The chiefs of Ma and the autonomous rulers in the Delta would have been reluctant to relinquish jurisdiction over their territories to a neighbouring polity, although they may have been willing to join an alliance in opposition to the Assyrians. Thebes at this time was controlled by the priests of Amun-Re, many of whom were related to the Kushites, and among them a number of powerful individuals exercised power, chief of whom was Montuemhat. The Kushites, although having fled from Egypt in the face of the Assyrians, still retained the loyalty of the Thebans, and may have had lingering ambitions to control both Kush and Egypt once again.

Economically the fledgling Saite state was quite weak, and Psamtek sought to improve his economic base by establishing trading relations, particularly with the Aegeans and the Phoenicians. Possibly this was a case of rebuilding the trading network that earlier had been established by Bakenrenef. Psamtek moved away from the traditional Egyptian land trade routes to the Near East where he would have been beholden to the eastern governors for access to the Levant. Instead he started looking to the Mediterranean where an extensive trade network already existed and which he could access via the western Nile mouths. Foreign trade which originally had passed through Bubastis, Mendes and Tanis was now moving to Sais. It is also possible that the Nile feeding Tanis was silting up although the Pelusiac branch was navigable.

Military forces

Not least of the difficulties that Psamtek would have experienced was the military weakness of the Saite state, which, although stronger than its rivals in the Delta, was not yet powerful enough to impose its will throughout Egypt. Many of the Egyptian forces that Psamtek had at that time under his control seem to have originated from Libyan mercenaries, who had either settled in Egypt during the New Kingdom or had infiltrated into the country later. They inhabited the various principalities in the Delta, but the numbers in the Kingdom of the West may not have been sufficient to subjugate or indeed threaten the other territories of the Delta.[9]

The Assyrian sources for this period, the prisms and cylinders of Ashurbanipal, while providing an account of Ashurbanipal's second invasion of Egypt also point to where Psamtek was able to obtain additional military support. They make reference to Gyges, King of Lydia, who at that time was engaged in expanding his territory on the Anatolian peninsula. Gyges is chronicled as having a dream, the outcome of which influenced him to send an emissary to Nineveh taking gifts as well as a number of captive Cimmerian prisoners, who had been seized ravaging the Lydian countryside. Gyges was perhaps attempting to obtain Assyrian assistance in Lydia's battles with the Cimmerians. These gifts were specified as presents and not tribute as Assyria did not dominate Lydia nor was Lydia an ally of Assyria. Prism A then states: 'He (Gyges) placed his trust in his own strength and then became overbearing. So, he sent his troops to the aid of Psamtek, the king of Egypt, who had overthrown the yoke of my friendship.'[10]

The passage above states not only that Gyges supplied Psamtek with fighting forces but also that the earlier treaty between the Kingdom of the West and Assyria had been revoked by Psamtek. With Assyrian attention now focused on rebellions elsewhere in its empire it is, perhaps, not surprising that Assyria did not or was unable to respond to this declaration of independence by the Kingdom of the West, an outcome that Psamtek could well have anticipated and astutely timed. However, as indicated from the wording of the passage, Assyria was unhappy with this pronouncement. There is some uncertainty as to the dating of Prism A, so this source cannot be used to support a date for the alliance between Gyges and Psamtek.[11] Nor do Prism A or any of the other Assyrian prisms provide information as to the circumstances in which Gyges would have sent troops to Psamtek. It is possible that some form of trading agreement may have been established, although Gyges could well have been expressing his dissatisfaction with Assyria for not providing assistance in his struggles with the Cimmerians.

The Gyges incident is not mentioned in the *Babylonian Chronicles*, but Herodotus[12] states that, following the departure of the Nubians, Psamtek was driven from Sais into the Delta marshes by an alliance of Delta rulers, aggrieved with his support for the Assyrians.[13] Later he was told by an oracle that 'men of bronze' would come to his aid. While in the marshlands he met up with Ionian and Carian pirates who had been forced to put in to the coast of Egypt due to adverse weather conditions, and after befriending them persuaded them to enter his service. Some of these pirates were known to have worn bronze armour, either some form of sheet bronze or 'scale armour' made up of many individual pieces of iron or copper sewn on to leather.[14] According to Herodotus the mercenaries together with Psamtek's supporters in Egypt enabled him to defeat the Delta rulers and regain his throne.

Diodorus[15] also narrates these events, but in his version states that Psamtek had requested the Carian and Ionian mercenaries to assist him. It is possible that Psamtek began by recruiting casually arrived pirates and then, perhaps realising their worth, called upon further mercenaries from Caria and Ionia. An alternative passage is supplied by Polyaenus (VII, 3), who, writing in the second century AD, states that 'Psamtek overthrew Tementhes (i.e. Tanwetamani) the king of Egypt ... But Psamtek, who had Pigres of Caria with him ... having hired many Carians as mercenaries, he led them against Memphis.'

This brief passage has been interpreted by some Egyptologists[16] to mean that Tanwetamani had once again invaded Egypt and was defeated in battle by Psamtek and his mercenaries at Memphis. Further evidence to support these events is lacking, and it is possible that Polyaenus may have conflated the wars of Sais against Kush with those of the Delta kings.[17] However, as previously suggested it could well be that, following the withdrawal of the main Assyrian army from Egypt, and with Assyria involved with revolts elsewhere in its empire, Tanwetamani once again took the opportunity to return and invade Egypt.

Psamtek did take a number of measures to discourage further designs on Egypt by the Kushites. He dispatched to Thebes one of his senior military officers, General Djedptahiufankh, and he installed a garrison at Elephantine. He may also have sent a military expedition south into Kush to repel further attempts by the Kushites to intervene in Upper Egypt, or merely to suppress incursions by local tribesmen.[18]

Ionian and Carian mercenaries

Gyges seemingly possessed influence in Ionia and Caria and so was able to facilitate mercenary forces for Psamtek.[19] Egypt had been utilising Nubian, Asiatic and 'Libyan' mercenaries for centuries, and it had long been normal practice to settle foreigners and war captives on Egyptian soil and to enrol them in the army. Now perhaps for the first time there were Ionian Greek and Carian mercenaries in Egypt. These mercenaries were important in helping to meet

Psamtek's military requirements, particularly as they had a reputation as being an efficient fighting force.[20] In addition Psamtek may not have fully trusted his Egyptian forces and an independent mercenary force where he could pay for loyalty may have seemed a better alternative.

The small number of fragmentary sources relating to these mercenaries does not permit too detailed an examination of their activities and can lead to interpretations based on exceptional occurrences of mercenary activity, with much of the literary evidence being derived from Herodotus and Diodorus.[21] However, the mercenary forces would have had a crucial impact on the revitalisation of the Egyptian army, and although the Ionians and Carians were a separate fighting force, they were under the control of Egyptian commanders.[22]

It is difficult to speculate as to how many of these forces Psamtek commanded. Herodotus and Diodorus Siculus[23] state that at the time of Haaibra, a later Saite ruler, there were thirty thousand such troops in Egypt. Also, evidence from sources such as the Carian necropolis near Memphis, graffiti found throughout Egypt, funerary stelae at Saqqara and Carian inscriptions found in a number of Egyptian sanctuaries do support a substantial presence of mercenaries within the country.[24] However, it is likely that in the early days of Psamtek's rule the numbers were probably far fewer. There is evidence for one of these mercenary soldiers, a certain Pedon, the son of Amphinneos, from an Ionian inscription on a small basalt statue. The statue, although found near Priene in Ionia, is considered to be of Egyptian manufacture. The inscription, in archaic Ionian lettering, states that Psamtek gave Pedon 'a golden bracelet and an Egyptian "city" as a prize for his valour'.[25] This suggests that, following active duty as a mercenary, Pedon became a district governor, before then retiring to Ionia.

Herodotus (II, 154) also mentions that after the Greek and Carian mercenaries had helped Psamtek 'to gain the throne' they were rewarded with two sections of land, known as 'the camps' or *stratopeda*. These were located on either side of the Pelusiac branch of the Nile, although the actual location and foundation dates of these sites are uncertain.[26] The mouth of this particular Nile tributary traditionally served as a point of defence for Egypt against foreign invaders as it was the main access route from Egypt to the east,[27] so it is quite likely that this site was chosen in order to boost defences in the region. Herodotus continues with his account by stating that the mercenaries were well treated in the camps, that they were supplied with interpreters, and he describes how they came to settle in Egypt: 'They were the first foreigners to live in Egypt, and after their original settlement there, the Greeks began regular intercourse with the Egyptians, so we have accurate knowledge of Egyptian history from the time of Psammetichus onward'.

Expansion of Psamtek's rule in the Delta

It was not long after coming to the throne that Psamtek set about exerting his hegemony over the other Delta states. The Delta was an area where political unity had collapsed and principalities of Libyan origin ruled by the 'Great chiefs of Ma' (*wrw ꜥꜣ n Mꜥ*) were now the prominent model. How Psamtek achieved control over the other Delta states is not completely certain, although it is recognised that he favoured diplomacy over the use of military force but negotiations could well have been supported by the threat or use of military action.[28]

This expansion of the Saite state can be traced by examination of the numerous extant donation stelae, which record various allocations of land gifted for the support of religious institutions (Figure 3.2). This tradition originated in

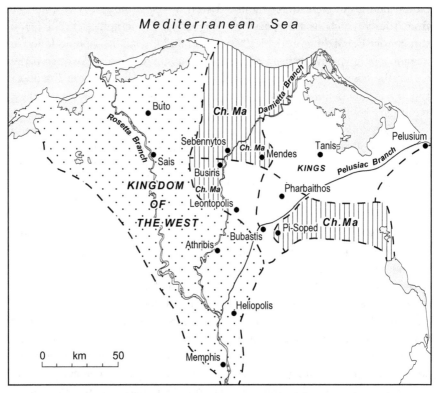

3.2 Delta region showing possible expansion of the Kingdom of the West: Kingdom of the West in 664 BC; Chiefdoms of the Ma at Sebennytos and Busiris subordinated to Psamtek early in his reign; chiefdom of Ma at Horbeit (Pharbaithos) recognised Psamtek by Year 8 (657 BC); by 656 BC the territories of Djanet (Tanis) and Per-Bastet (Bubastis) as well as the chiefdom of Pi-Soped and Mendes all appear to have submitted.

the New Kingdom, became common in the Third Intermediate Period but ceased later in the Saite Period.[29] Psamtek's name begins to appear on these donation stelae, rather than the names of local chiefs or kinglets as had previously been the case. An example of this reduction in status can be recognised in Busiris, the state immediately to the east of the Kingdom of the West which had been controlled by a 'Libyan' family since at least the reign of Piye. An inscription on a statue of Sheshonq F, a prince of Busiris, and dated to *c*. 670 BC, lists him as great chief of the Ma.[30] Pimay, a successor of Sheshonq F, bears the titles prince and mayor (*iry-pˁt ḥꜣty-ˁ*), servant of the God Osiris, Lord of Busiris, but he no longer bears the title of Great Chief of the Ma or army officer.[31]

Similarly, in Sebennytos, the chiefdom to the north of Busiris, and again adjacent to the Kingdom of the West a similar situation can be recognised. Akanosh A, a chief of Ma, is the earliest attested ruler of Sebennytos. His name appears on the Victory Stela of Piye, and his lineage can then be traced throughout the 25th Dynasty.[32] Akanosh B (perhaps his grandson) records on a donation stela, dating from Year 2 of the reign of Nekau I, that an endowment of fields was made by him to the Osirian triad of Per-Hebyt. Akanosh B disposed of the land within his chiefdom, and he used the royal iconography of the 'gift of the countryside'.[33] Akanosh C, the last known representative of this line of rulers, dedicated a statue to Osiris[34] which bears the cartouche of Psamtek I. Here Akanosh C is count and governor, god's servant of Onuris-Shu, Son-of-Re, Lord of Sebennytos, but he is no longer a Great Chief of the Ma and army officer, and significantly he now recognises the authority of Psamtek. Akanosh C retains the title of Lord of Sebennytos, so a compromise seems to have been reached between Sais and Busiris and illustrates how the descendants of the high chiefs of Ma were gradually being integrated into the Saite state. However, at this time Akanosh C is more than a mere mayor and could have been a member of the 'Council of Nobles' (*sḥ n srw*).

The 'Council of Nobles' was an organisation which existed during the period when Psamtek was consolidating his power within the Delta region and appears to have been a transitional arrangement before he was later able to impose a more absolute form of monarchy. The council, rather than being a consultative group, seems to have been an organisation in which the king had to defend his point of view and gain adherence, perhaps based on the model of a 'Libyan' tribal meeting. An inscription on the statuette of Djedptahiufankh[35] mentions 'pronouncing wise judgements in the council of nobles', and a further inscription on a fragmentary statue of Harsiese[36] states: 'in whose word the king trusts during the council of nobles'.[37]

Consequently, early in his reign both Busiris and Sebennytos, two of the four great chiefdoms of the Ma which bordered on the Kingdom of the West, recognised the sovereignty of Psamtek. The territory under the control of Sais now extended across more than half the Delta. For the chiefdom of Mendes, this transitional arrangement does not appear to have been used as here the title High Chief of the Ma suddenly disappears and is no longer attested during the 660s BC.[38]

Elsewhere in the Delta recognition of Psamtek as overlord may have taken longer. At Djanet (Tanis), Pedubast II remained in power for a number of years, and it is not certain when he submitted to Psamtek's rule. Nominally within the territory ruled by Djanet was the chiefdom of Ma at Horbeit (Pharbaithos), and here there is evidence that by Year 8 Pedikhons, the local ruler, had recognised Psamtek. A donation stela set up there by Pedikhons shows Psamtek in the relief rather than Pedikhons, although it was Pedikhons who originally made the donation and dedicated the stela.[39] With the defection of Horbeit, the territories of Djanet and Per-Bastet (Bubastis) as well as the chiefdom of Pi-Soped all appear to have submitted soon afterwards.[40]

There is little evidence of the Assyrian reaction to Psamtek's annexation of the Delta states. It is possible that Psamtek could have secured the authority of Assyrian troop-commanders, who may have still been stationed in the Delta, to help gain control of these territories. Psamtek could have assured Assyria that his actions were designed to help maintain order and loyalty for it; by such negotiations Psamtek was, of course, extending his own power base.[41] It is also possible that the Assyrians could have left or had very little presence in the Delta during this period, as they were faced with a civil war in Babylonia, and the pressure of a new movement of peoples along their northern borders. Finally, Psamtek could even have used his mercenary forces to help expel the remnants of the Assyrian troops, as the expression 'who had overthrown the yoke of my friendship' perhaps could imply.

Consolidation in Middle Egypt

Meanwhile in Middle Egypt Psamtek had strong allies, the rulers of the Herakleopolitan kingdom, first Petiese until Psamtek's fourth year and Somtutefnakht thereafter.[42] Petiese, son of Ankhsheshonq, is known from a statue in Stockholm where he bears the title 'Governor and Chief of Buto' (ḥȝty-ꜥ wr m Ntr).[43] Petiese was probably a descendant of a family of Delta chiefs who supported Psamtek, later becoming governor of the Herakleopolitan nome, and eventually being appointed 'Leader of the fleet' or 'Shipmaster' (ꜥȝ n mryt).[44]

Petiese married Tasherientaihet, considered to be a member of the Saite royal family, an older relative of Psamtek, and on chronological grounds possibly a daughter of Bakenrenef. Petiese and Tesherientaihet are suggested to be the parents of Somtutefnakht, although this is not universally accepted.[45] Information from both Papyrus Rylands IX[46] (col. 10.4) and the Nitiqret Adoption Stela

(l. 9) indicates that Somtutefnakht grew up at the court at Sais, and in Year 4 of Psamtek, Somtutefnakht was appointed 'Leader of the fleet' at Herakleopolis, succeeding his father, Petiese.[47]

The function of 'Leader of the fleet' can be deduced from a passage in Papyrus Rylands IX (col. 6.5) spoken by Psamtek: 'You inspected the Southern Land, you will (now) be responsible for its accounting' (*di.k mšd r p3 t3-rsy i.iry r di.t ip.w s irm.k*), implying that the role was associated with the collection of taxes.[48] The position can be equated to *rab kãrì* 'the master of the quay' a title first attested when the Assyrians administered Egypt, and whose primary task was to collect taxes for the Assyrians. However, the position of 'the master of the quay' may also have included some involvement with the administration of the city.[49] Papyrus Rylands IX and a statue of Somtutefnakht also indicate that Somtutefnakht was 'Overseer of the Priests of Heryshef' as his father had been before him.[50] The 'Southern Land' mentioned above is again explained in Papyrus Rylands IX (col. 5.13–15), and corresponds roughly to Upper Egypt, but has been interpreted as also including Middle Egypt as far as Memphis.[51]

Somtutefnakht dedicated a number of statues of himself in various temples across Egypt, extending from Thebes to the Mediterranean. The inscriptions on these statues provide an insight not only into his position at Herakleopolis but also into his relationship with the king, and in a wider context illustrate the tradition of self-presentation at this time. The paramount status of Somtutefnakht and possible examples of archaism can be demonstrated from the inscription on the base of a statue in Richmond, Virginia (51–19–4 + 64–60),[52] where the titles 'Count of Counts, Princes of Princes, Chief of Chiefs, Noblest of Courtiers' are inscribed. Also of interest are the epithets that follow these titles which demonstrate the privileged relationship that Somtutefnakht enjoyed with the king: 'a member of the inner circle of the king, one to whom the king speaks in private ... who loves his lord and who is beloved of his lord ... who is dressed as a pure one of the king, in the king's own cloth'.[53] This range of titles and epithets cited together portray a senior figure in Psamtek's administration, a trusted confidant and administrator. The other seven known statues and a statuette provide little in the way of further information about Somtutefnakht, but their discovery in centres both north and south of Herakleopolis suggests that he had influence both in the Delta and the Nile Valley.[54]

The apparent prominence of Herakleopolis at this period is perhaps explained from a commercial viewpoint, in that the city, situated between the Nile and the Faiyum, not only offered river access throughout Egypt but was also at the centre of a number of caravan land routes to the western desert oases.[55] One of the titles that Somtutefnakht possessed was 'Overseer of Northbound and Southbound River Traffic' (*imy-r ḥd ḫnt*), which was often linked with 'Overseer of the Southern Land' (*imy-r p3 t3-rsy*), indicating the commercial and administrative importance of the city. Perhaps Herakleopolis, a key 'Libyan' centre and the administrative focus of the Faiyum, can be viewed as a balance or bulwark between Upper and Lower Egypt, as during the Kushite period Herakleopolis was a vassal of Kush and had resisted Saite annexation.[56]

Upper Egypt and God's Wife of Amun

By about Year 8, with the Delta under his control and an able ally in Middle Egypt, Psamtek was able to turn his attention to Upper Egypt. In the south he achieved his greatest success, with the adoption of his eldest daughter, Princess Nitiqret, as heir to the powerful position of God's Wife of Amun. In doing so he was able to return the Thebaid to Egyptian (rather than Kushite) central royal authority and strengthen his claim to the kingship of Egypt, with the legitimacy conferred by close association with the Amun cult.

The office of God's Wife of Amun[57] first came to prominence during the 18th Dynasty and the title reflects the notion of the marriage of Amun to a mortal woman. Her function was that of consort to the deity in various temple ceremonies, and, similarly to the higher priests, she was able to enter the sanctuary of the god. This female priestly title was held by members of the royal family and was endowed with its own domain which created an economic powerhouse for whoever controlled it. The role continued during the New Kingdom, and by the time of Ramesses VI the holder of the office was a celibate daughter of either the King or the High Priest of Amun.

With the collapse of the New Kingdom, Pharaonic administration was centred in the north of Egypt, with the south being under the authority of the Chief Priest of Amun at Thebes. During the 23rd Dynasty the political role of God's Wife of Amun was elevated when Osorkon III appointed his daughter Shepenwepet I to this position. The God's Wife of Amun was now at the head of a college of priestesses or votaresses.[58] She exercised significant secular, economic and spiritual power, and would therefore have had considerable political influence.[59] At this same time the position of First God's Servant of Amun disappears from prominence and may even have been left vacant in the second half of the eighth century BC. The affairs of the cult of Amun were then conducted by the Second, Third and Fourth God's Servants of Amun together with the God's Wife.[60] The God's Wife was now the celibate daughter of the King, with each God's Wife succeeding by adoption. The office could not, therefore, produce a schismatic dynasty as the priesthood of Amun had been able to during the New Kingdom. In addition, the position could be used by the northern-based kings to maintain some authority in Thebes. The estates and affairs of the God's Wife were managed largely by chief stewards, whose importance and wealth is demonstrated by the very large size of their tombs.[61]

Later, with the extension of Kushite authority into southern Egypt, Kashta seemingly persuaded the incumbent God's Wife, Shepenwepet I, to adopt his daughter, Amenirdis I, as her heir. The office of God's Wife then continued under Kushite control with Amenirdis I adopting Piye's daughter, Shepenwepet II, and she in turn adopting Taharqa's daughter, Amenirdis II.[62] Meanwhile, the high priesthood was revived, but its power base diminished by stripping its holders of the military and civic authority they had previously possessed.[63] The high priests were now Kushites, appointed from within the ruling family, with Haremakhet, son of Shabaqo, becoming the first High Priest of Amun to hold office at Karnak in some forty years.[64] Haremakhet's son, Harkhebi, was later to take over this role, and served as High Priest of Amun until at least Year 14 of Psamtek. The reduction in power of the high priesthood is attested by the order of the list of Thebans who were later to make donations to Nitiqret, with the influential Montuemhat, the Fourth God's Servant of Amun, together with his family preceding the First God's Servant of Amun.[65]

This was the situation in Thebes during the early 660s BC when Psamtek was consolidating his position in the Delta, and when, presumably, major negotiations were being conducted between Sais and Thebes for Psamtek's daughter to be adopted as next in line to the office of God's Wife of Amun. The sources that describe this important event are a damaged red granite stela (Nitiqret Adoption Stela)[66] and a series of reliefs in the temple of Mut at Karnak.[67]

Nitiqret Adoption Stela

The Adoption Stela is recognised as one of the more important records surviving from the Saite Period documenting the taking of power by Psamtek in Upper Egypt, nine years after ascending the throne at Sais. The stela, which was originally positioned in the first court of the Amun temple at Karnak, is 1.45 m wide, and although now damaged would originally have stood some 2.90 m tall. It would have been an imposing monument and a prominent symbol of both the establishment of Saite authority at Thebes and Psamtek's recognition of the authority of Amun.[68] Conspicuous display of the stela in the temple would have ensured public and divine acceptance of the decree.[69] The stela is a record of one of the important decisions of Psamtek's reign and had significant consequences for the whole of Egypt, so much so that it is possible that copies were set up in other temples throughout Egypt.[70]

The beginning of the text of the stela is lost, but the first recognisable section is a speech by Psamtek in the royal court, at Sais or possibly Memphis, presumably after the negotiations with Thebes relating to the adoption had reached a satisfactory conclusion. Psamtek is using this opportunity to formally declare the legitimacy of his right to be king of Upper and Lower Egypt to his courtiers, as well as affirming his moral integrity in relation to his conduct towards the gods:[71]

> [Psamtek has dedicated his daughter Nitiqret as God's Wife to Amun] in order to play the sistrum [before] his face in […] to see his goodness, since he knows him to be weighty of wrath. I acted for him through the desire to act for my father. I am his first-born son, whom the father of the gods made successful in performing the divine rituals. He begat him for himself to satisfy his heart. I have given to him my daughter specifically to be the God's Wife. I have endowed her better than those who existed before her. Surely, then, he will be pleased by her worship and protect the land of the one who gave her to him. (ll. 1–3)

In the next section of the text, Psamtek recognises the inviolability of the office, as the Nubian ruler Kashta had done a century previously. He clearly states that he does not wish to remove the present god's wife, Shepenwepet II, or her heiress, Amenirdis II, from this agency, but merely have his daughter adopted as next in line.[72] He will respect the rules of succession and states that he would not do anything against Maat:

> Now, I have heard that a king's daughter is already there, of the Horus 'Exalted of Daidems', the good god Taharqa, the justified, whom he hath given to his sister to be her eldest daughter and who is there as Divine Votaress. I shall not do the very thing that should not be done and expel an heir from [her] seat, because I am a king who loves Maat, while my special abomination is falsehood, being a son and protector of his father, who has seized the inheritance of Geb and united the two parts (of Egypt) as a youth. Thus, I shall give her (Nitiqret) to her (Amenirdis II) to be her eldest daughter likewise, as she (Amendiris II) was made over to the sister of her father. (ll. 4–5)

The courtiers respond to Psamtek's speech and after asserting the usual respectful endorsements they state that Nitiqret is to receive 'the beautiful name' (*rn-nfr*) of Shepenwepet. This name was previously borne by two god's wives of different dynasties and can probably be seen as another diplomatic move on the part of Psamtek aimed at reassuring Theban sensibilities.[73]

Consequently, in Year 9, the first month of Akhet, on the 28th day (2 March 656 BC) Nitiqret left the king's palace in the north: at Memphis or possibly Sais, as the actual departure point is not stated. She travelled south up the Nile, with the description on the stela describing her procession as a fleet of richly fitted-out vessels under the command of Somtutefnakht. The voyage appears to have been an elaborately organised event with the nomarchs of the various districts through which the flotilla sailed being responsible for the provisioning[74] of the party: 'Her supplies were obtained from each nomarch who was in charge of his provisions and was furnished with every good thing, namely bread, beer,

'The great boat of Sais'

'The great boat of Amun carrying gold'

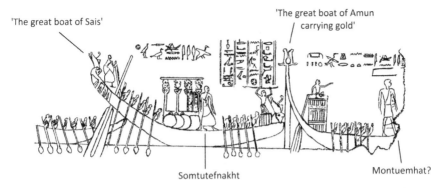

Somtutefnakht

Montuemhat?

3.3 Relief inscribed on blocks from the temple of Mut at Karnak, the so-called 'Pi(ankh)y blocks' depicting the arrival of a flotilla at Thebes conveying the God's Wife of Amun.

oxen, fowl, vegetables, dates, herbs, and every good thing; and one would give (way) until she reached Thebes' (l. 10).

The impressive flotilla passing up the river must have been a remarkable spectacle for the bystanders along the banks of the Nile, and it has been suggested that such a display would have helped to unite the north and south of the country in a 'symbolic' manner.[75] After sixteen days the party arrived at the quay at Thebes, and Nitiqret was welcomed by a great crowd of cheering well-wishers who brought with them oxen, fowl and abundant provisions intended for the new arrival. There is a tone of celebration and national jubilation woven within the text, while it also stresses the importance of this event for the whole of Egypt.

Further evidence for the arrival of the flotilla at Thebes is attested in a series of blocks excavated from the temple of Mut at Karnak, the so-called 'Pi(ankh)y blocks' (Figure 3.3). Although only one register survives in its entirety, there may formerly have been three registers portraying the fleet, with perhaps as many as twenty ships depicted. The original suggestion that the scenes illustrated on these blocks portray the arrival of Nitiqret at Thebes[76] has recently been challenged. The alternative interpretation proposes that the name of Somtutefnakht is a later addition to the scene, being cut in a different style from the reliefs depicting the ships. The conclusion then is that the scenes date back to the reign of Piye and record the arrival of the God's Wife Amenirdis I at Thebes. Later Somtutefnakht changed this representation into an account of the arrival of Nitiqret, by prominently adding his own name to the original inscription.[77]

After disembarking, Nitiqret was escorted to the temple of Amun where she was welcomed by Amun and the other gods, probably in the form of a spoken oracle. Importantly, with the Thebans now accepting Nitiqret they were also accepting Psamtek. After her presentation to Amun, Nitiqret was proclaimed to the reigning God's Wife, Shepenwepet II, and her heiress, Amenirdis II:

> Now after she came to the God's Wife Shepenwepet, the latter saw her and was pleased with her; she loved her more than anything and made over to her the testament which her [Shepenwepet's] father and her mother had executed for her; and her eldest daughter Amenirdis, daughter of King Taharqo, justified did likewise. Their bidding was done in writing: 'Herewith we give you all our property in country and in town. You shall be established upon our throne firmly and enduringly till the end of eternity'. (ll. 16, 17)

Shepenwepet had therefore given Nitiqret her official approval, but this was more than a mere verbal gesture as the 'testament' or 'transfer document' (*imyt-pr*),[78] the legal document that Shepenwepet had received from her father and her adopted mother (the God's Wife of Amun, Amenirdis I), was now endorsed in favour of Nitiqret. The *imyt-pr* unambiguously transferred the land-holdings with their respective rights to Nitiqret. Similarly, Amenirdis II, the successor to Shepenwepet, also signed her acceptance, and the document was witnessed by the various ranks of the temple priesthood.[79]

This extensive and detailed list of land and daily foodstuffs that were part of Nitiqret's endowment are itemised on the Adoption Stela and take up nearly half of the preserved text. Psamtek claimed that he had endowed Nitiqret 'better than those who were before her', which seems quite probable judging by the sizeable inventory detailed on the stela. The list comprises 1400 arourae of land (946 acres) from four nomes in the Delta, and the unspecified donor is assumed to be Psamtek, as here his control of land-holdings would have been secure. A further 1900 arourae (1,284 acres) of land-holdings from seven nomes in Upper Egypt were also assigned to Nitiqret, but here the benefactor is specified as being the King.[80] Interestingly, these fields are scattered over the northern section of Upper Egypt only, perhaps indicating that Psamtek was not yet secure in his position to be able to donate land in southern Egypt, as he was only just beginning to exercise control there. This would again appear to be an example of diplomacy on the part of Psamtek and indicative of his cautious policy towards the Theban administration.

The land-holdings of Shepenwepet II and Amenirdis are also listed on the stela as being made over to Nitiqret, but are not included in the itemised list of donations. It is probable that these estates remained under the control of Shepenwepet II and Amenirdis during their lifetimes. Among the detailed list of daily foodstuffs donated to Nitiqret are quantities from Psamtek himself, from the nomes, from the temples in Egypt and also from specified members of the clergy at Thebes. Conspicuously, the prominent Kushite officials at Thebes are also listed as contributors to this dowry: the Fourth God's Servant of Amun, Mayor of Thebes and Governor of Upper Egypt, Montuemhat; his eldest son, inspector of priests at Thebes, Nesptah B, and Montuemhat's wife, Udjarenes, are among the contributors. Similarly, the Kushite High Priest of Amun, Harkhebi, and the Third Priest of Amun, Padiamunnebnesuttawy, provided various foodstuffs on a daily and monthly basis.[81] Politically, it could appear that the officials were being penalised or alternatively made concessions based on negotiations, having to make this continuous payment to maintain their positions in Thebes. This would also be a demonstration of loyalty to the new regime, perhaps necessary after previously being so closely allied to the Kushite rulers.[82]

Montuemhat

Montuemhat,[83] the most important of the Theban officials listed on the stela, first achieved high office under Taharqo, and his subsequent career continued under the Assyrians when in *c.* 671 BC he was appointed *šarru*[84] (Figure 3.4). His role now continued into the Saite era, by which time he had become a powerful and influential figure in Upper Egypt, sometimes even being considered its *de facto* ruler. Ashurbanipal records him as the 'King of Thebes' (*Mantimeanhê Niʾ*) on the Rassam Cylinder.[85] Although he was based at Thebes, the territory that Montuemhat controlled extended from Elephantine in the south to Hermopolis in the north. The fact that he survived the Assyrian invasions and was still in office when the Kushites were finally expelled from Egypt is testament to his political acumen and long experience of Theban politics, and is a remarkable story of tenacity in the face of political turmoil. It seems likely that Montuemhat would have been party to the preliminary negotiations with Sais concerning the adoption of Nitiqret to the office of God's Wife of Amun prior to the agreement of terms, as specified on the Adoption Stela and the *imyt-pr*. Little is known about the terms of these discussions, although it would probably have been part of the agreement that Nitiqret was to serve only after the deaths of Shepenwepet II and Amenirdis II.

Montuemhat was born into one of the major Theban families, with his father, Nesptah, being Mayor of Thebes and a God's Servant of Amun before him, these titles having been handed down within the same family for generations from father to son. Although he was only Fourth God's Servant of Amun, the combination of a series of priestly titles that Montuemhat possessed, which included 'Inspector of Priests' (*šḏ ḥmw-nṯr*), 'Overseer of the Priests of the Temples' (*imy-r ḥmw-[nṯr] m ḥwwt*) and 'Overseer of Priests of all the gods in the Southern and Northern lands' (*imy-r ḥmw-nṯr nṯrw nb(w) tꜣ-rsy tꜣ-mḥw*), suggests that Montuemhat directed all the Theban clergy.[86] Collectively, all these titles indicate the pre-eminent position that Montuemhat enjoyed within the Theban hierarchy.

3.4 Seated group statue of Montuemhat on the right and his son, Nesptah B, on the left. Black granite. H. 34 cm (Egyptian Museum, Cairo).

Funerary cones from the tomb of Montuemhat (TT 34) attest to him having had three wives, the first of these being Neskhons, as it was her firstborn son, Nesptah B, who became heir to Montuemhat's several offices. Montuemhat also married a Nubian princess, Udjarenes, whose father was the 'King's son Pi(ankh)y-har'.[87] Montuemhat may have entered into this marriage as a demonstration of his loyalty to the Kushites under whose rule he had originally entered office. The union would not only have strengthened his family ties to the ruling regime but would also have the benefit of helping to promote his personal ambitions. Additionally, it would probably have suited the Kushite ruler, Taharqo, in reinforcing his position in Thebes, as not only were the God's Wives of Amun Kushite but now one of the most important of its officials was related to him through marriage.[88]

Udjarenes is represented in the first and second courts of Montuemhat's tomb by a niche statue, in which she sits next to her husband, and she is further depicted in a relief in which she is shown accompanying Montuemhat in his pilgrimage to Abydos. Such prominent portrayals in the tomb suggest that she

3.5 Tomb of Montuemhat (TT34) at the Asasif at Thebes showing the sunken court.

was the most important of his three wives as Montuemhat's other wives are not given anything like this same status. It is Udjarenes who is listed on the Adoption Stela as having to provide '100 deben of bread in the course of every day', and, although the smallest of the Kushite contributions, it was a permanent daily commitment, while Montuemhat's contribution of '200 deben of bread, 5 hin of milk, 1 cake, 1 bundle of herbs in the course of every day; monthly due: 3 oxen and 5 geese' was a greater pledge.[89]

The tomb of Montuemhat at Thebes is one of largest and most sumptuous tombs on the west bank of Thebes, although today it has suffered considerable destruction and is poorly preserved[90] (Figure 3.5). The tomb has an extensive substructure consisting of two large sunken courts and more than fifty subterranean rooms. It is decorated with exceptionally fine reliefs and displays a number of architectural innovations such as a second additional court, pylons at the entrance to the tomb and large elegant representations of Montuemhat.[91]

Montuemhat's lengthy biographical inscription is not in his tomb but is recorded on the walls of a chamber in the temple of Mut at Karnak. This biography relates mainly to how he claimed to have restored and rebuilt the great temples of Thebes, following the Assyrian destruction of the city in 663 BC, and how he 'placed Upper Egypt on the path of its god, when the whole land was in upheaval'.[92] He also left a large number of high-quality statues, often recognised as some of the masterpieces of the Kushite–Saite Period.[93] However, the inscriptions on the statues provide little in the way of historical detail, and again no mention is made of his role in the adoption of Nitiqret.

Montuemhat was retained in office by Psamtek, and his extensive political experience would have been an asset to Psamtek in the new political order of Upper Egypt. Having Montuemhat and his colleagues loyal to Psamtek within the administration would have been more beneficial than having factions agitating in the background. Similarly, many of the other Theban dignitaries seem to have initially retained their posts. The Saite Oracle Papyrus (47.218.3) dated to Year 14 of Psamtek records the petition of a man named Pemou who requests a favour on behalf of his father, Harsiese, who wished to leave the service of Amun for that of Montu Re-Horakhty. The petition was granted and the events recorded on a papyrus that was witnessed by fifty priests.[94] Many of these priests are known to have still been active at the time of Nitiqret's adoption in 656 BC.

Montuemhat is known to have taken part in this oracular ceremony in 651 BC, and there is evidence of him sending a mining expedition to the Wadi Gasus in Year 16 of Psamtek (649 BC).[95] P. Vienna 12.002 attributes the titles of Fourth God's Servant of Amun to Nesptah B, Montuemhat's son, one year later in Year 17,[96] suggesting that Montuemhat was now dead. A second papyrus, P. Vienna 12.003, dated to Year 25 of Psamtek records Nesptah's name followed by $m3^c$-$ḥrw$ indicating that Nesptah B himself had died by Year 25.[97] Thereafter, Montuemhat's family disappears from the leading offices at Thebes.

Consolidation of power

As other Upper Egyptian officials died or left office they were gradually replaced by Northerners, many being members of Psamtek's own court. Nesnaiu,[98] a senior Saite dignitary, was appointed mayor of eight separate cities in the Delta and Upper Egypt, including Edfu and el-Kab where he bore the title of 'governor' ($ḥ3ty$-^{c}). In Thebes he was merely a rsw here translated as 'observer', with the role being probably that of monitoring affairs, as Saite control was not yet secure at this time.[99]

From the outset high stewards of northern origin such as Ibi, Pabasa and Padihorresnet were appointed by Nitiqret, or were appointed on her behalf.[100] Harkhebi, the High Priest of Amun, who is last attested in the Saite Oracle Papyrus of 651 BC, appears not to have been replaced, although it is possible there may have been some unattested successors.[101] The shipmasters of Herakleopolis were gradually marginalised and these positions do not appear to have survived past the seventh century BC,[102] perhaps reflecting the growing

3.6 Scene from the west wall of the tomb of the Vizier Nespakashuty D (TT 312) at Deir el-Bahri, Thebes, showing the Abydos pilgrimage. The ritual *nsmt*-boat, carrying the deceased and his wife Ketykety, is being towed by a sailing boat (not shown). (Brooklyn Museum of Art, New York).

importance of Naukratis as the Saite port. Similarly, the position of Vizier of Upper Egypt was dissolved or fell into abeyance, and noticeably there is no mention of that role in Papyrus Rylands IX, with the last holder of this title appearing to be Nespakashuty D[103] (TT 312) (Figure 3.6).

The tomb of Nespakashuty can be dated to about 656–650 BC as Nespakashuty signed the Oracle Papyrus as the fourth witness in 651 BC, in Year 14 of Psamtek, indicating that he was then still in office. Other than vizier, Nespakashuty's titles included 'Overseer of Priests of Amun-Re, King of Gods' (*mr ḥmw-nṯr 'Imn-rˁ nswt nṯrw*), 'Overseer of Upper Egypt' (*mr Šmˁw*) and 'Overseer of the City' (*mr niwt*), revealing that he was an important official in Thebes at that time. Following the demise of Nespakashuty the functions of the vizier were probably then executed by other officials such as the Governor of Thebes and the Chief Steward of the God's Wife.[104]

Progressively, Psamtek's formal acceptance as overlord in the southern part of Egypt was being translated into real power, but the numbers of officials being replaced may have been limited. There is no evidence of a massive transfer of Delta people to Upper Egypt, more a paced installation of selected Saite loyalists. Moreover, the administration of Egypt included men from all areas of the country, and it would seem that Psamtek was careful not to antagonise the status quo, illustrating his deliberate internal political strategy and shrewd diplomacy.[105] By Year 26 with the appointment of Ibi to be Chief Steward of the God's Wife, there appears to be little remaining opposition to Psamtek's rule. Finally, in Year 31 the last known evidence for a 'chief of the Meshwesh', once a powerful local ruler, is to be found in the role of a police official in the vicinity of Herakleopolis.[106]

Succession of the God's Wives

It is not known at what date Shepenwepet died or when Nitiqret was inducted into the office, but it is unlikely to have been later than 639 BC, Year 26 of Psamtek, on the basis of the autobiography of her Chief Steward, Ibi.[107] It is also uncertain what happened to Amenirdis II – did she ever actually occupy the office of God's Wife; did she meet an unnatural or premature death, or was she excluded from the post once Nitiqret became established at Thebes, contrary to the terms of the Adoption Stela? No known tomb or funerary artefacts have been found in the Theban area. It is quite possible that Amenirdis returned to Kush, and the suggestion has been put forward that she became the wife of Montuhotep, the vizier and son-in-law of Taharqo.[108] On the basis of an inscription from a stela of Aspelta, a later Kushite ruler, found at Gebel Barkal, she is suggested to have had a daughter, Nasalsa, who was the mother of Aspelta's mother.[109] Finally, she could have remained in Thebes, retaining a junior position in the college of Amun, but never becoming God's Wife.[110]

In c. 595 BC, Year 1 of the reign of Psamtek II, Nitiqret adopted Ankhnesneferibre, the daughter of Psamtek II, as her heir apparent to the position of God's Wife. Nitiqret stayed on as God's Wife until her death in 586 BC, having retained her position for some seventy years, her death being recorded on the stela of Ankhnesneferibre (JdE 36907). The office of God's Wife remained in Saite hands until the Persian conquest in 525 BC when the role was abolished.[111]

Conclusion

Thus, within a period of some nine years, through what would appear to be largely peaceful means, Psamtek I had imposed his will throughout Egypt. In the Delta, he had by his eighth or ninth year, either gradually removed the local rulers or entered into interim alliances with them, in which he established himself as the dominant partner. In Middle Egypt, he had promoted relations with the powerful Herakleopolitan family of Petiese by his fourth year, and by his ninth year he gained the recognition and adherence of Thebes and Upper Egypt, by the adoption of his daughter as God's Wife of Amun. Accordingly, by 656 BC, therefore, it can be said that he had completed the political reunification of Egypt and he could justifiably regard himself as 'King of Upper and Lower Egypt, Lord of the Two Lands, Wahibre, Son of Re, Psamtek'. However, overall consolidation of his power and full reintegration of the state of Egypt was some time away.

Notes

1   For foundations of day-exact chronology see Depudyt 2006b.
2   Louvre C 101.
3   Malinine 1975; Jansen-Winkeln 2014b: vol. 1, 67; Muhs 2016: 186, 204.
4   Vittmann 1975: 376–77; Dodson and Hilton 2004: 244.
5   Ayad 2009: 26.
6   Hölscher 1939, 1954: 23–28; Dodson and Hilton 2004: 246.
7   Koch 2017: 243–44.
8   Leahy 1996: 162.
9   Lloyd 1983: 284, 309–10.
10 Prism A, col. II, 113–15; Luckenbill 1927: 298.
11 Spalinger 1976: 133–37; Younis 2002.
12 Herodotus II, 152.
13 Perhaps a mythological allusion: see Blouin 2014: 285–88. The mention of the marshes may relate to them being considered places of resistance where mythological and historical figures regenerated themselves, sheltered from external aggression. In Egyptian mythology, Horus hid from Seth on the floating island of Chemnis, not far from Buto. This reappearance of the mythological story now being cited as 'fact' may be an attempt to emphasise Psamtek's claim to the throne.
14 Boardman 1999: 114.
15 Diodorus I, 66.1–7.
16 See Sauneron and Yoyotte 1952; De Meulenaere 1965; Burstein 1984.
17 Spalinger 1976: 138.
18 Inscription on a block found at Edfu. See Sauneron and Yoyotte 1951: 201 n. 3; Kitchen 1996: 405–6; Bonnet and Valbelle 2006: 153.
19 Roebuck 1959: 50ff.
20 Lloyd 1983: 279–88.
21 Smoláriková 2006; Iancu 2016: 15.
22 For a discussion on mercenaries during the Late Period see Austin 1970: 15–22; Smoláriková 2006 with references p. 245 n. 1; Kahn 2007a and Iancu 2016.
23 Herodotus II, 163; Diodorus Siculus I, 68.2–5.
24 Masson et al. 1978; Vittmann 2001b: 40–41 and 2003: 161–79; Iancu 2016: 22.
25 Inscription SEG 37.994, 39.1266. See Masson and Yoyotte 1988: 171–80; Vittmann 2003: 203–5.
26 Cf. Smoláriková 2006.
27 Sullivan 1996: 186.
28 Agut-Labordère 2013: 975.
29 Ritner 2009a: 3.
30 JdE 25572. See Maspero 1884: 93; Kitchen 1996: 287 n. 250; Yoyotte 2012: 74–76.
31 Kitchen 1996: 400 n. 930; Yoyotte 2012: 68–69, H.
32 Perdu 2004: 102.
33 Perdu 2004: 98; Agut-Labordère 2013: 975–76.
34 Cairo CG 567.

35 JdE 36949 see De Meulenaere 1965; Josephson and el-Dalmaty 1999: 87–90, pl. 37.

36 Phil. Univ. Mus. E 16025; De Meulenaere 1982.

37 Agut-Labordère 2013: 969–71.

38 De Meulenaere et al. 1976: 173.

39 Louvre C. 297; Revillout 1892: 237–38; Yoyotte 2012: 10, nos 22, 31.

40 Kitchen 1996: 402.

41 Kitchen 1996: 402 n. 934.

42 De Meulenaere 1964: 99–101.

43 Medelhavsmuseet NME 081; De Meulenaere 1956: 251–53; Perdu 2006: 152–53.

44 Agut-Labordère 2013: 982.

45 See Kitchen (1996: 402–3) and Morkot (2000: 275), but contra Leahy (2011: 219) who considers that Somtutefnakht may have been a ward rather than the biological offspring of Petiese and Tesherientaihet.

46 Attempts to trace the political history of Middle Egypt during this period are frustrated by the scarcity of local monuments; however, the discovery of nine papyri in the ruins of el-Hibeh, and later sold to the John Rylands Library in Manchester, shed some light on this period. Of these papyri it is P. Rylands IX, known also as 'The Petition of Petiese', which has attracted the attention of Egyptologists. See Griffith 1909 and Vittmann 1998.

47 Kitchen 1996: 235; Leahy 2011.

48 Agut-Labordère 2013: 983.

49 Spalinger 1974a: 314–16.

50 For P. Rylands IX see Spiegelberg 1911: 176. The statue of Somtutefnakht known as the Sharia Wagh el-Birket statue was seen at Cairo in 1905 by Spiegelberg, and later published by him (Spiegelberg 1915: 112).

51 Morkot and James 2009: 30. Agut-Labordère (2013: 981) considers that Psamtek sought to merge Middle and Upper Egypt into a single administrative region known as the 'Southern Land', ignoring the traditional division into nomes. However, Pope (2014: 248 nos 97–99) suggests that this region does not include Middle Egypt.

52 An 'alabaster' statue of a man in a cross-legged position in the Museum of Fine Arts, Richmond.

53 Leahy 2011: 210.

54 Leahy 2011.

55 Mokhtar 1983: 18–25.

56 Pope 2014: 235–55.

57 For discussions of God's Wife of Amun see Robins 1993: 149–56 and Ayad 2009.

58 Various titles are used by the God's Wives and their heirs. 'God's Wife' (*ḥmt-nṯr*) designates the senior member of the Amun clergy, whilst the meaning of the title 'God's Adoratrix' (*dwȝt-nṯr*) is more problematic, on occasions implying the heir to the position of God's Wife, but this title is sometimes also used by a reigning God's Wife. The final title 'God's Hand' (*ḏrt-nṯr*) is related to that of God's Wife, but again the distinction between the titles is not clear (Dodson 2002: 180–1; Ayad 2009).

59 Caminos 1964: 97.

60 Vittmann 1978: 66–100; Kitchen 1996: 197, 480; Broekman 2011: 66.

61 Eigner 1984: 40–58; Aston 2009: 411–16; Pischikova 2014.

62 Ritner 2009a: 575–76.

63 O'Connor 1983: 243; Leahy 1996: 158.
64 Lefebvre 1925; Ayad 2009: 14.
65 Leahy 1996: 158.
66 JdE 36327. The stela was unearthed by Georges Legrain (1897) from the forecourt of the temple of Amun at Karnak, and is now in the Egyptian Museum in Cairo. See Caminos 1964: 71–101; Der Manuelian 1994: 297–321; Kitchen 1996: 172–73, 403–44, 480 table 13; Gozzoli 2006: 87–92; Ritner 2009a: 575–82.
67 Benson and Gourlay 1899: 257–58, 370–79, pls XX–XXII.
68 Caminos (1964: 72) considered that, because the back was uncut, the stela was a panel embedded in a wall, while Legrain (1897: 12) thought that, because of a round cavity cut into the stela, it was 'le montant gauche d'une porte monumentale'. However, Leahy (1996: 154) considered it more likely to have been a freestanding monument, which does appear to be the more likely alternative.
69 Ayad 2009: 25.
70 Leahy 1996: 156.
71 Gozzoli 2006: 87–88.
72 Morkot 2000: 299.
73 The name Shepenwepet was conferred on both the daughter of Osorkon III and the daughter of Piye (Leahy 1996: 161 n. 64).
74 Ritner (2009a: 582 n. 1) suggests that 'supplies' means 'tackle' in association with ships, and is distinct from 'provisions' arranged in advance by royal messengers, which is the normal interpretation of these sentences.
75 Wilson 2010: 242.
76 Daressy 1919: 31–32; Kitchen 1996: 236–39; Morkot 2000: 299–300.
77 Broekman 2009: 100–1; Pope 2014: 224–25 n. 262. Contra Perdu see Broekman 2009: 101, n. 50.
78 For a discussion on the *imy-pr* document see Logan 2000.
79 Leahy 1996: 156; Ayad 2009: 25.
80 Caminos 1964.
81 Caminos 1964: 75–76, ll. 17–31
82 Russmann 1997: 39.
83 The standard work on Montuemhat is Leclant 1961; for information on his family see Bierbrier 1975: 104–8 and 1979; Taylor 1987; Pope 2014; for his history see Kitchen 1996: 230–33, 390–405.
84 Šarru can refer to monarch or king, but perhaps corresponds to 'mayor of the city' in this case (*ḥꜣty-ꜥ n niwt*) see Naunton 2011: 110.
85 Luckenbill 1927: 293–94.
86 Bierbrier 1979: 116–18; Leclant 2001: 436.
87 This family connection is known only from an offering table found in the First Court of Montuemhat's tomb, see Barguet et al. 1951: 493–94, pl. 2. The full title of Udjarenes is *špst nswt wꜥtt nbt-pr Wḏꜣrns sꜣt sꜣ-nswt P-ꜥnḫ-y hꜣrw*, see Leclant 1961: 264 and Russmann 1997.
88 Russmann 1997.
89 Russmann 1997.
90 Early work on the tomb was carried out by Leclant (1961), and later in the 1980s and 1990s the Egyptian Antiquities Organisation undertook the enormous task of clearing and restoring the tomb. Since 2006 Gomaà has been investigating this site, see Gomaà 2006: 62–64; Gestermann and Gomaà 2014: 201–3.

91 Russmann 1994.
92 Mut Temple inscription of Montuemhat (text B, l. 11), Ritner 2009a: 556–64. Also see Kitchen 1996: 397–400 who considers that the inscription refers to the earlier Assyrian invasion of 667/666 BC.
93 Lichtheim 1980: 29.
94 Parker 1962.
95 Leclant 1961: 192.
96 Parker 1962: 24.
97 Parker 1962: 192.
98 For Nesniau see Ranke 1907–8: 42–54; Kitchen 1996: 405 n. 952.
99 De Meuleunaere 1965: 31; Agut-Labordère 2013: 978.
100 Kitchen 1996: 405 n. 953 relating to Russmann 1971: 5.
101 Kitchen 1996: 480; Leahy 1996: 158.
102 Wessetzky 1963.
103 Pischikova 1998.
104 Ritner 1990: 104; Vittmann 2009: 94.
105 Spalinger 1976: 139; Kitchen 1996: 404–5; Ritner 2009a: 589.
106 P. Rylands IX, 11, 12 (Griffith 1909; Vittmann 1998: 148–52). See Ritner 1990 for discussion and Dodson 2012: 175.
107 The date is based on an analysis of the stela of Ibi (JdE 36158) in which Ibi describes his installation as Chief Steward in Year 26 of Psamtek I and which includes a reference to a festival in honour of the God's Wife. This is suggested to have been in honour of Nitiqret's accession to full status as God's Wife (Graefe 1998: 96–97; Leahy: 1996: 163; Pope 2014: 211. Dodson (2002) queries whether the event recognised as Nitiqret's accession has been correctly interpreted and tentatively suggests that this event may have been as early as 654 BC.
108 Based on a carnelian scarab in Moscow and an abraded stela currently in the garden of the Egyptian Museum in Cairo, see Habachi 1977: 165–70.
109 Cairo JdE 48866 published in Grimal 1981: 21–35, pls V–VII and discussed in Morkot 1999: 196–200.
110 This suggestion by Dodson (2002) is based on a number of monuments which list Amenirdis as 'God's Adoratrix' (*dwꜣt-nṯr*), 'God's Hand' (*ḏrt-nṯr*) but never as 'God's Wife' (*ḥmt-nṯr*). Also a lintel inscription (JdE 29254B) shows a later God's Adoratrix, Shepenwepet IV, with Nitiqret and Amenirdis together at what Dodson considers to be a single point in time.
111 Leahy 1996: 157–58.

4

Egypt, a new beginning: foreign relations and internal reforms

I Foreign and commercial relations

Invasion from the west

Shortly after the investiture of Nitiqret as God's Wife of Amun at Thebes, and with Psamtek now effectively in control of Upper and Lower Egypt, a threat was posed by the desert tribes who were attempting to infiltrate Egypt through the western border. A series of seven stelae, discovered along the ancient Dahshur road at South Saqqara between the pyramid of Pepy II and the modern Cairo–Faiyum road, are witness to this event.[1] These stelae are suggested to have been road markers or possibly victory memorials set up along the route that the Egyptian army took into the western desert.[2] Many of these stelae are badly preserved and now almost illegible, displaying only a few epithets. Stelae III and V furnish a few details concerning the victory of the king's army, but it is Stela VII dating to Year 11 of Psamtek on which the text, although fragmentary, preserves a report of a campaign against the western tribes.

The inscription indicates that the trouble had started in Year 10 of Psamtek and seems to suggest that this could well have been a full invasion rather than just a series of skirmishes, although the extent of the incursion could well have been exaggerated. The level of the threat can be identified by examining the geographical boundaries of the invading forces described on the stelae, 'who are in the Oxyrhynchite nome northward to the Mediterranean Sea',[3] suggesting that the western forces had penetrated Egypt from the Faiyum northwards to the Mediterranean coast. Two different groups are listed as forming part of the invasion group, the Tjehenu and the Ma, and additionally documented are 'both men and women from every district of the west'. Diodorus (I, 66.12) comments that some of the disaffected Delta leaders, who had fled when Psamtek took control of Lower Egypt, may have joined the invading forces.

The tone and structure of the text inscribed on the stela, resembles those seen some five hundred years earlier when Merenptah and Ramesses III faced the earlier invasions from western groups.[4] The stela describes how Psamtek had to call upon all his nome leaders to provide troops, perhaps suggesting that his mercenaries and standing army were not powerful enough to withstand the threat. In addition, special desert 'hunters' (*nw ḥ3st*) were summoned to support the army. Another possible interpretation is that the motivation of Psamtek for calling on the nome leaders was as much political as it was military, as the impact of troops from different parts of Egypt fighting together as a unified force could help in transferring local loyalties into national ones and help promote the concept of a united Egypt.[5]

The stela further describes how Psamtek went on to defeat the western tribes and following the victory there is then no further evidence of such a threat during the remainder of his reign. Importantly, the central cartouche on the stela carries the heading 'Wahibre, who smites the Tjehenu' (*W3ḥ-ib-rˁ ḥw(i) Tḥnw*), now indicating the full legitimacy of Psamtek as an Egyptian ruler and also allowing him to display his prowess as a military leader.

Fortresses at the borders

Within a few years, possibly soon after the war with the western tribes, Psamtek set up a series of fortified structures and restored existing strongholds at key points in his kingdom, securing his frontiers and stationed his mercenaries there. Herodotus in his *Histories* (II, 30) provides some textual information as to the location of some of these structures: 'The Egyptians had guard posts in various parts of the country: one at Elephantine against the Ethiopians, another in Daphnae at Pelusium against the Arabs and Assyrians, and a third at Marea to keep a watch on Libya'. Additionally, he mentions 'the camps' set up for the Carian and Ionian mercenaries at the Pelusiac mouth of the Nile.[6]

Tell Dafana (Daphnae) in the eastern Delta has long been considered a typical Saite fort, and when Petrie excavated it in the 1880s he identified it as the location of Herodotus's 'the camps' or *stratopedia*, and he further described a palace and Greek settlement at the site.[7] More recent research and interpretation identifiy the site as a Classical Egyptian temple town functioning as a frontier post[8] (Figure 4.1). A more definite Saite fortress exists on the north-eastern frontier at Tell el-Kedua, the 'Migdol' fortress,[9] and possibly at Tell el-Balamun.[10] Herodotus refers to a fort at Marea in the west, built as a safeguard against potential 'Libyan' incursions, and which may have been associated with the western campaign of Year 11.[11] This could refer to a 'gate' and likely fortress, named the 'door of the foreign lands of the Tjehenu' (*ˁ3-n-ḥ3st-Tḥnw*). This was probably located in the north-west of the area of Lake Mareotis and can be identified with the ancient town of Khaset-Tjemehou.[12]

4.1 Site of Tell Dafana (Daphnae) in the eastern Delta. Showing Casemate Building A after excavation by Flinders Petrie in 1886. In antiquity, the locality occupied a strategic position near the end of the ancient caravan land route from Syria–Palestine and would have been an ideal and easily provisioned starting point for expeditions towards Asia.

Late in Psamtek's reign a series of citadels and strongholds were constructed on the Levantine coast during the short period of Egyptian occupation there.[13] One such garrison is that at Mezad Hashavyahu, on the coast, not far from Ashdod, where Greek pottery of the period 625–600 BC attests the presence of Greek occupants (see p. 82). An earlier suggestion that the fortification may have been constructed by Josiah[14] now appears unsubstantiated.[15] Other examples of these fortified structures were situated in the south-east such as at Tell Melah in the Negreb and at Arad.

Relations with Syria-Palestine
Following the western campaign of Year 11 there seems little further evidence of foreign related activity until the later years of Psamtek's reign. Whilst it is likely that Psamtek concentrated on consolidation of his rule and reforms to the administration during the middle period of his reign, it would be expected that there would be some indication of military or commercial activity, particularly in Syria–Palestine, Egypt's traditional sphere of influence. Possibly this is due

to a lack of preserved evidence, especially as archaeological material, particularly from Sais in the Delta is not preserved to the same extent as that found in the drier conditions of Upper Egypt. Also, the tradition of proclaiming foreign campaigns and successes in reliefs and texts on temple walls and other monuments, a practice prominent during the New Kingdom, was no longer a tradition in Saite Egypt.[16]

An event which may have occurred during these poorly attested middle years of Psamtek's reign is the siege of Ashdod in Philistia, where according to Herodotus (II, 157) Psamtek spent twenty-nine years besieging the city before eventually capturing it: 'The reign of Psammetichus lasted for fifty-four years, during twenty-nine of which he was engaged in the siege of Azotus (Ashdod), a large town in Syria, until he finally took it. Azotus held out longest of any city known to us' (Figure 4.2).

Ashdod was of considerable strategic value, being on the main route to the coastal cities of the Levant and the north, and not only would the seizure of the city gain control of Philistia but its occupation would be a barrier to any force attempting to travel south and threaten Egypt. Ashdod also had considerable commercial importance, controlling both north–south and east–west trade routes as well as the local maritime commerce.[17] Securing its allegiance would have provided Egypt with a key foothold in the dynamic commercial world of the Levant. Egyptian motives in attacking the city may well, therefore, have been commercially as well as strategically orientated.

Archaeological evidence lends support to this offensive, as excavations carried out at Ashdod have associated the siege and subsequent conquest with the destruction evident in Stratum VII. Then the subsequent city (Stratum VI) is considered to have come under Egyptian control as attested by hieroglyphic inscriptions found there.[18] The figure of twenty-nine years has often been called into question, with even Herodotus appearing surprised at it, and one suggestion has been that it might refer to Psamtek's twenty-ninth regnal year (635 BC).[19] It is difficult to be certain exactly when the siege took place as there is little further archaeological evidence, although it would seem probable that Ashdod came under Egyptian control between 655 and 630 BC.[20]

Ashdod had previously been under Assyrian control, but by this time the power and influence of Assyria had been diminishing for a number of years. It had been weakened by constant warfare, corruption, a deteriorating political structure and internal struggles for leadership, and so was no longer the power that it once was. In Palestine, the latest datable evidence points to a gradual disintegration of Assyrian rule. Assyrian deeds of sale relating to 651 BC and 649 BC have been found at Gezer, there was an Assyrian governor in Samaria in 646 BC and Ashurbanipal campaigned in the Levant in 644 BC to put down revolts in Ushu, Tyre and Akko. It would appear that, by the 630s BC, Assyrian

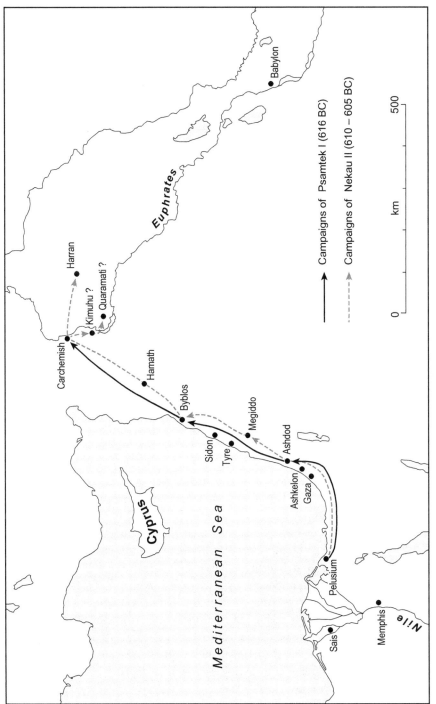

4.2 Campaigns of Psamtek I and Nekau II in the Near East.

rule had come to an end, and both Egypt and Judah were now rivals to fill this political vacuum. Judah took advantage of this and by *c.* 620 BC it had extended its territory into Samaria (II Kings 23.15, 19) and possibly even further.[21]

Following the siege of Ashdod, the next textual evidence for Egyptian forces campaigning abroad is recorded in Nabopolassar's *Babylonian Chronicle*, and, whilst the chronicle covers only the periods 626–623 BC and 616–610 BC, the entry for 616 BC (Chronicle 3) states that[22] 'In the month of Tishri, the army of Egypt and the army of Assyria went after the king of Akkad (Babylon) as far as Gablini[23] but they did not overtake the king of Akkad (so) they withdrew'.

Although there is no further textual evidence of Egyptian activity in the Levant before the 616 BC date, there are a number of archaeological finds that relate to this period. An ostracon which had originally been ascribed to the reign of Ptolemy II has now been redated to Year 28 of Psamtek (637 BC).[24] The text states how Psamtek was in Daphnae and planning to march to Kharu, indicating that Egypt was preparing to enter the Levant region. A number of artefacts such as scarabs, amulets and 'New Year's Flasks' (Figure 4.3)[25] dating to the reign of Psamtek I have been excavated from the coastal plain of the southern Levant.[26]

At the Philistine city of Ashkelon various Egyptian cultic objects such as a bronze offering table and bronze setulae, also dating to this period, have been discovered. It is possible that the nature and combination of these objects could indicate that Ashkelon had an Egyptian enclave with its own shrine.[27] These finds are contemporaneous with material found at Ekron and the southern Philistine territory. Discoveries at sites such as Tell el-Far'ah, Tell el-Ajjul, Ruqeish and Tell Abu Salima show a strong Egyptian influence and have been dated from 640 BC onwards.[28] At Ekron a sequence of two phases of use can be detected in the Stratum I level, with the first predominately Assyrian (IC) and the second mainly Egyptian (IB), the change being suggested to have occurred about 630 BC.[29]

Similarly, different cultural phases have been detected in southern Philistia.[30] A scarab with the name Psamtek, not in a cartouche but thought to be a royal person, has been found at Khirbet el-Maqatir in Israel; the scarab has been ascribed to Psamtek I but may possibly relate to Psamtek II.[31] If it does belong to Psamtek I it is the only one so far discovered in Israel, and may hint at military or economic activity in this region. During this period, considerable quantities of Greek pottery begin to appear in the southern Levant, particularly on the coastal plain.[32] In a few sites, such as Tell Kabri and the fortress at Mezad Hashavyahu, pottery items of everyday use, such as cooking pots, have been found, pointing to the presence of Greek traders, colonisers or possibly mercenaries residing there.[33]

4.3 New Year's Flask, inscribed for the God's Father Amenhotep, son of the God's
Father Iufaa. Filled perhaps with perfume, oil, or water from the Nile, it would
have been a gift associated with the celebration of the beginning of the year.
Around the shoulders of the vase are incised bands of floral patterns, meant to
echo the vegetal collar that would have been worn by a participant in a ceremonial
or festival event or draped around the neck of a jar of wine or oil. Two baboons
flank the tall neck of the flask, which is made to echo a bundle of papyrus and lotus
plants. Faience. H. 21 cm; Diam. 18 cm (Metropolitan Museum of Art, New York).

The archaeological evidence discussed above tends to suggest that Psamtek
with his mercenary forces gradually advanced into previously held Assyrian
territories in the Levant, following their withdrawal from the region. Initially
focusing on Ashkelon and the coastal plain, Psamtek's forces later occupied Ekron
and established a number of bases in the region. At least one of these, the fortress
at Mezad Hashavyahu, was garrisoned with Psamtek's Greek mercenaries.[34]

Egypt's reasons for establishing its rule in the region of Syria–Palestine would have been twofold. From a commercial viewpoint, control of the Mediterranean ports and access to the cedar and fir trees from Lebanon would have been important. Strategically, with the demise of Assyrian power and the increasing peril posed by the rise of the Babylonian Empire, there was now a need to create a buffer zone to prevent the Babylonians directly threatening Egypt.

The Babylonian textual evidence indicates that Egypt therefore not only campaigned in the Levant in 616 BC but was now fighting alongside Assyria, its one-time overlord, against the Babylonians. Chronicle 2,[35] which is a report on the early years of Nabopolassar's rule, contains no reference to Egypt when recording the conflict between Assyria and Babylonia in the years up to 623 BC. Therefore, between 623 BC and 616 BC it can be assumed that relations between Egypt and Assyria changed markedly, although it is unclear whether Psamtek came to Assyria's aid as part of a treaty or whether he sought Assyria's help in curbing the Babylonians.[36] Psamtek's relations with Assyria had, therefore, changed markedly during his rule, firstly as a vassal, then as an independent ruler, who subsequently began to fill the power vacuum in the Levant caused by diminishing Assyrian power, as attested by the siege of Ashdod and Egypt's later control of the cities of the Levant (see below). Finally, Psamtek fought alongside Assyria against the expanding Babylonian Empire.

In 616 BC the *Babylonian Chronicle* records that the Egyptian army travelled to Gablini on the Middle Euphrates, a city that was some considerable distance from the borders of Egypt. Psamtek must have previously secured the eastern Mediterranean seaboard and adjacent coastal plain before the Egyptian troops crossed the Kingdom of Judah, suggesting sufficient Egyptian control in Syria–Palestine to operate freely throughout the region. Such a deployment of troops indicates a period of ever-increasing involvement in the region prior to this 616 BC date.[37]

As regards Judah, the implication is that some form of alliance or understanding would have had to be agreed between these two states, although the Bible, an important source of information for the Kingdom of Judah, is silent on any such agreement.[38] The relevant sections in Chronicles and Kings referring to these dates do not discuss an anti-Egyptian or an anti-Assyrian policy but merely concentrate on religious reforms that Josiah, the King of Judah, was undertaking.[39] With Assyria no longer the threat to Judah that it once was, Egypt was now the greater military force in the region.[40] Egypt displayed no hostile intentions towards Judah and, with Egypt being more powerful militarily, Judah was not perceived as a threat, although Judah did control the trade routes through the Negev, an area of commercial interest for Egypt.[41] It is possible that at this time Judah may have tacitly supported Egypt against the increasing Babylonian threat.

The Scythians

Another possible threat to Egypt at this time were the Scythians, the first of the great nomadic cultures to emerge from the Eurasian Steppe. The Scythians had no written language and left no discernible record of any possible attacks on Egypt, and so reliance has to be placed on Herodotus (I, 105), who states that 'The Scythians next turned their attention to Egypt but were met in Palestine by Psammetichus the Egyptian king, who by earnest entreaties supported by bribery managed to prevent their further advance. They withdrew by way of Ascalon in Syria.'

This passage has been the subject of much analysis and interpretation, but there is little additional evidence to support this account.[42] Previously, Herodotus and other Classical authors had described the displacement and persecution of the Cimmerians by the Scythians, and the rise of the Medes to prominence followed then by their defeat at the hands of the Scythians. The date of the encounter between the Scythians and Egypt is not certain and the confrontation appears to have had little effect on ongoing Egyptian policy in the Levant.[43] There is no other reference to a Scythian–Egyptian encounter in either the Babylonian or the Assyrian sources. Pompeius Trogus, the Gallo-Roman historian, wrote about Scythian invasions and their domination of Asia.[44] Later Classical authors such as Arrian, Photius, Strabo and Justin also describe a confrontation between the Egyptians and the Scythians, but their accounts are similar to that of Herodotus and add little further information regarding this possible conflict.[45] Archaeological evidence does support the suggestion of warlike Scythian activity in the eastern regions of Eurasia, but such finds in the west are not as plentiful.[46]

Herodotus (I, 104, 106) refers to the twenty-eight years of Scythian supremacy in Asia, but again there is no other archaeological or textual evidence to support this, and few conclusions can be drawn from his generalised account. While raiding parties from the northern steppes were a problem for the settled civilisations of Western Asia, and the Scythians may have embarked on periodic plundering raids, sources do not support the suggestion of a period of stable Scythian domination or rule.[47]

The rising power of Babylon

In contrast, the rising power of Babylon under Nabopolassar did pose a threat to the region in the 620s, and with Assyria in decline the Babylonians were now beginning to endanger Assyrian territory.[48] The Babylonians allied themselves with the Medes in c. 614 BC, and by 612 BC the major cities of the Assyrian Empire – Ashur, Nimrud and Nineveh – had been destroyed by allied Babylonian and Median forces (Figure 4.4). The Egyptians were campaigning once more against the Babylonians in 610 BC, as again attested by the *Babylonian Chronicle*,

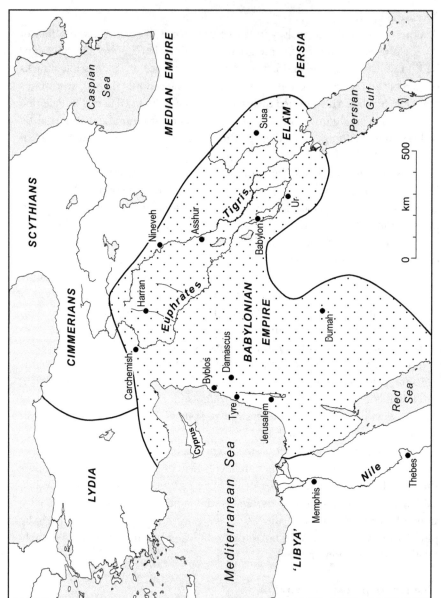

4·4 Babylonian Empire 612–538 BC.

according to which a combined Assyrian and Egyptian force was forced out of the city of Harran by the Babylonians and their Median allies (called here the *Umman-Manda*).[49] The Assyrians and Egyptians attempted to retake the city but failed, and so withdrew:[50] 'As for Assuruballit (the Assyrian ruler) and the army of Eg[ypt] which had come [to his help], fear of the enemy fell upon them; they abandoned the city and ... crossed [the river Euphrates]'.[51]

Despite this setback, by the end of his reign Psamtek controlled the Levantine coast up to and including Phoenicia, and probably the Kingdom of Judah, territories previously held by Assyria. Control of such territories is attested by the king's Second Serapeum Stela[52] which records the burial of the Apis bull in 612 BC and is dated to Year 52 of Psamtek. The inscription on the stela includes the following passage: 'Every craftsman was occupied with his task, anointing the body with unguent, wrapping it in royal cloth of every god; his casket was of *ḥr*, *mr*-wood and cedar, the choicest of every terrace. Their chiefs were subjects of the palace, with a royal courtier placed over them; and their taxes (*bꜣk.w*) were assessed for the Residence, as though it were in the Land of Egypt.'

The inscription indicates that craftsmen were manufacturing the casket for the Apis bull out of cedar wood, timber known to originate from Lebanon. The chiefs referred to in the passage are described as being subject to Egypt and paying taxes accordingly, thus signifying that the region was under Egyptian control at this time. The so-called Wadi Brisa Inscription set up by the Babylonian King Nebuchadnezzar describes the Levant, prior to his conquest of the territories, as a region 'over which a foreign enemy (probably referring to Egypt) was ruling and robbing it of its riches'.[53]

A source of interest concerning Egyptian relations with these areas is a greywacke Middle Kingdom statuette,[54] reinscribed in the Saite Period by 'the king's messenger to Canaan (and) to Philistia, Pediese son of Apy' (Figure 4.5). The role of such a messenger would have been to conduct diplomatic relations between Egypt and Syria–Palestine, to either neighbouring or vassal states. In addition, there is the so-called 'Adon-letter', a fragmentary papyrus, found at Saqqara and sent from Adon, the King of Ekron, to an unnamed king of Egypt.[55] The contents describe a request from Adon for military assistance from his overlord, Egypt, in fulfilment of Egypt's vassal obligations to protect his kingdom from the threat of the Babylonians, whose forces had advanced as far as Aphek. The date of the letter is not established with certainty, and the unnamed king could also be the later Saite ruler Nekau, the son of Psamtek. However, it is likely that Egyptian control of Ekron was established some years previously, and probably during the reign of Psamtek. The letter is also significant from the perspective of the language being used since this is the earliest attested example of Aramaic to come from Palestine.[56]

4.5 Middle Kingdom statuette originally carved to commemorate an unknown
official. During the 26th Dynasty the inscription naming this man was erased, and
a carved scene was added depicting its new owner, Pediese, son of Apy,
worshipping the gods Osiris, Horus and Isis. Greywacke. H. 30.5 cm; W. 10.25 cm;
D. 11.5 cm (Walters Art Museum, Baltimore).

End of Psamtek's reign

It is likely that by the end of Psamtek's reign treaties would have been signed
with a number of Phoenician and Philistine cities. Some of these cities may
have voluntarily ceded control in view of the weakening authority of the Assyrian
Empire, the aftermath of Scythian raids and the resurgence of Egyptian power
in the region. Although there is an absence of textual sources relating to Egyptian
influence in the southern Levant, the artefacts described above, which date to

the reign of Psamtek I and later Saite rulers, support the suggestion of Egyptian presence in the region. It would seem that Egyptian expansion under Psamtek gradually advanced into territories previously controlled by Assyria, including the Kingdom of Judah, a process that appears to have been largely peaceful. For the first time since the New Kingdom Egypt controlled vassal states in the Levant which contributed taxes to Egypt.[57]

Psamtek died in 610 BC and his death may have occurred beyond the borders of Egypt. A Demotic papyrus[58] preserves a tradition that a King 'Psamtek' died in the lands east of *N₃y-w-ˁ₃m-p₃-nḥs*. It would seem likely that the Psamtek referred to is the first king of this name as there is later textual evidence for the deaths of both Psamtek II and Psamtek III.[59] The location of *N₃y-w-ˁ₃m-p₃-nḥs* is possibly a frontier post close to Tell Dafana (Daphnae) on Egypt's north-eastern border, as the papyrus describes how a priest of Tell Dafana inscribed mortuary texts at the entrance of the embalming place of Psamtek. Perhaps at the end of his reign Psamtek was travelling abroad to the Levant campaigning with his troops. Herodotus (I, 105 and II, 157) and Diodorus Siculus (I, 67) record similar journeys by Psamtek earlier in his reign when he besieged Ashdod and again later when he confronted the Scythians.

Papyrus Berlin 13588 states that the embalming house (*wˁbt*) of Psamtek was located at *N₃y-w-ˁ₃m-p₃-nḥs*, so it is possible that Psamtek was embalmed before his body was transported back to Egypt for burial, but no evidence of his burial has been discovered.[60] Herodotus (II, 169–70) states that he saw the tombs of Wahibre Psamtek and Ahmose II in the complex of Neith at Sais, and that all the kings of Sais were buried there; the burials may also have included those of the earlier 24th Dynasty.[61]

Trade and the city of Naukratis[62]

Pottery, trade goods and other foreign artefacts found in Egypt indicate that throughout history Egypt was trading with its neighbours in the eastern Mediterranean, but during the Saite era it increasingly engaged with these cultures, motivated by shared interests in trade and military security. Key to early commercial contacts were traders from countries such as Phoenicia and the Greek states. An important factor relating to early commerce in Egypt was the city of Naukratis, a centre where Greeks and to a lesser extent other foreigners are attested, and where processes of cultural interaction can be recognised.[63]

Naukratis is situated on the Canopic branch of the Nile in the western Delta some 16 km from Sais. It was one of the earliest instances of an organised Greek presence in Egypt, and it was an important hub for trade and cross-cultural exchange. Archaeological fieldwork was first undertaken at the site by Petrie in 1884, continued by Gardner and then later by Hogarth in 1899. Coulson and Leonard investigated the site in the 1970s and 1980s, and more recent research and fieldwork were carried out by the British Museum during 2012–14.[64]

The recent British Museum reports indicate that the settlement was much larger than previously recorded with an area exceeding some 60 hectares.

Naukratis was accessed from the Mediterranean via the Canopic branch of the river Nile and was able to be navigated in Saite times by seagoing vessels. The western area of the city is where the busy port's main harbour facilities were located, whereas in the east a substantial industrial quarter existed. In the north was the Hellenion, a group of Greek sanctuaries which the different Greek communities were allowed to establish during the later reign of Ahmose II. Here inscriptions indicate that the Greeks worshipped a number of gods such as Herakles and Aphrodite, and it has been suggested that the temple was a place where Greek identity and culture were maintained and developed.[65] Excavations have also revealed details of religious practices from the earliest periods at Naukratis, indicating close links with Cyprus, Phoenicia and the Levant, as well as a greater degree of cultural mixing between Greeks and Egyptians than previously assumed.[66]

There has been considerable debate over many years relating to the date of the foundation of Naukratis, particularly when attempting to reconcile the early Classical evidence with the results of the excavations.[67] Textual and archaeological evidence suggests that Naukratis was established during the reign of Psamtek I, perhaps as early as 625 BC, as attested by the presence of Greek pottery, such as Corinthian 'Transitional', Attic, East Greek and Carian types that were discovered there.[68] Strabo (XVII, 1.18) also appears to indicate that Naukratis was founded during the reign of Psamtek whereas Herodotus (II, 178) comments that it was established during the later reign of Ahmose II. It is possible that the city, although founded earlier, may not have developed into a thriving commercial centre, an emporium, until the reign of Ahmose, and then continued to flourish even after the establishment of Alexandria during Ptolemaic times.[69]

It is likely that Naukratis was the site of an Egyptian town before the first Greeks arrived.[70] The presence of the 'Great Enclosure', in the south, which has been identified as the brick enclosure wall of an Egyptian temple complex dedicated to Amun, would support this, as a local temple would form the core of any Egyptian town. Although foundation deposits and surviving sculptural decoration of the Great Enclosure date to the reigns of Ptolemy I and II, Egyptian epigraphic and archaeological evidence indicates that a predecessor to this temple may have existed early in the 26th Dynasty.[71] The earliest Greek presence at Naukratis may relate to its original establishment as a military settlement and base, occupied by mercenaries engaged by Psamtek I who were later rewarded for their service by being allocated land-holdings. The base, with its access to the Mediterranean, would have had an important strategic role, with navy vessels being able to berth there.[72]

Naukratis was part of the complex trade network that linked the Mediterranean and connected the two civilisations of Greece and Egypt,[73] with Greek ships docking at Naukratis to trade such goods as silver, wine and oil in exchange for grain, linen, papyrus and natron.[74] Pottery finds indicate that the trading connections of Naukratis were quite extensive, not only involving the Greek states, Phoenicia, Cyprus and Cyrene but also extending as far as Italy and Spain. Large numbers of weights conforming to a variety of different standards (Egyptian, Greek and Phoenician) provide evidence for thriving commercial activities in both Naukratis and the similar centre of Thonis-Heracleion.[75]

What effect did this cross-cultural trade and interaction at Naukratis have on Egypt and the Greek states? The Egyptians appear to have adopted few Greek elements into their culture during the early Saite Period whereas, in contrast, the Greeks were influenced by Egyptian ideas and the Egyptian way of life. A significant degree of acculturation is evident amongst the Greek and Ionian mercenaries, as attested by their adopting Egyptian names and burial customs.[76] Greek mercenaries and traders took Egyptian goods to dedicate in local sanctuaries back in their homeland.[77] Egyptian architectural and technological developments had a strong influence on Greek monumental architecture, as demonstrated in the remains found at Didyma and Samos. Greek sculpture was similarly affected by Egyptian style, with Egyptian motifs and iconography appearing in Greek vase paintings,[78] and Egyptian scarabs have been discovered not only in the Greek world but throughout the Mediterranean region.[79]

Related to the foundation of Naukratis is the question of whether Egyptians and Greeks lived together in the city. To date over fifteen hundred inscriptions on pottery and stone have been unearthed during the various excavations, with the majority of these being Greek, although as the early excavators retained only the inscribed material it is not certain what overall percentage was Greek. Evidence from the faience workshop or 'Scarab Factory' located in the vicinity of the sanctuary of Aphrodite, which specialised in the mass production of scarabs and amulets, indicates that the moulds that were used in their manufacture were different from others found in Egypt. Errors are demonstrable in the hieroglyphs, which could imply that production of these faience objects was by the Greeks resident in Naukratis. It is likely that there was a continuing core Egyptian administrative and policing presence,[80] and Herodotus (II, 154) writes that Egyptians were trained as interpreters to communicate with the Greeks.

Naukratis remained an important hub for trade and cross-cultural exchange for much of its history and survived until at least the seventh century AD.[81] Naukratis was not the only site of this type; the harbour town of Thonis-Heracleion (Hone), which was the first point of entry into the Delta, was also established during the 26th Dynasty. Both these cities may have been acting as ports for Sais, as at that time river traffic would have been able to navigate inland via the Canopic branch of the Nile, and then perhaps onwards to Sais via ancient river branches or canals which have long since silted up.

Both Naukratis and Thonis-Heracleion were taxed and regulated by Egyptian officials, and the 'Overseer of the Gate of the Foreign Lands of the Great Green' would have been responsible for security as well as for administering taxes.[82] In the wider Mediterranean there were several such emporia such as the Greek city at Cyrene, thought to have been founded about 600 BC, and Milesian trading posts on the shores of the Black Sea. Artefacts and pottery finds at Cyrene suggest that they had trading links with Naukratis.[83]

Recent fieldwork at Kom el-Nugus (Plinthine) on Lake Mareotis has excavated not only local Egyptian material but significant amounts of Near Eastern imports dating to the Saite Period. Pottery has been identified as coming from Greek centres such as Miletus, Samos, Lesbos and Corinth as well as from the Levant and Cyprus. The diversity of this material would suggest that Plinthine acted as another trading centre and entrance into Egypt.[84] According to Herodotus (II, 179), Ahmose II required Greek trading vessels to travel to Naukratis in an attempt to control trade. However, the finds at Plinthine would indicate that the Naukratis monopoly may not have been totally observed.

II Internal reforms in the early Saite Period

Psamtek I was at the centre of the Egyptian administration as the king had traditionally been throughout Pharaonic history. The role of the monarch was, as in previous eras, to preserve the continuance of ordered life in Egypt by maintaining the power of the gods, through administration of the realm and by repelling the enemies of Egypt. Although he was still designated as 'His Majesty' (*ḥm.f*), and 'Lord of the Two Lands' (*nb t3wy*), the royal titulary was written in a manner found in certain Old Kingdom inscriptions. In addition, a number of decrees, such as the Wahibre stela at Mit Rahina[85] in their phraseology, language and writing resemble Old Kingdom compositions. These texts suggest that the rulers of the Saite Period, saw their role as not only that of embodying the ideal of kingship but also now linking Egypt to its ancient greatness.[86]

By the end of his reign, Psamtek appears to have largely achieved political reunification of Egypt, a process that had involved the reorganisation of the administration to better serve the needs of a united country. As in previous periods officials who controlled the country were theoretically appointed by the king and were responsible to him for the day to day running of the state. Similarly, the tradition of hereditary claims to these offices still applied. The king appears to still have had very much a hands-on approach, as demonstrated in Papyrus Rylands IX and other texts, where he is attested as administering justice, rewarding servants and having an active role in making governmental decisions.[87] Such participation could result in decisions being given merely by obtaining an audience with the monarch, a feature of court life that is stated throughout much of Pharaonic history. Access to the king to make an appeal is not only attested in Papyrus Rylands IX but can also be seen in the earlier Middle Kingdom *Tale of the Eloquent Peasant*.[88]

However, in practice many of the decisions regarding the day to day running of the administration may have been delegated, and detailed information relating to the protocol of the royal court is lacking.[89] The thirteenth maxim of the *Teaching of Ptahhotep* narrates how rank was important in the audience chamber, and biographies and literary tales throughout Pharaonic history stress how people in high positions could obtain access to the king while others would be left waiting in the outer courts.[90]

The small statue of Djedptahiufankh, an official during the reign of Psamtek I contains an inscription that sheds some light on court advisers to the king during this period (see p. 59). The text refers not only to the 'Council of Nobles' operating at court but also to a 'High Council' (*sḥ ʿȝ*), this later body appearing to have been a group of prominent officials summoned to advise the monarch on affairs of government.[91] A later example of a Saite monarch in consultation with a council or group of advisers is attested on the Bentehhor Stela,[92] where Nekau II describes to his courtiers the deteriorating condition of the Theban monuments. Again, in the Elephantine Stela[93] Ahmose II is informed by his council of an attack by Haaibra and his Greek mercenaries (see p. 149).

During the Saite Period court titles such as 'Sole Companion' (*smr wʿty*) and 'Acquaintance of the King' (*rḫ-nsw*), titles that had been in use since the Old Kingdom, were still conspicuously employed, but now probably in an archaising manner. However, the *rḫ-nsw* title fell into disuse at the end of the 26th Dynasty as did the title 'Hereditary Prince and Count' (*iri-pʿt ḥȝty-ʿ*).[94] Other titles such as 'Overseer of the Antechamber' (*imy-r rwt*), also found in Papyrus Rylands IX, are now evident for the first time. This official was a prominent member of court and is attested from the reign of Psamtek I to that of Ahmose II, but then disappears during the later Persian Period.[95]

The primary role of the 'Overseer of the Antechamber'[96] was that of organising access to the monarch by scheduling royal audiences, but he had a further function in resolving disputes and mediating in matters that were brought to the attention of the sovereign. Such a position is attested in the Petition of Petiese, and from this source it is evident that the authority of the office was quite far-reaching. The overseer employed scribes who operated throughout the country and these scribes had the power to investigate and arrange arrests of suspects.[97] The monarch would therefore have had to be in a position to trust such a powerful official. Such confidence is demonstrated in the example of Neferibrenefer, 'Overseer of the Antechamber' to Nekau II, as he was additionally assigned the tutorship of the royal children.[98]

The position of Vizier of Upper Egypt had been abolished early during the reign of Psamtek, but in Lower Egypt an alternative arrangement seems to have been in place, as several different holders of the title Vizier coexisted in different localities at the same time.[99] The function of the holders of these 'local' titles is not certain but some responsibility for regional administration seems likely.

At a provincial level, the nome system that had been in operation throughout much of Dynastic history continued to function. The system is attested at the beginning of the reign of Psamtek I in the Nitiqret Stela (l. 10) where it is recorded that every nomarch had to ensure supplies for the ships transporting Nitiqret to Thebes while the flotilla passed through their territory. There is also a reference in the biography of Peftuaneith, the late Saite high official who served under both Haaibra and Ahmose II, where the author lists the standard title 'Revered One (*imꜣḫw*) of his Nome'.[100] Psamtek initially administered Middle and Upper Egypt by merging them into the 'Southern Land', a region controlled by the 'Leader of the Fleet' who had a supervisory role in the administration of the nomes. This system appears to have been short-lived, as a passage in Papyrus Rylands IX (15.3) refers to Horudja, son of Hortheby, a priest of Sobek, being Governor of Herakleopolis in Year 4 of the reign of Psmatek II (*c.* 592 BC). This suggests that by this date a governor was now in control of Herakleopolis, rather than the previous 'Leader of the Fleet', and the traditional system of the nomes being administered from a major city had now been restored'.[101]

III Culture and funerary practices

Art, sculpture and archaism in the Saite Period
Egyptian visual culture of the Saite Period was little influenced by the brief Assyrian occupation or indeed by early contacts with the Greek city states.[102] One of the most salient features of the arts of this period is archaism,[103] a conscious return to past styles and models. Archaism has been much discussed in the literature relating to ancient Egypt, and a number of definitions[104] have been proposed to account for this concept. Many older and somewhat unsatisfactory terms have in the past been used to discuss this phenomenon[105] such as 'a pitiable and unhealthy return to a long lost since abandoned cultural era',[106] 'a replacement for the lack of contemporary creativity'[107] and 'longing for a Golden Age of Egyptian history'.[108] These rather disparaging expressions, combined with the notion that a lack of imagination and innovation was evident in the artistic representations of the period, are now disappearing in more

modern interpretations of Saite culture. Even the popular term 'renaissance',[109] with its undertones of the great European Renaissance of the fourteenth to seventeenth centuries AD, does not fully explain the artistic character of this era. Perhaps the overriding understanding of archaism is more of a deliberate attempt to reproduce older facets of Pharaonic civilisation that had been long been out of use and whose line of tradition had been interrupted. These relate not only to visual culture but also to language, titles, literature and other cultural elements.[110]

However, it is important to recognise that the practice of deriving inspiration and utilising styles from previous periods was common at all times in ancient Egypt. For example, following the reunification of Egypt, artistic styles during the Middle Kingdom broke with the Theban artistic tradition and returned to copying the Memphite Old Kingdom canon.[111] In architecture, the 18th-Dynasty temple of Queen Hatshepsut at Deir el-Bahri is clearly modelled after the adjoining 11th-Dynasty temple of Mentuhotep.[112] Approaches other than archaism were also used to draw inspiration from the past, such as restoration, reuse of building materials, ancestor cults and the reconstruction of historical events.[113] Archaism is a concept that was often utilised to reinforce claims to legitimacy for aspiring rulers. The use of the past as a guarantor of authority, the past representing an accumulation of experience, was a long-established tradition in ancient Egypt. This is particularly evident in the Late Period where the rulers were of 'Libyan' descent, and again in the previous Kushite period when the kings were of foreign birth and therefore may have had a lack of confidence about their ancestry. These rulers, who were often in control during unsettled periods and unable to claim legitimacy through Egyptian descent, had a need to establish their authenticity as pharaohs, and therefore made particular use of archaism.[114]

There can be difficulties in identifying archaising Egyptian artwork as examples are never exact copies of earlier works but were adapted to conform to the current stylistic trends. There is always some degree of reinterpretation and modification, and, although inspiration from older models is the overriding characteristic, there is also a degree of innovation.[115] The new styles can create problems for the art historian in recognising and categorising artefacts, particularly when through accidents of survival few similar comparable examples are known to exist for a particular era. Only relatively recently has it been realised that some private statues originally dated to the 25th Dynasty but supposedly conforming to the late Middle Kingdom style were in fact created during the Middle Kingdom.[116] Similarly, a colossal head once thought to be a representation of Psamtek II has now been reattributed to Thutmose I.[117]

It is during the Late Period that archaism was most conspicuous in the surviving evidence and particularly during the Saite and earlier Kushite Dynasties.

This trend is generally recognised as commencing during the Third Intermediate
Period in the Delta where representations of the local rulers were modelled on
older works, originally drawn from Old Kingdom patterns.[118] This archaising
style was later continued by the Kushites in their monuments in what may be
an attempt to legitimise their kingships.[119] These rulers embarked on an extensive
building programme that included elements of Old, Middle and New Kingdom
styles. The temple of Kawa, a typical example of the later New Kingdom style
which was built by Taharqo, has architectural and sculptural features based
on Old Kingdom models. Artists were sent to Kawa from Memphis to undertake
this work.[120] A relief depicts Taharqo as a sphinx trampling a 'Libyan' chief
while his family look on, a standard theme in Old Kingdom royal mortuary
temple complexes.[121] Similar scenes are seen in the Old Kingdom temples of
Sahura and Nyuserra at Abusir[122] and that of Pepy II at Saqqara.[123] The Berlin
sphinx of Shepenwepet II with its Hathorian wig is based on 12th- or early
18th-Dynasty models[124] (Figure 4.6).

During the Saite Period, examples such as the tomb of Petamenopet (see
below), perhaps dated to the end of Kushite and beginning of Saite power,
has full-scale architectural forms based on Old and New Kingdom models.[125]

4.6 Berlin Sphinx of Shepenwepet II, who was the daughter of Piye and held the
office of God's Wife of Amun. Here she is seen in the form of a sphinx, offering a
ram-headed vessel to the god Amun. Dated to c. 660 BC. Discovered at Karnak.
Black granite. L. 82 cm (Neues Museum, Berlin).

The tomb of Bakenrenef, Vizier to Psamtek I, at Saqqara,[126] one of the earliest Saite-Memphite tombs, rivals the size and elaboration of those on the Asasif at Thebes. The tomb has an entrance chamber decorated with archaising scenes of daily life, and an extensive rock-cut interior with religious texts, such as those derived from the Book of the Dead. Later, during the reign of Haaibra, the fortress of Memphis was converted into a palace, the main gate of which was embellished with temple scenes copied from Old Kingdom examples (see p. 155).

Archaising art did not necessarily refer back to a single period in ancient Egyptian history but often took eclectic inspiration from several earlier models. For example, in the tomb of Montuemhat[127] certain scenes depict various offering bearers, while other nearby scenes show cattle being slaughtered, all of which are copied from scenes in the upper terrace of Hatshepsut's temple at Deir el-Bahri.[128] Similarly, scenes from the New Kingdom Theban tombs of Menna (TT 69) and Rekhmire (TT 100) are also replicated in the tomb of Montuemhat.[129] Fragments of raised relief from porticoes in the second court of the tomb of Montuemhat depict scenes of swamps, cattle-tending in the marshes and other agricultural activities, these being based primarily on Old Kingdom activities.[130]

On the basis of stylistic observations such as the muscular legs and smooth surface to the wigs of the offering bearers in the reliefs of the first court of Montuemhat's tomb, this element of the tomb has been recognised as primarily 25th Dynasty in its decorative style. The reliefs in the second court, however, demonstrate slimmer figures, longer limbs and more animated faces with the suggestion of a smile, and may be assigned to the early 26th Dynasty. This latter date is confirmed by various prominent representations of Psamtek I, such as in the first room and in the lintel above the large central doorway of the first court of the tomb. These stylistic differences in decoration allowing a 25th or 26th Dynasty date to be determined is also represented by significant changes in the decorative programme, suggesting that a later extension was added to the tomb when the Saite Dynasty took control.[131]

The sculpture of the Saite Period was generally of very high quality and was marked by the use of fine-grain hard stone such as schist and diorite. The sculpture favours smooth surfaces that almost create the impression of softness even in hard stones.[132] There was a change in the canon of proportions resulting in a longer torso and neck area although discoveries in the South Asasif tombs of Karabasken and Karakhamun indicate that the 'Saite Canon' was already in use in the early 25th Dynasty.[133] During the Saite Period figures were modelled after Old Kingdom examples, with the Saite torso thinner than the preceding Kushite torso. One of the masterpieces of the early Saite Period, illustrating this slimmer pattern, is the standing grey granite statue of Montuemhat[134] which he dedicated at Karnak.

In statuary seated figures are less commonplace than in previous periods, but the traditional symmetrical cross-legged 'scribe' statue or squatting statue was revived during the reign of Psamtek.[135] The majority of these examples are without back pillars and were created in Memphis, harking back to Old Kingdom examples. The squatting figure with knees drawn up to the chest and arms crossed on the knees, simplified into a cubic form and known as the block statue, already extensively employed in the 25th Dynasty, became even more widespread during the remainder of the Late Period.[136] Similarly, theophorous and naophorous statues were popular, especially in the Delta region.[137]

Another characteristic feature of Saite sculpture is the appearance of a 'smile' in the facial expression, which is typified by a deep sickle-shaped curve along the bottom of the lower lip turning upwards; often referred to as the 'Saite smile', it is not necessarily an indication of an emotional state. The expression is not present on all the statues created during the reign of Psamtek I, but when present gives a benign appearance to the face. Although the smile is typical of the Saite Period, it was not an innovation of this era as Old Kingdom statues offer the illusion of a smile, Middle Kingdom examples display careful modelling of the mouth area, and in 18th-Dynasty statues the mouth tends to be upturned.[138] Thus, the Saite smile is yet another example of archaism, being a revival and reinterpretation of previous styles.

Although there are a number of examples of private statuary, usually placed in temples, there are few reliably dated intact royal statues from the Saite Period, although a number of fragments and incomplete sections have survived. This is possibly because the activities of the Saite kings were predominately in the Delta region, an area where environment, lack of excavation and subsequent history are not conducive to the survival of artefacts. There is also the inherent difficulty in dating extant uninscribed statues of this period.[139]

Other than in artistic representations, archaism can also be recognised in the royal titularies and titles in use. Piye modelled his throne name on that of Thutmose III, as is attested in the temple at Gebel Barkal, later changing it to Usermaatre, a name which had been used first, and famously popularised by Ramesses II, also in the temple at Gebel Barkal.[140] Later the fifth ruler of the 26th Dynasty was to take the name Ahmose, harking back to the powerful founding member of the 18th Dynasty. Additionally, titles which had not been in use for centuries, with their original meaning and function sometimes obscure, were revived during the Saite era. These titles were used as a source of prestige in a new context, and the meaning of the title perhaps now related to a completely different activity. This deliberate restoration of old titles communicated the ideological message that the new administration was the heir to the ordered world of the past, particularly relevant if this restoration followed recent periods of political turmoil and division.[141] Although on occasions there appeared to be no functional weight to these titles, they may well have been modelled on much older sources.

Sais and the buildings of the early Saite Period

Sais, the present name of which is Sa el-Hagar, is located on the eastern bank of the Rosetta branch of the Nile river in the Egyptian Delta. Sais was the provincial capital of the fifth Lower Egyptian nome and main cult centre of the Warrior-goddess Neith. Although it is first mentioned in inscriptions in the Early Dynastic Period, there are few archaeological remains that show how the city developed to become in the Third Intermediate Period the centre of the Kingdom of the West and then later the capital city of Egypt during the 26th Dynasty.[142]

The total destruction of Sais over the millennia has, unfortunately, resulted in the loss of all the representative buildings of the 26th Dynasty from this site. Attempts at reconstructing these buildings rely, therefore, on early accounts of visitors to Egypt and surviving textual and archaeological evidence, together with the results of modern archaeological surveys.

The commanding mud-brick walls noted by earlier visitors to Sais have, over the years, been removed by the *sebakhin* and used as fertiliser by generations of farmers. The almost complete lack of any remaining stone buildings in Sais is not surprising as the continual rebuilding of Egyptian temples, constantly making use of the existing stone blocks, is recognised throughout the Dynastic age. Stone blocks in existing buildings were a ready target once the buildings were being replaced or no longer in use. This is particularly noticeable in the Delta where all new stone would have to have been transported from distant quarries, making it a valuable commodity. There are inscriptions, dating to the reign of Psamtek I and Psamtek II, in the quarries at Wadi Hammamat[143] demonstrating the distances that certain types of stone were transported.

There are accounts by Classical authors such as Herodotus,[144] who is considered to have visited Sais and Memphis in the middle of the fifth century BC. He described the palace of Wahibre Psamtek at Sais as 'a large and noteworthy building' (II, 163) and the temple court at Sais as 'a great cloistered building of stone, decorated with pillars carved in imitation of palm-trees, and other costly ornaments' (II, 169). He also mentioned the obelisks within the temple enclosure and a stone-bordered lake upon which were enacted festivals (II, 170–1). Although Herodotus's accounts mainly relate to the temple of Neith complex there is a brief mention of a 26th-Dynasty palace. Strabo[145] in his *Geography* mentions the location of Sais and the buildings, and, similarly to Herodotus, places the tomb of Psamtek within the walls of the Neith temple complex.[146]

A number of medieval and Arabic authors later wrote about Sais, but it was not until Napoleon's expedition of 1798 that the first full description, measurements and plans of what was, by then, left of Sais were compiled. Later, in the middle of the nineteenth century, a number of other travellers, such as Edward Clarke and Henry Salt, visited the site and described the ruins they observed. Of all these early visitors, it was perhaps Champollion who provided the most detailed plans and descriptions of the various architectural remains, including documenting the large extent of the necropolis, thought to be associated with the cult of Osiris Hemag.[147] Similarly, other travellers such as John Gardner Wilkinson, Lepsius and other early Egyptologists visited Sais and recorded their findings.[148]

Study of surviving blocks and monuments, sometimes now located some distance from Sais, has aided in attempts at reconstructing ancient Sais. Building blocks inscribed with the names of Psamtek I and other Saite kings have been found in many locations and would suggest an extensive building programme initiated by Psamtek. They have been found used as building materials in the Fort of Rosetta, and at villages such as Dibi, Foua and el-Nahhariya. In addition, museums around the world have artefacts, including statues and blocks, that have been assigned a Saite provenance.[149]

This information combined with the results of more current archaeological fieldwork has shed some light on ancient Sais. The recent 'Royal City of Sais Project' under the direction of Dr Penny Wilson[150] has been able to identify two separate areas of development. The first is the Northern Enclosure, which includes the last traces of an enclosure wall about 750 m by 700 m in area, and contains two protected areas of antiquities called Kom Rebwa, perhaps the area of the 26th-Dynasty Royal Palace and main temples. The other is the 'Great Pit', an area approximately 400 m by 400 m. These two zones were perhaps linked by a processional route and within this combined area a number of temples and buildings have been recognised. The chief sacred complex was that of the Temple of Neith as well as the temple of Osiris and the temple of Atum, although their exact location has not yet been positively determined. Some form of enclosure wall may have existed around the temple sites, but not necessarily around the whole settlement, as was the case with other Delta towns such as Tanis and Mendes[151] (Figure 4.7).

The Survey of Sais has been able to propose a site plan for the cult centre of the goddess Neith using information from a range of monuments and objects such as a wooden label,[152] dating to the reign of King Aha of the 1st Dynasty, a 26th-Dynasty stela describing festival buildings,[153] and the later statue of Udjahorresnet.[154] Similarly, the temple of Atum has also been recognised, and it is from here that a number of black basalt slabs with cornices of uraei have survived. It has been suggested that these once formed part of a balustrade at the temple.[155] One of these is inscribed with the name of Psamtek and displays two sunk relief representations of him (Figure 4.8).

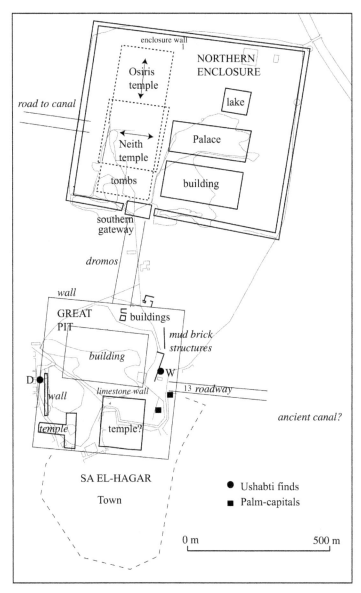

4·7 Sais: reconstruction of Saite buildings superimposed over the modern area of
Sa el-Hagar.

Surviving archaeological evidence from other Delta cities has similarly
provided information relating to their appearance in antiquity. As many as
thirty blocks inscribed with the name of Psamtek have been found as part of
the retaining walls of the sacred lake at Tanis; originally, these blocks may have

4.8 Block with cornice of uraei displaying the cartouches and Horus-name of Psamtek I and a sunk relief representations of the king kneeling and offering bread to two bull-headed deities (not shown). The treatment of the head recalls the royal iconography of the 25th Dynasty. Excavated at el-Rashid (Rosetta), Lower Egypt, Nile Delta. Black basalt. H. 1.21 m; W. 1.03 m; D. 25 cm (British Museum, London).

been part of a colonnaded building in the city.[156] According to Herodotus (II, 153), Psamtek added a temple for the Apis bull to the sanctuary of Ptah at Memphis. Building work was carried out at Heliopolis, from where fragments of a colossal statue of Psamtek I have been recovered as well as a temple screen wall fragment and a stela from the Serapeum all suggesting that Psamtek restored a temple at this site.[157] This recent discovery of the colossal statue highlights

4.9 Colossal statue of Psamtek I found at site of the temple of Ramesses II at Heliopolis. The quartzite statue is estimated to have been about 7.9 m tall and he is depicted with his left arm in front of his body. (Egyptian-German Mission at Matariya).

the existence of very large royal Saite statues, a feature that Herodotus (II, 175–76) described for Sais (Figure 4.9).[158]

Some well-preserved foundations of Saite temples survive at Mendes and Buto, and there are remains of the temple of Ahmose II at Athribis. Such groundworks allow an understanding of building methods of the 26th Dynasty which demonstrate the desire of the Saite builders for strength and support. Foundations pits were constructed, these being retained by thick mud-brick walls, and into the pits limestone blocks were placed on a sand fill. A number of examples are extremely well constructed, such as the foundations for the sanctuary area of the temple of Mendes, which extends down some 11 metres.[159]

Tombs of the officials in western Thebes

The Asasif in western Thebes is one of the principal areas of the Theban necropolis and located there is a remarkable group of tombs of the local high officials of the 25th and 26th Dynasties.[160] The radical design of these extensive tombs marks a break with previous burials of the past, and these large structures were to dominate the Asasif for over a hundred years. The tombs are typified by their archaising characteristics, incorporating reliefs that not only imitate those from a number of nearby tombs but also copy those from mortuary temples of preceding dynasties. Therefore, in creating 'copies' the tomb builders also created a 'new style' which was both innovative and imitative at the same time. Tomb decoration increased during this period, and traditional motifs such as fishing and fowling, butchery and bee-keeping are seen displayed alongside established funerary texts.

The tombs are notable for their size and complexity and share a number of common features including massive mud-brick superstructures with entrance pylons, descending passages leading to open sunken courtyards[161] and multi-level burial chambers. Originally the complexes were surrounded by mud-brick enclosure walls but much of these structures has now been lost.[162] The conspicuous nature of these tombs with their large mud-brick superstructures probably resulted in them being robbed at an early stage in antiquity. Consequently, many details of their burial equipment have been lost, but it is known that some individuals were buried in anthropoid stone coffins.[163] The elaborate subterranean parts of the tombs were used for intrusive burials during later periods. Among the main tombs at the Asasif are those belonging to Chief or High Stewards of the God's Wives of Amun, all of which are to be found in the (northern) Asasif, the principal tombs being those of Harwa, Petamenopet, Ibi, Pabasa and Padihorresnet.

Harwa

The earliest of these tombs to be built on the North Asasif is that of Harwa (TT 37), although the tomb of the First ꜥk-priest Karakhamun (TT 223) on the South Asasif was perhaps constructed a little earlier.[164] Harwa was one of the principal dignitaries of the Kushite Dynasty and was Chief Steward to Amenirdis I and then later to Shepenwepet II. His badly damaged incomplete tomb has numerous funerary scenes and texts inscribed on the walls, some of which are based on those observed in earlier tombs, including a depiction of bee-keeping similar to that seen in the tomb of Rekhmire (TT 100).[165] There are certain analogies with the nearby earlier tomb of Karakhamun, but Harwa also introduced some architectural and decorative innovations of his own, such as changing the location of the Book of the Dead spells and Pyramid Texts, modifications which were to influence later tombs built nearby.[166]

Other than his tomb at Thebes, Harwa is known through an offering table found at Deir el-Medina, eight statues[167] and a number of shabtis. His inscriptions list his many titles and offices, as well as affirming his virtues and the esteem in which he claimed he was held, both by his mistress, the God's Wife of Amun, and also by the King. The inscriptions are conspicuous for the combination of traditional phrases and the innovative choice of new metaphors.[168]

Petamenopet

The tomb of Petamenopet (TT 33),[169] the largest tomb in the group, is differentiated from its neighbours by its imaginative design. With its twenty-two rooms, spread over three levels, it is the most extensive private tomb in Egypt; the walls are elaborately decorated and covered with funerary texts. The vaulted entrance hall is decorated with offering scenes in raised relief, a number of these displaying similarities with those found in the tomb of Hatshepsut at Deir el-Bahri.[170]

Petamenopet was a 'Chief Lector' (*ḥry-ḥbt ḥry-tp*) and possessed the title 'in charge of the royal archives' (*sš nswt ʿ n ḥft-ḥr*), perhaps likened to being a private secretary to the king. He also had a number of epithets such as 'Beloved Sole Companion' (*smr wʿty n mrwt*), 'Overseer of all the King's Affairs' (*mr sp nbt nt nsw*) and 'who is in the heart of his lord' (*imy ib nb.f*), all of which suggest a close relationship with the monarch.[171] A number of additional and as yet not fully published titles were discovered in Corridor XII of the tomb during the 2010s: at the entrance to the corridor are 'Master of Secrets of the Morning House', 'Master of Secrets of the Two Diadems', and 'One who Adorns the Great of Magic'. Such titles suggest that Petamenopet was also an expert in royal rituals and so more than just a royal secretary. His high status and importance are also demonstrated by the large number of surviving statues of him. At least twelve are known, some of which were inspired by more ancient works.[172]

Unlike his neighbours in the same necropolis Petamenopet does not appear to have any connection to a God's Wife or her household. But he did carry a number of priestly titles including 'he controls the secrets of the divine words' (*ḥry-sštз n mdwt-nṯr*) and 'scribe of the divine books' (*sš mdwt-nṯr*). These together with the title of chief lector would indicate someone who was a specialist in rituals and competent in the field of religious literature. The entirety of the walls of rooms XII–XVI is covered with funerary texts, some of which seem to have been updated in antiquity, and it is suggested that these rooms represent a library using the medium of stone.[173] Thus, Petamenopet can perhaps be considered in modern terminology as an intellectual, a compiler of ancient texts and an exceptional antiquarian with comparisons to the earlier Prince Khaemwaset.

All of these titles indicate his importance and suggest that he was an influential figure in Upper Egypt and go some way to explain a tomb whose size exceeds that of most of the tombs of the pharaohs in the Valley of the Kings. Because of the absence of cartouches both in his tomb and on his statues, an unusual but seemingly deliberate oversight at this period, it is difficult to pinpoint the monarch he served. Being a contemporary of Montuemhat he perhaps belonged to the transition phase between the end of Kushite rule and that of Psamtek I.[174]

Ibi

The tomb of Ibi (TT 36),[175] Chief Steward to Nitiqret, God's Wife of Amun, is located close to that of Petamenopet. The decoration of the tomb displays a blending of Old and New Kingdom influences with many of the scenes derived, probably indirectly, from ones in the 6th-Dynasty tomb of an official with the same name, the nomarch Ibi at el-Gabrâwi.[176] Inscriptions on a stela of Ibi (see p. 76 n. 107) include details of the induction of Nitiqret in Year 9, as well as his appointment as Chief Steward in Year 26. Ibi further describes how he helped restore the palace of the God's Wife of Amun and the tomb of Osiris at Thebes, and how he helped to build a chapel to Osiris-Wennefer.[177]

Pabasa

Pabasa (TT 279)[178] was also Chief Steward to Nitiqret and was probably the successor of Ibi, and so his tomb belongs to the latter part of the reign of Psamtek I. Similarly to Ibi, he was Governor of Upper Egypt and carried many of the titles that Ibi possessed. Psamtek is the only king mentioned in Pabasa's tomb so it seems that he died either before or shortly after the accession of Nekau II. The tomb of Pabasa is in a good state of preservation but the substructure, although penetrated in the nineteenth century to extract Pabasa's stone coffin, has never been explored archaeologically. Of particular note are the reliefs of bee-keeping and the collecting of honey from pottery bee-hives, scenes which are widely published.[179] These scenes are either imitated from the New Kingdom tomb of Rekhmire or copied from the later tomb of Harwa. Among the texts inscribed on the walls are the Ritual of the Hours of the Day and the Hours of the Night. This latter text found in the pillared hall of the tomb is particularly well represented and is recognised as one of the best sources for the extended version of this Ritual.[180]

Padihorresnet

Padihorresnet (TT 196)[181] was the great-grandson of Ibi, and was to become Chief Steward to Nitiqret, occupying this office from late in the reign of Psamtek I to the beginning of the reign of Psamtek II. Both his father and grandfather had served in the administration of the God's Wife of Amun, and thus Padihor-resnet came from an old well-established and well-respected Theban family. Again, many of the titles possessed by Padihorresnet, including that of 'Governor of Upper Egypt', were similarly held by his predecessors.

Tomb chapels of the God's Wives of Amun at Medinet Habu

The God's Wife of Amun, Nitiqret, continued the tradition of building a chapel for herself within the temple precincts at Medinet Habu, as her predecessors Shepenwepet I, Amenirdis I and Shepenwepet II had done before her (see pp. 52–53). Nitiqret completed the tomb chapel of her immediate predecessor, Shepenwepet II, and then added another for herself between the tomb of Shepenwepet and that of Amenirdis I. Some time later, Nitiqret extended the building further west to accommodate a tomb chapel for her mother, Queen Mehytenweskhet C.[182] Located nearby was a cemetery for the female members of the cult of Amun who were closely associated with the God's Wives. These tombs were frequently found to be grouped together, in groupings of mother and daughter, sisters or servants and mistresses.[183]

Again, Nitiqret adopted the practice that previous God's Wives had assumed, that of building a small chapel dedicated to Osiris. This was erected north of the temple of Amun at Karnak and was called 'The Lord of Life who gives Sed-festivals'. Also, north of the Amun temple, Nitiqret built a columned building, and inscribed on the walls are her own cartouche and that of her father, Psamtek I.[184]

Northern elite burials

The practice of royal burials within cult-temple enclosures, a feature of the Third Intermediate Period, was maintained during the Saite Period. Although there is no archaeological evidence of these burials at Sais, Herodotus refers to them in his *Histories*.[185] Similarly, the revival of monumental tomb building for high officials that was initiated during the 25th Dynasty continued into the Saite Period, particularly as described above, at the Asasif at Thebes.

As well as the tombs on the Asasif, another new style of tomb design appeared in the Memphite region, the shaft-tomb, perhaps based on or influenced by the Step Pyramid at Saqqara. In these tombs, the architectural emphasis was on the substructure, which consisted of a large chamber built at the bottom of a deep shaft, often accessed from a secondary shaft. The tombs were designed to be completely filled with fine sand after the burial, in order to safeguard the body and burial equipment from tomb robbers. Very little remains of the perhaps once imposing superstructures of these shaft-tombs and so it is difficult to determine their shape or structure, and there seems little consensus as to what form that took. The inscriptions in the burial chamber of such tombs are largely formulaic, including references from the Pyramid Texts, Coffin Texts and Book of the Dead as well as prayers to Osiris, Re, Ptah-Sokar and Anubis. These inscriptions are often copies of these texts but some have innovative additions, such as the 'new' texts added to the Pyramid Texts in the tomb of Padinisis and one of the first appearances of the god Tutu.[186] Also included on the tomb walls are extensive offering lists.

A number of sites were chosen to build these tombs in the Memphite region, such as at Giza, Saqqara, Heliopolis and Abusir. These particular locations were already 'sacred landscapes' where previous generations were buried and where the site had become recognised as a centre for worship and communion with the ancestors.[187] The shaft-tombs were often placed in close proximity to important ancient monuments of the past such as the pyramid fields and Sun Temple at Heliopolis. Sometimes they were even cut into these structures so that they could become a part of this wider group of monuments and have close association with the past. Other than the religious consideration was the desire on behalf of the deceased elite for an element of conspicuous display in the design of their tombs. They built large prominent tombs, lavishly decorated, intending that their name and deeds would impress and live on in the memories of those who followed.[188]

Certain features of the shaft-tombs may have been influenced by the Step Pyramid of Djoser, further illustrating the theme of archaism during the Saite era. The Saites are known to have explored the substructure of the Step Pyramid, as attested by the copy grids that are visible on two of the three reliefs of Djoser in the galleries. The grids conform to the later grid system that came into operation in the Late Period rather than the one in use during the Old Kingdom.[189] They also created a new long 'Southern Gallery', perhaps designed for access to inspect the monument, or possibly the Saites had intended to carry out some renovations. Examples of such tomb complexes at Memphis are Saqqara, Heliopolis and Abusir.

Saqqara

At Saqqara there is the impressive rock-cut tomb of Bakenrenef (see p. 97) dated to the reign of Psamtek I as well as a number of shaft-tombs, including the tomb of Amuntefnakht built during the reign of Haaibra, and Djanehibu during the reign of Ahmose II. Amuntefnakht was responsible for the recruitment of the royal guard, the troops who safeguarded the monarch, and he possessed the title 'Commandant of Recruits of the Royal Guard' (*ḥrp-nfrw n mḥ-ib nswt*).[190] The main shaft of his tomb descends 22 metres below ground level to where his sarcophagus was placed. Inside the shaft was a greenish slate anthropoid coffin within which was found a wrapped body, presumably that of the deceased.[191]

Heliopolis[192]

Heliopolis, ancient Iunu, was important as a religious centre and burial ground in Predynastic times and is frequently associated with creation in the Coffin and Pyramid Texts. The proximity of the sacred site of the Sun Temple would have been a desirable burial place for the elite of the 26th Dynasty. At Heliopolis it was not shaft-tombs that were constructed but vaulted chamber tombs, in which a short access led to a rectangular or square vaulted chamber that housed the burial. The quality of the rock at Heliopolis was not suitable for the construction of rock-cut and shaft tombs, and the tombs were all of small size and similar shape owing to a lack of space in the already crowded burial ground.[193] Many of the tombs are now below the modern north-east Cairo suburbs, and because of this building construction many details of these structures have disappeared, including the funerary chapels which were built above the burial chambers. In addition, some of these Late Period tombs appear to have been dismantled and reused in Ptolemaic and Roman times.

One example where the decoration and inscriptions have survived is that of Panehesy, an important official during the reign of Psamtek II who possessed the titles of 'Chancellor of the King of Upper and Lower Egypt' (*sḏꜣwty bity*), 'Sole Companion' (*smr-wꜥty*) and 'Royal Acquaintance' (*rḫ nswt*), as well as the priestly title 'God's Father of Heliopolis' (*it-nṯr ꜣwnw*).[194] The tomb walls are decorated with chapters from the Book of the Dead, Pyramid Texts and Coffin Texts, but had the innovative addition of 'new' texts added to the Pyramid Texts in an example of textual archaism.

Abusir

Abusir, an important Old Kingdom site, was brought to prominence by Udjahorresnet towards the end of the Saite Period when he commenced construction of his tomb there in Year 40 or 41 of Ahmose II. A new cemetery then came into being located some 200 metres from the Old Kingdom monuments. The necropolis contains at least five large shaft-tombs and several smaller ones, but other than the tomb of Udjahorresnet these tombs date to the Persian Period and later, with the cemetery probably still in use in Ptolemaic times.[195]

It is difficult to say why Udjahorresnet should have chosen this remote site for his burial, but it is possible he may have wished to start a new cemetery centred on his tomb.[196] However, his tomb does lie in a sacred area overlooking the Serapeum and 5th-Dynasty Sun Temples and there was a ready supply of ancient stone available from the Old Kingdom monuments. The impressive tomb that Udjahorresnet constructed was probably visible from Memphis and its size and lavish nature would have provided a conspicuous display for such an important individual.[197] Excavations have revealed that the tomb had a considerable superstructure of limestone blocks, although its form is uncertain. One suggestion is that the main shaft was covered with a truncated pyramid with a flat roof and that the whole tomb was surrounded by an enclosure wall.[198] The main shaft is also encircled by a trench more than 11 metres deep, possibly having a religious function, perhaps with the intention of imitating the design of the Step Pyramid or the Osireion at Abydos.[199] At the bottom of the 20-metre shaft rested the massive white limestone sarcophagus of Udjahorresnet.[200]

From the structure, decoration and importantly the titles inscribed in these elite tombs, it is apparent that it was the highest ranks of society that were buried in the Memphite region, with the largest and most visible tombs being built by those at the top of the social hierarchy.[201] The priesthood and military are represented but many of these elite tombs were occupied by individuals possessing high administrative titles, indicating the importance of Memphis as an active and key administrative centre during the Saite Period. Examples being those of Panehesy mentioned above, Bakenrenef,[202] who was 'Director of Upper and Lower Egypt' (*ḥrp wr šmˁ mḥw*), and Psamtek, son of Meramuntabes, who was not only 'Overseer of the Great House' (*imy-r pr wr*) but 'Overseer of all Bureaucracy' (*imy-r sˁḥ nbt*).[203]

Changes in funerary practices

Funerary equipment

A new type of anthropoid coffin was developed during the 25th and the 26th Dynasties with the coffin representing the deceased in mummy form, standing on a pedestal with a pillar supporting the back, clearly copying the pattern normally seen on statues.[204] Both wooden and stone examples are attested, with ornamentation and inscriptions which included the funerary deities. Decorated inner coffins of wood replaced earlier cartonnage models, and the design of these inner coffins allowed more space for inscriptions.[205]

Stone sarcophagi,[206] often substantially decorated, saw a revival during the Saite Period. A typical example is that of the God's Wife Ankhnesneferibre, which bears extensive texts and has a raised two-dimensional depiction of Ankhnesneferibre on the lid (Figure 4.10). Similarly, the sarcophagus of Nitiqret has a recumbent body portraying the God's Wife upon the flat lid, a depiction which displays archaising features of the New Kingdom royal examples.[207]

Large numbers of canopic jars survive, with the solid dummy jars of the Third Intermediate Period now being replaced, in the archaising manner of the Saite Period, by a return to the traditional style of 'open' vase with human-headed stoppers. Each jar now had its own particular formulation rather than merely differing in the deities invoked. The canopic equipment was now no longer placed at the foot of the body as previously, but usually placed in niches in the walls of the burial chamber.[208]

4.10 Detail of the lid of the sarcophagus of Ankhnesneferibre, God's Wife of Amun, daughter of Psamtek II. The upper surface is decorated with a figure of Ankhnesneferibre in low relief, shown in full regalia, with double-plumed headdress. Discovered at Deir el-Medina. Black siltstone. L. 2.59 m (British Museum, London).

Ushabtis (Shabtis)[209]

Shabtis, the mummiform funerary figurines which were first introduced around 2100 BC, become a standard element of burials by the first millennium, and saw further development during the Saite, and the Late Period in general. The full significance of the shabti figure was complex but overall it was intended to be a servant of the deceased once activated in the afterlife.[210] From the New Kingdom onwards, the deceased was supplied with 365 shabtis representing one for every day of the year as well as overseers to organise the workers. A total of 401 was not uncommon in the Late Period, as attested in the tombs of Hekaemsaf and Tjanehebu, although the overseers became harder to distinguish during the Saite Period[211] (Figure 4.11). The figurines were usually stored in wooden boxes, sometimes placed in niches in the walls of the tomb or standing in ranks around the tomb chamber.

During the Late Period they became known as *ushabtis*, after the verb 'to answer' (*wsb*), referring to the shabtis' reply to the summons to work. They were then usually fabricated out of faience, in pastel tones of mainly green and less often blue, and often very carefully modelled. Faience production witnessed

4.11 Shabti of Hekaemsaf who was a high official during the reign of Ahmose II. The inscription on the back pillar: 'Shabti of the Osiris, Overseer of Royal Ships, Hekaemsaf, behold you shall answer at any time'. Discovered in his tomb, near the Pyramid of Unas at Saqqara. Faience, pale blue-green glaze. H. 18.6 cm (Private collection).

a revival in the Late Period and the standard of artefacts produced was high. The greater degree of detail and clarity of form are indications of this higher level of craftsmanship. The figurines became slender in form, were usually male and often displayed the Saite smile. An important feature was a dorsal pillar and trapezoidal base which was inspired by these elements appearing in statuary of the period, emphasising the essential 'statute-ness' of the figurines (Figure 4.12).[212] The majority of the shabtis of the Saite Period have been found at sites in the north of Egypt. There are relatively few from Thebes, and those are of an inferior type, such as that of Ankhhor, Chief Steward of the God's Wife,

4.12 Shabti of Psamtek born of a woman named Sebarekhyt. Mummiform shabti wearing a striated tripartite wig, and a plaited divine beard which is curled at the tip. The arms are crossed right over left on the chest, and the hands emerge from a shroud to hold a hoe in the right, and a pick in the left. On the shabti figure Psamtek has the title 'God's Father'. Probably from Saqqara. Faience, bright blue glaze. H. 18.6 cm (Private collection).

who was buried about 586 BC – another example of the steady decline in the importance of Thebes following the reunification of Egypt.[213]

The functioning of the figurines was dependent on a magical incantation known as the shabti spell, based on chapter 6 of the Book of the Dead, and which developed over time. In the Late Period this was sometimes inscribed on the dorsal pillar of the shabti, although many display a short text, often merely 'illuminating/glorifying the Osiris' (*sḥd Wsir*) followed by the name of the deceased.

Animal mummies

Animal cults existed in ancient Egypt as early as the Predynastic Period, probably beginning as manifestations of regional symbols, with the animals then acquiring divine associations and becoming a focus of religious piety. The animal gods became national deities, and, while the animal associated with a particular deity was not worshipped, it was regarded as a representation of a particular deity, embodying certain characteristics of the god, the notion of divinity resident within an animal. Although animal cults gained in popularity in the New Kingdom, it was during the Saite and subsequent Persian and Ptolemaic Periods that the cult of divine animals underwent a considerable degree of development and proliferation. It is considered that the king had a central role in founding and maintaining estates and buildings for the divine cults and it is probable that such foundations were given such status by royal decree during the reigns of Psamtek I and Ahmose II.[214]

Why this progression of the sacred animal cults occurred is not completely certain,[215] but it could have been related to a manifestation of resurgent national pride and cultural consciousness, after periods of foreign occupation, also associated with an increase in personal piety that was evident at this time.[216] Again mummification techniques now became less expensive and hence more accessible to the general populace. Also, there was a need for the temples to raise income by the sale of votive offerings as temples were now no longer so well endowed.[217]

Increasingly, all examples of a particular species of animal were regarded as sacred to the deity to which the animal was associated, and this led to the keeping of large numbers of animals at the temple of that deity. It was at death that they acquired their main significance when their bodies were mummified and ritually buried in animal catacombs, such as that at North Saqqara where the underground chambers have yielded millions of mummies (Figure 4.13). The numbers of officials serving such cults increased considerably during the Saite Period and the sale of these offices, together with the taxation of the cult centres, would have yielded additional revenues for the state.[218] Examples of

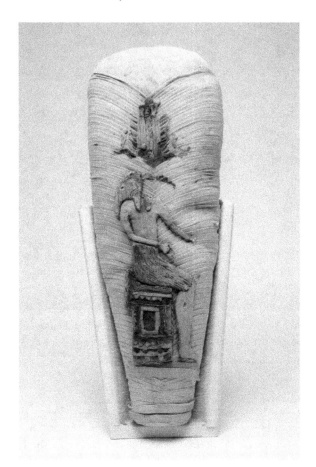

4.13 Animal mummy from the Sacred Animal Necropolis at North Saqqara. A CT scan and radiograph taken at Manchester showed the bundle to be that of an ibis bird. The tight herringbone pattern of the wrappings, typical of the Saqqara necropolis, has been enhanced with an embossed appliqué image of the god Thoth. H. 48 cm; W. 18 cm; D. 15.5 cm (Manchester Museum, Manchester).

the day-to-day activity of these institutions during the Ptolemaic Period is attested in a set of documents known as *The Archive of Hor.*[219]

Although these animal mummies were used as votive offerings, the manner in which they were considered to function has been widely debated,[220] but a common understanding is that the souls of the animals acted as messengers between the people on Earth and the Gods. It was believed that the animal mummy would carry a message requesting intervention in a human problem, as attested by the large numbers of such oracular questions and responses that

4.14 Chamber Y of the underground galleries of the Serapeum, North Saqqara, the burial place of the Apis bulls. The sarcophagus shown is for Apis XLI, buried in Year 23 of Ahmose II.

have survived.[221] Certain sites such as Saqqara show evidence of pilgrim activity where an individual would visit the temple, make a donation and dedicate an animal. Archaeological and literary evidence indicates that the first ibis burial place in Egypt was at Tuna el-Gebel and that mummified animals which originated from locations all over Egypt were brought to Tuna el-Gebel for interment.[222]

Another category of sacred animals was the 'temple animal', and of particular note was the cult of the Apis bull, one of the oldest and most prominent cults in ancient Egypt. The Apis bull was the most important of the sacred animals and was regarded as an incarnation of the Memphite Creator-god, Ptah, a receptacle in which the non-physical essence of the deity was manifested. The Apis bulls, selected from among the cattle of Egypt by means of specific body markings, lived within the temple complex at Memphis, and, upon their natural deaths, their remains were mummified and buried in massive granite sarcophagi in the Serapeum (Figure 4.14). The deceased Apis became identified with Osiris and was referred to as Osiris-Apis, becoming a symbol of Osirian resurrection. Osiris-Apis or Osarapis was shortened to Serapis in the Ptolemaic Period, and from this the burial galleries became known as the Serapeum.[223]

The earliest known burial at the Serapeum, which is located north-west of the Step Pyramid of Djoser, dates to the reign of Amenhotep III but the tradition of the ceremonial burial of the Apis may date further back to an earlier reign.[224] The first bull to die under Psamtek I, in his Year 20/21, was interred in a set of galleries first founded under Rameses II (the 'Lesser Vaults'), in a chamber that already held the mummy of a bull that had died in Year 24 of Taharqo. However, for the next, which died in Year 52, a new sequence of chambers, the 'Greater Vaults', was begun, which would be subsequently enlarged progressively, reaching 350 m in length as attested by a stela Psamtek erected.[225] The Serapeum went out of use at the end of the Ptolemaic Period.

Many of the stelae found in the tombs of the Apis bulls have provided detailed dates for the birth and death of the Apis and their lifespan to the day, as well as details of the dedicator of the stela. From this information a chronological list of the bulls' burials can be created that permits links to the regnal dates of the ruling monarch.[226] Such precise dating information is rare from Pharaonic Egypt and provides key data for establishing fixed points in Egyptian chronology during the Late Period.

Notes

1   Published by Goedicke 1962; Basta 1968; Moussa 1981 and Perdu 2002b. For discussion see Spalinger 1982: 220–21; Der Manuelian 1994: 323–32 and Gozzoli 2006: 92–95.
2   Spalinger 1982: 221.
3   Stela VII, l. 7.
4   Gozzoli 2006: 94.
5   Boast: 2007: 22.
6   Herodotus II, 154.
7   Petrie 1888.
8   Leclère and Spencer 2014.
9   Oren 1984; Smoláriková 2008: 48–54.
10 Spencer 1996, 1999, 2003; Smoláriková 2008: 65–70.
11 Dodson 2012: 175.
12 Redon and Dhennin 2013.
13 Smoláriková 2008: 28.
14 Tadmor 1966: 102; Redford 1992: 444.
15 Miller and Hayes 2006: 460.
16 Redford 2000: 183.
17 Lloyd 1983: 338.
18 See Malamat 1973, 1974 and for excavations Dothan and Freedman 1967, Dothan 1971
19 See Tadmor 1966: 101–2. Spalinger (1977: 223) comments that this figure is often regarded as mere fiction. Also see Kienitz 1953: 17.
20 Lloyd 1988: 148.
21 Malamat 1973: 270–2; Kahn 2015.

22 BM 21901, ll. 10 and 11, Grayson 1975: 91.
23 Gablini is a city on the mid-Euphrates while the location of Akkad is uncertain, and was originally considered to be on the river Euphrates. More recent discussions site Akkad on the river Tigris (Wall-Romana 1990: 205–6; Reade 2002: 69).
24 Chauveau 2011.
25 Round bottles having an inscription wishing the owner a good new year. They contained incense or water from the Nile, a symbol connected to the regeneration of the land.
26 Schipper 2010: 204–12.
27 Stager 1996: 69–70.
28 Oren 1993: 103–4.
29 Na'aman 1991: 38; Gitin 1998: 173.
30 Oren 1993.
31 Stripling et al. 2017.
32 Lehmann 1998: 7–9; Fantalkin 2001.
33 Naveh 1962: 99; Wenning 2001: 262.
34 Schipper 2010: 204–12.
35 BM 25127, Grayson 1975: 87–90
36 Spalinger 1977: 224; Na'aman 1991: 39; Schipper 2010: 203.
37 Miller and Hayes 2006: 452.
38 The early relations between Egypt and Judah are referred to in chapter 2 of Jeremiah. See Milgrom 1955 and Spalinger 1977: 223.
39 Cogan 1971: 70–71; Kahn 2015: 512.
40 Zawadski 1995.
41 Schipper 2010: 214.
42 See Spalinger 1978c and n. 3 for extensive bibliography; for a history of the study and bibliography see Grantovskii 1994; Ivantchik 1999; West 2002.
43 Spalinger (1978c: 49) deduced that the conflict between the Egyptians and the Scythians must have occurred after 623 BC, whereas Lloyd (1983: 338) suggests earlier at between c. 637 and 625 BC. Zadwadski (1995) considers that the Scythian peak of their success, if it existed, was c. 630–620 BC.
44 Ivantchik 1999.
45 Spalinger 1978c: 50.
46 Chugunov et al. 2017.
47 Ivantchik 1999: 517–18; West 2002: 437 n. 4.
48 As described in the *Babylonian Chronicle* 3, BM 21901, Grayson 1975: 90–96.
49 The *Umman-Manda* is often used to refer to semi-nomadic hordes from northern Mesopotamia or Asia, with early authors recognising them as the Scythians, whereas more recently they are suggested to be the Medes. In the *Babylonian Chronicle* referring to the conflict at Harran in 610 BC, the term is considered to refer to the Medes. See Spalinger 1978c: 50 and particularly the discussion in n. 9. For a comprehensive analysis of the *Umman-Manda* see Zawadzki 1988 and Addah 2011.
50 Spalinger 1977: 224.
51 Chron. 3, BM 21901, ll. 61ff, Grayson 1975: 95–96.
52 Louvre E 3335. See Freedy and Redford 1970: 477; Redford 1992: 442; Perdu 2002b 39–41; Schipper 2010: 201.

53 *ANET* 307; Miller and Hayes 2006: 447.
54 Walters Art Gallery, Baltimore No. 22.203. See Steindorff (1939), who dated the later inscription to the 22nd Dynasty. However, see Porten (1981: 44) and Schipper (2010: 213) for a 26th Dynasty date.
55 For discussions on the Adon letter and the location of Ekron which is often assumed to be Ashkelon but could perhaps be Gaza, see Fitzmyer 1965; Freedy and Redford 1970: 477 n. 77; Porten 1981.
56 Fitzmyer 1965: 43; Krahmalkov 1981.
57 Schipper 2010: 220.
58 P. Berlin 13588. See Erichsen 1956: 49–81 and Smith 1991.
59 See Smith 1991: 101–9. There is an account of the death of Psamtek II in P. Rylands IX (15.8–15), and of Psamtek III in Herodotus (III, 15).
60 Little funerary equipment can be attested to the reign of Psamtek I, but Wilson (2016) discusses shabti figures dating to his reign and describes a recent shabti fragment found near the Great Pit at Sa el-Hagar (Sais) which she attributes to Psamtek I. Also see Aubert and Aubert 1974: 210–15 and Schneider 1993.
61 Wilson 2006: 27 and 2016: 75.
62 See Villing 2017.
63 Wilson and Gilbert 2007.
64 See Leonard (1997: 1–35) for a comprehensive overview of previous excavations at Naukratis. Also for excavation reports and bibliography from the British Museum Project 'Greeks in Egypt' see: www.britishmuseum.org/research/research_projects/all_current_projects/naukratis_the_greeks_in_egypt.aspx
65 Höckmann and Möller 2006.
66 Thomas et al. 2014.
67 For discussions of the evidence see for example: Möller 2000; James 2003; Demetriou 2012: 109–23; Villing and Schlotzhauer 2006.
68 Boardman 1999: 121; Villing and Schlotzhauer 2006: 5.
69 Möller 2001; Redon 2012.
70 Yoyotte 1983; Leclère 2008: 117; Spencer 2011: 35.
71 Spencer 2011.
72 Coulson and Leonard 1981: 11; Malouta 2015: 3.
73 Villing and Schlotzhauer 2006: 7.
74 Boardman 1999: 129–30; Villing and Schlotzhauer 2006: 1.
75 Van der Wilt 2010.
76 Villing and Schlotzhauer 2006: 7.
77 Kouriou 2004; Ebbinghaus 2006.
78 For discussions of Egyptian influences on Greek architecture and sculpture see Bietak 2001; Tanner 2003; Höckmann 2005; Villing and Schlotzhauer 2006: 7–8.
79 Webb 1978; Gorton 1996; James 2003: 251–56.
80 Demetriou 2012: 106.
81 Thomas and Villing 2013: 82.
82 See Villing and Schlotzhauer 2006: 5 and n. 22 for bibliography on this topic.
83 Schauss 2006; D'Angelo 2006; Villing and Schlotzhauer 2006: 5.
84 Redon and Dhennin 2013.
85 Gunn 1927.
86 Lloyd 1983: 288–89.

87 In P. Rylands IX, 8.19 Petiese was granted priesthoods in various temples by Psamtek; in 10, 6 Somtutefnakht was made Master of Shipping; in 10.15–18 Psamtek allowed Petiese to retire and rewarded him with a property and in 11.19 he administers justice by causing two priests to be punished.

88 Parkinson 1997: 54–88.

89 For discussions on political decision-making see Loprieno 1996; Jansen-Winkeln 1998; Hofmann 2004; Beylage 2002: 553–618; Quack 2010: 5.

90 Jansen-Winkeln 1985: 317–20; Vernus 1999: 146–47; Kloth 2002: 158–59; Quack 2010.

91 Agut-Labordère 2013: 969.

92 Louvre A 83; see Vittmann 1978: 74–75.

93 Leahy 1988; Ladynin 2006

94 De Meulenaere 1982: 569; Vittmann 2009: 99.

95 Pressl 1998: 17–19; Agut-Labordère 2013: 973–74.

96 For attestations of this title during the Late Period see Vittmann 1998: 654–60.

97 P. Rylands IX, 19.1–3 and 8–13.

98 As mentioned on statue CG 658 dedicated by the future Psamtek II. See El-Sayed 1974; Agut-Labordère 2013: 974.

99 Vittmann 2009: 94.

100 Bassir 2013: 8.

101 Lloyd 1983: 335; Agut-Labordère 2013: 983.

102 Smith 1998: 238–39.

103 For discussions on archaism see Brunner 1975; Der Manuelian 1994; Russmann 2001; Morkot 2003b; Kahl 2010; Stammers 2016.

104 For a study of the various definitions of archaism see among others Der Manuelian 1994; Neureiter 1994, and Jurman 2010.

105 Der Manuelian 1994: 408.

106 Erman 1934: 321.

107 Anthes 1953: 213.

108 Otto 1969: 100–1.

109 The term Renaissance has been used widely to explain the Saite phenomenon; see for example Grimal (1994: 354–59). However, see Spalinger's comments (1978b: 12–14) and those of Agut-Labordère (2013: 966) relating to the problems in using this term.

110 Brunner 1975; Jurman 2010: 75–76.

111 Freed 1997.

112 Peterson 1967.

113 Kahl 2010: 1.

114 Russmann 2001: 44.

115 Robins 1997: 212.

116 Josephson 1997.

117 BM EA 1238. See Müller 1979: 29; Leahy 1984d: 59; Lindblad 1984: 53–54 [B], pl. 32.

118 Fazzini 1972: 64–68. Morkot and James (2009) have suggested that the development of this trend can be dated precisely to the end of the reign of Sheshonq III of the 22nd Dynasty, but on a proposed lowering of the accepted chronology. Contra Broekman 2011.

119 Spalinger 1978b: 12; Der Manuelian 1994: 2.

120   See stela of Taharqo, Year 6, l. 21–3 in Macadam 1949, I: 16 n. 51 and II:
      pls 7, 8.
121   O'Connor 2003: 177–78.
122   Morkot 2003b: 81; Kahl 2010: 2.
123   Leclant 1980.
124   ÄM 7972; Morkot 2014: 15.
125   Traunecker 2014.
126   Tomb LS 24. See El Naggar 1986; Bresciani et al. 1988; Pressl 1998: 168–70.
127   Der Manuelian 1994; Russmann 1994, 1997; Smith 1998: 238–44; Morkot 2003b:
      89–92; Kahl 2010: 6.
128   Der Manuelian 1994: 28–51.
129   Der Manuelian 1994: 18–21, figs 1–3.
130   Russmann 1994: 13.
131   Russmann 1994; Morkot 2003b: 89–93.
132   Robins 1997: 226; Smith 1998: 238, 244; Mendoza 2015: 209, 408–10. An example
      of this is the statue of Nespekashuty, Cairo JE 36665.
133   Pischikova 2014: 84.
134   Egyptian Museum, Cairo. CG 442236.
135   Robins 1997: 226.
136   Levin 1964: 16.
137   A theophorous statue portrays the individual holding or supporting a deity while
      a naophorous statue portrays the subject holding a naos shrine usually containing
      a divine image.
138   Levin 1964: 21–23; Mendoza 2015: 409–10. For a Middle Kingdom example see the
      seated statue of Mentuhotep II which demonstrates a hint of an expression (JdE
      36195, Russmann and Finn 1989: fig. 18). In the New Kingdom see the statues of
      Tuthmosis III (e.g. BM EA 986, Russmann 2001: 118–19) and early sculptures of
      Amenhotep III (e.g. BM EA 7, Russmann 2001: 132–33).
139   Saite royal sculpture is reviewed in Leahy 1984d, which includes a catalogue and
      associated bibliography.
140   Morkot 2000: 169–70.
141   Moreno Garcia: 2013a: 7.
142   Wilson 2006, 2010.
143   See Couyat and Montet 1912: 33 (inscription 2) and 58 (inscription 59) for Psamtek
      I; 100 (inscription 71) for Psamtek II.
144   For translation of Herodotus see Herodotus 1996 and for commentaries on Herodotus
      see Lloyd 1975, 1976, 1988. Also see Leclère 2008: 159–96.
145   For Strabo see Jones 1982.
146   I, 17, 18.
147   Wilson 2006: 55.
148   For a detailed description and bibliography of all the early accounts and the
      various visitors who travelled to Sais see Wilson 2006: 35–85.
149   Wilson: 2002: 571.
150   See Habachi 1943 and Wilson 2006 for a history and bibliography of more recent
      fieldwork at Sais.
151   Wilson 2006: 233–66.
152   Label of King Aha, Dynasty I, see Petrie 1901: pl. III A5.
153   BM EA 1427 (808), see El-Sayed 1975: 61–72, pl. IX.

154 Wilson 2006: 19–33.
155 It was discovered at Rosetta and is now in the British Museum (BM EA 20). See Habachi 1943; Smith 1998: 244–5; Arnold 1999: 71; and www.britishmuseum.org/research/collection_online/collection_object_details.aspx?objectId=120153&partId=1&searchText=Psamtek+1&page.
156 Montet 1966.
157 Arnold 1999: 70–74.
158 Ashmawy and Raue 2017a and b: 40–41.
159 Arnold 1999: 66–67.
160 There is an extensive publication list for these tombs: see Eigner 1984 and Smith 1998: 239ff n. 31 (for bibliography). Also Pischikova 2014 for tombs of the South Asasif.
161 These courts form a prominent and essential element of architecture in these monumental 'temple-tombs' of the Kushite and Saite Periods. See Eigner 2017: 73–74.
162 Robins: 1997: 218; Thomas 2000: 38.
163 See Buhl 1959: 151–52 for stone sarcophagi and Aston 2003: 138–66 for the Theban West Bank.
164 Einaudi 2014.
165 Tiradritti 1998: 3–6; Dodson and Ikram 2008: 52; Kritsky 2015: 45–60.
166 Einaudi 2014: 328–35.
167 For publication of the statues see Gunn and Engelbach 1931: 791–815 and Gunn 1934.
168 Lichtheim 1980: 25.
169 For the tomb of Petamenopet see PM I, I 50–56; Anthes 1937; Thomas 2000 with bibliography; Traunecker 2014: 205–34; Price 2017a
170 Smith 1998: 240.
171 Anthes 1937: 31; Traunecker 2014: 209–10.
172 Traunecker 2014; Price 2017a: 397–99.
173 Régan 2014.
174 Traunecker 2014: 210.
175 Kuhlmann and Shenkel 1983.
176 PM IV, 244 (12–13); Davies 1902: 8–24, pl. 14.
177 Breasted 1906: 4, 488–91; Graefe 1990.
178 Graefe 1981: 63–64; Dodson and Ikram 2008: 284; Broekman 2012b: 119; Corsi 2017; Griffin 2017: 279.
179 Kritsky 2015: 45–60.
180 Griffin 2017.
181 Graefe 1981: 80 and 2003; Broekman 2012b: 119–20.
182 Hölscher 1954: 16–29; Ayad 2009: 26.
183 Elias 1993: 72–74; Aston 2003: 145.
184 PM I, I (1972) 13–14, 19–20; Arnold 1999: 72; Dodson 2012: 175.
185 II, 169–70.
186 Gesterman 1994: 89; Stammers 2016: 86–87.
187 Buikstra and Charles 1999: 204.
188 Stammers 2016: 1, 94.
189 Lauer 1972: 12–13; Robins and Fowler 1994: 160–70; Baines and Riggs 2001: 111–15; Smoláriková 2010.

190 Saad 1947: 386; Pressl 1998: 282; Stammers 2016: 73, 164.

191 Saad 1947: 389–90; Stammers 2016: 104, 164.

192 Gauthier 1921a, 1921b, 1922a, 1927, 1933; Bickel and Tallet 1997; Dodson and Ikram 2008: 286–87.

193 Stammers 2016: 45.

194 El-Sawi and Gomaa 1993: 7; Stammers 2016: 127.

195 Bareš 1999: 108 and 2000: 13.

196 Verner 2002: 188.

197 Stammers 2016: 27–28, 111–12.

198 Bareš 1999: 48.

199 Bareš 1999: 63 n. 314;

200 Bareš 1999: 54; Verner 2002: 179.

201 Stammers 2016: 45.

202 Vittmann 1978: 146.

203 Stammers 2016: 76.

204 For images see Taylor 2001: figs 174, 175; Aston 2009.

205 Ikram and Dodson 1998: 236–40; Taylor 2001: 236–41.

206 See Buhl 1959 for examples of anthropoid stone sarcophagi.

207 Ikram and Dodson 1998: 268–69.

208 Dodson and Ikram 2008: 286.

209 Aubert and Aubert 1974; Schneider 1977; Taylor 2001: 112–35; Janes 2002; Milde 2012 (with bibliography).

210 Taylor 2001: 112.

211 Janes 2002: 207, 210.

212 Aubert and Aubert 1974: 208; Janes 2002: xvii; Price 2017a.

213 Taylor 2001: 131–32.

214 Kessler and Nur el-Din 2015: 124; Atherton-Woolham and McKnight 2015: 23.

215 Quirke 2015: 40.

216 Davies and Smith 1997: 122; Taylor 2001: 246; Ikram 2005: 10.

217 Dunand and Lichtenberg 2006: 122, 206; McKnight et al. 2018.

218 Taylor 2001: 246–47.

219 Hor of Sebennytos was an important functionary at the sanctuary of the Ibis at Saqqara, as well as at other institutions. He was a priest and scribe and interpreted dreams as well as foretelling events. He had contact with the Ptolemaic rulers during his career and was active 170–145 BC. The *Archive*, consisting of approximately 70 ostraca, which are mainly personal notes and drafts of documents, is an important source of information of the events at that period (Ray 1976; Prada 2017: 5).

220 Kessler 1989; Ikram 2005; Atherton-Woolham and McKnight 2015: 23–24.

221 Bleiberg 2013; Atherton-Woolham and McKnight 2015.

222 Kessler and Nur el Din 2015: 120–26.

223 Taylor 2001: 247–50; Marković 2015: 135–36.

224 Taylor 2001: 244–63; Nicholson 2005: 46.

225 Stela E 3339; Devauchelle 1994: 100.

226 Von Beckerath 1997: 85–87; Depuydt 2006a: 267–68 and 2006b: 466.

5

The heirs of Psamtek I: Nekau II and Psamtek II

I Nekau II

Levantine policy

Following the death of Psamtek I in 610 BC, his only known son, Nekau, born by Mehytenweskhet C, was crowned king as Nekau II. The earliest evidence relating to him is of his campaigning east of the river Euphrates against the Babylonians, in an action either previously sanctioned by Psamtek or already under way at the time of Psamtek's death. Nekau and the Egyptian army marched north and together with their Assyrian allies confronted a combined force of Babylonians and Medes at Harran, an engagement in which Nekau was defeated and forced to withdraw west of the Euphrates.[1]

A year later Nekau was back campaigning in Syria–Palestine, and he returned to Harran to challenge the Babylonians and their Median allies once again. On the march through Judah at Megiddo he encountered Josiah, the ruler of Judah, and in a confrontation that ensued Josiah was killed. The circumstances of Josiah's death are described in II Kings (23.29–30): 'In his days, Pharaoh Nekau king of Egypt went up to the king of Assyria to the river Euphrates, King Josiah went to meet him; but when Pharaoh Nekau met him at Megiddo, he killed him. His servants carried him dead in a chariot from Megiddo, brought him to Jerusalem, and buried him in his own tomb.'

A more detailed but considerably later account of this incident is provided in II Chronicles (35.20–24). Whereas the story in II Kings is neutral in its description, II Chronicles introduces changes in the terminology, implying a military encounter, an incident which Nekau seemingly tried to avoid through negotiation.[2] Josiah persisted with the altercation, which eventually resulted in him being shot by Egyptian archers. He was then taken to Jerusalem where he later died.

The circumstances of the encounter are not clear as to whether there actually was a military clash, and, if there was, why Josiah would choose to oppose the Egyptians who were superior in both numbers and military capability. Prior to this, Josiah is believed to have been an Egyptian vassal after Egypt's gradual takeover of southern Lebanon, following the Assyrian withdrawal. Subsequently, in 609 BC it is possible that Josiah switched sides and now supported the Babylonians, anticipating Babylon's eventual conquest of Syria–Palestine. Possibly Judah was now acting with the Babylonians in attempting to slow down or halt the Egyptian progress northwards.[3] Also with the Egyptian defeat at Harran, and a new untried ruler on the throne of Egypt, Judah may have considered Egypt would now be weaker militarily.[4] Biblical sources relate how Josiah had received specific assurances from the prophets and the priests that divine aid would be afforded in any encounter.[5] Other factors that may have had a bearing on this incident were an upsurge of Judean nationalism in wishing to establish Judah's independence from Egypt[6] or even vying for control of territories recently annexed by Judah.[7]

Whether there was a military conflict or whether Josiah had been summoned to attend some form of 'court-martial' are topics which have been much debated, together with the subject of Josiah's death.[8] The II Kings passage does not necessarily relate to a meeting on the battlefield, although the Chronicles passage has been interpreted as evidence that a military confrontation took place. Neither account provides a reason for any kind of action; both merely state that Nekau was passing through Judah on his way to assist the Assyrians. There were probably similar movements of Egyptian troops during the earlier reign of Psamtek I, but there is no evidence of Judah then attempting to prevent their passage.

A number of scholars reject the suggestion that a battle between Josiah and Nekau did take place and provide alternative explanations for Josiah's arrival at Megiddo. Josiah may have been called to give an account of the religious reforms, which he had previously carried out, and with which Egypt was unhappy.[9] These reforms had been enacted a number of years previously, however, and there is no evidence that religious freedom in the vassal states was contrary to Egyptian policy.[10] Perhaps Josiah was summoned to meet the new monarch to explain the earlier annexation of territories adjoining his kingdom, but as long as he paid his taxes on these territories it is unlikely that Egypt would have considered this a major problem. If Josiah failed to pay these taxes to Egypt then he may have been punished by execution.[11] The tragedy of the loss of Josiah was so deeply felt in the Judean kingdom that a day of remembrance was commemorated for generations.[12] Until further evidence is uncovered, the circumstances surrounding the death of the Judean leader remain difficult to explain.

According to II Kings (23), following Josiah's death, Jehoahaz, his son, succeeded to the throne of Judah, but after ruling for only three months was deposed by Nekau for his anti-Egyptian sympathies. It would seem that Nekau was exercising personal control over the vassal state by appointing a ruler of his choice. He replaced Jehoahaz with another son, Jehoiakim, an action that served their mutual interest, as Jehoiakim, the eldest son, was the legitimate heir to the throne of Judah, and he was to become Nekau's vassal and loyal ally.[13] Nekau then adopted a conciliatory policy towards Judah, and other than a small tribute being imposed, of 100 talents of silver and one of gold,[14] Judah was left alone. This was perhaps a result of the Babylonian threat as Egypt did not want to lose a potential ally in Palestine. In addition, Egypt was more concerned with the coastal plain of the Levant where commercial activity was based, whereas its principal interest in the state of Judah related to its control of the trade routes through the Negev.[15]

Following the events in Judah, Nekau resumed his campaign against the Babylonians, and in 609 BC, the seventeenth year of the reign of Nabopolassar, the Babylonian king, Nekau with his Assyrian allies was successful in retaking Harran:[16] 'In the month Tammuz, Ashur-uballit (II), king of Assyria, the large army of Egypt [...] crossed the river (Euphrates) and marched against Harran to conquer (it). [...] they [captured] it. They defeated the garrison which the king of Akkad had stationed inside. When they had defeated (it) they encamped against Harran. Until the month Elul they did battle against the city but achieved nothing. [However] they did not withdraw.' Interestingly, this is the last time that Assyria is referred to in the *Babylonian Chronicles* and Assyria disappears from the world stage with Egypt then having to fight alone against the Babylonians.[17]

The *Babylonian Chronicle*, the main source for events at this time, is silent with regard to Egypt for the eighteenth and nineteenth years of Nabopolassar (608–607 BC), while Herodotus makes no reference to Nekau's campaigns in Syria–Palestine. The Egyptians based themselves at Carchemish, and in the summer of 606 BC they besieged Kimuhu for four months before taking it, a city that had in the previous year been captured by the Babylonians.[18] Later they successfully defeated the Babylonian army at Quramati.[19]

Loss of the Levant

This was the peak of Egyptian successes in the Levant and was not to last, as Nekau and his forces were defeated in 605 BC by the Babylonians under the command of the crown prince Nebuchadnezzar, at the celebrated battle of Carchemish on the Euphrates, located close to the present Turkish–Syrian border (Figure 4.2). The Egyptian army was forced to retreat and was once again attacked and comprehensively defeated by the Babylonians at Hammath, as described in the *Babylonian Chronicle*:[20]

> In the 21st year the King of Akkad (i.e. King Nabopolassar of Babylon) stayed in his own land. Nebuchadnezzar, his eldest son and crown prince mustered (the Babylonian army) and took the lead of his troops; he marched to Carchemish which is on the banks of the Euphrates and crossed the river (to go) against the Egyptian army which lay in Carchemish. [...] they fought with each other and the Egyptian army withdrew before him. He effected their defeat and utterly annihilated them. The rest of the Egyptian army which had escaped from defeat sped quickly, not having yet joined battle in the environs of Hamath, the army of Akkad overtook them and defeated them so that not a single man [escaped] to his own country.

From the *Chronicle*, it seems possible to suggest two scenarios. The Babylonian attack was sudden, and part of the Egyptian army already encamped at Carchemish was unable to reach the main battle, possibly then panicked and withdrew southwards. Alternatively, the main Egyptian army marching north from the Delta was unable to arrive in time, and was later attacked at Hamath and destroyed. What is perhaps surprising is that in the previous encounters between Egyptian and Babylonian forces the Egyptians had acquitted themselves creditably, but in contrast the battle at Carchemish seems to have been an overwhelming victory for the Babylonians. Nebuchadnezzar was reputably an excellent tactician and so superior strategies by the Babylonians may have helped to achieve their victory.[21] At about this time Nebuchadnezzar was crowned king of Babylon as Nebuchadnezzar II (605–562 BC) following the death of his father Nabopolassar.

Following the Egyptian defeat and the subsequent withdrawal of Egyptian forces back to the borders of Egypt, the Babylonians moved southwards and gradually took control of all the Egyptian dependencies in Syria–Palestine. By the winter of 601–600 BC they had reached the eastern frontier of Egypt. However, Nebuchadnezzar's domination over these newly conquered territories was not assured as long as Egypt remained independent, and so Nebuchadnezzar decided to launch an attack on Egypt itself. He took the coastal route along the eastern Mediterranean seaboard, reaching Tell el-Kedua, the 'Migdol' fortress in the eastern Delta, where the Egyptian army was drawn up and waiting. According to the *Babylonian Chronicle*,[22] in the ensuing battle, both sides suffered severe losses, causing Nebuchadnezzar to withdraw back to Babylon without achieving his objective: 'In the month, Kislev (November–December 601 BC) [Nebuchadnezzar] took the lead of the army and marched to Egypt. The king of Egypt heard of it and mustered his army. They fought one another on the battlefield and both sides suffered severe losses. The king of Akkad and his army turned and [went back] to Babylon.'

Egypt is absent from the *Babylonian Chronicle* between 600 and 594 BC, but a number of Babylonian campaigns to the Levant are mentioned, although they do not appear to be of any great military significance. Nebuchadnezzar attacked the Arabs (see p. 181 n. 11) in the Syrian Desert in 599 BC, and Jerusalem surrendered to the Babylonian army without resistance in 598/7 BC. In 597 BC he went to Hattu, the area west of the Euphrates, which included states in Anatolia and Philistia to the south, and then returned to Babylon.[23]

Following the Babylonian withdrawal of 601 BC and before its reappearance in Syria–Palestine in 597 BC, Egypt may have attempted to re-establish its influence in the region. It is possible that in the 597 BC campaign the Babylonians travelled further south than some sources suggest and destroyed Gaza and Ekron, resulting in Egypt losing its final holdings in the southern Levant.[24] However, according to Herodotus (2, 159), Nekau captured Kadytis (Gaza) in Palestine, but no date is given for this conquest. It has been suggested that this occurred towards the end of his reign: if this is correct it would mark a resurgence of Egyptian influence in southern Palestine.[25] Other than this possible expedition to Gaza, there is no evidence that Egypt ventured into the Levant for the remainder of Nekau's rule. This new political state of affairs is stated in II Kings (24.7): 'The king of Egypt did not march out of his country again, because the king of Babylon had taken all his territory from the Wadi of Egypt to the Euphrates River'. Perhaps recognising the dominance and strength of the Babylonians on land, Nekau began to place emphasis on naval activity, not only aimed at defence but also in an effort to maintain some commercial activity or economic control in the eastern Mediterranean.

Kush

Information relating to any possible Egyptian contact with the Kushites since their expulsion by the Assyrians in 663 BC is sparse, although it would seem likely that the Kushites still harboured ambitions to reconquer Egypt. There is evidence from the Egyptian fort on the island of Dorginarti at the Second Cataract of an Egyptian presence from as early as the reign of Psamtek I, which would suggest that exchanges between Egypt and Nubia continued after the expulsion of Tanwetamani.[26] Dorginarti was originally built as a fortress to guard and warn against advancing Kushite armies, but in Saite times its function appeared to be one of controlling trade routes to the south.

There is some evidence of a campaign to Nubia during the reign of Nekau as attested by an inscription on a fragment of stela excavated from the Satis temple precinct at Elephantine.[27] The text is incomplete but suggests a 'rebellion' (*m bštw*) and the transportation of an Egyptian force: 'the ships went south carrying them, and [they] reached …' (*ʿḥʿ(w) ḫnti(w) ḥr.sn pḥ [.sn?]*). The text then lists the type of shipping involved and later includes a reference to Kush. This campaign may have occurred after 600 BC following Nekau's departure from the Levant and was aimed either at curbing nomadic infiltration or at putting down some form of rebellion in Upper Nubia.[28]

Building activities

Nekau's building activities were not extensive during his fifteen-year reign, which may be partially explained by the effort involved in sustaining his considerable military activities and developing his naval forces. Also, some of his unfinished buildings may later have been completed and inscribed by Psamtek II, and, similarly, some of the completed monuments are known to have been usurped by Psamtek. Building projects which can be assigned to Nekau are the renovation of the earlier Hyksos fortress at Pithom as part of the Wadi Tumilat canal scheme, and continued work at the Neith temple at Sais, inaugurated by Psamtek I.[29] The cartouches of Nekau as well as those of Psamtek II and Ahmose II have been found on reused blocks in the Roman-Period temple dedicated to Thoth at the Dakhla Oasis. It would appear, therefore, that the Roman temple was constructed using some of the building blocks from the earlier 26th-Dynasty temple.[30] Additionally, reliefs in Baltimore and Copenhagen are suggested to have come from the temple of Hathor at Kom el-Hisn.[31] There is also evidence of Nekau II being active at Karnak, where a statue, a fragmented stela and a number of reliefs have been attested from his reign.[32]

The only named possible sculpture of Nekau II is a celebrated bronze statuette showing the king kneeling with both arms stretched forward with palms turned in (Figure 5.1). On the back of his belt he has the inscription 'Son of Re, Nekau, living forever'. Characteristically, the statuette displays a triangular face, a slant to the eyes and a curved smile, the so-called 'Saite smile'.[33] A number of shabti figures,[34] mostly fragmentary, are attributed to Nekau II, although it is possible they could relate to Nekau I.

The wife of Nekau is generally considered to have been Khedebneithirbinet I, on the basis of circumstantial evidence: the form of her sarcophagus is appropriate for this period, the titles inscribed on her sarcophagus are those that would be expected of the wife of a monarch, and also no wife of Nekau is otherwise attested[35] (Figure 5.2). Nekau fathered a son, Psamtek, who succeeded him, and three daughters, Isetemkheb, Meryetnebti and Meryetneithites. They are known from a fragmentary naophorous statue dedicated to their tutor, the chief of the antechamber, Neferibrenefer.[36] Nekau survived to perform the rituals for the burial of the Apis bull in 594 BC[37] and died later in the same year. He was reputedly buried within the precinct of the temple of Neith at Sais,[38] a location perhaps supported by a scarab allegedly found there.[39]

The Saite navy

Dedicated fighting ships had been part of the Egyptian navy since at least the 20th Dynasty, but during the Saite Period technical advances are known to

5.1 Figure of a kneeling king, suggested to be that of Nekau II. The figure's hands
are held above his knees as if to present an offering. Inscribed on the belt is the
name of Nekau; the rest of the belt is decorated with a herringbone pattern.
Bronze. H. 14 cm; W. 5.7 cm; D. 7 cm (Brooklyn Museum, New York).

have been achieved in Egyptian naval shipping. There was significant naval
activity throughout the Saite Period: naval resources became an important part
of the Egyptian military machine and played an increasing role in defence as
well as being a factor in foreign policy.[40] Naval shipping is mentioned in
Ashurbanipal's invasion of Egypt[41] and again later in the 26th Dynasty where
the phrase 'royal ships of war' (*ꜥḥꜥw nsw n ꜥḥꜣ*)[42] occurs. Although these may
have been large seagoing vessels used as warships, there may also have been
Egyptian ramming war-galleys operating in the Mediterranean. These vessels
were perhaps present as early as the reign of Psamtek I and similar to those
being used by the Greeks and Phoenicians.[43]

5.2 Stone sarcophagus lid of Queen Khedebneithirbinet I, probable wife of Nekau
II. The identification as Nekau's wife is based on the fact that her sarcophagus
dates to the 26th Dynasty, that her titles as King's wife and King's mother fit, and
that no other wife is attested for the king. Granite. (Kunsthistorisches Museum,
Vienna).

A much celebrated and discussed passage in Herodotus (II, 159.1–2) mentions
naval activity during the reign of Nekau II: 'Having given up his canal Nekau
turned his attention to military campaigns, and triremes were built, some for
the northern sea and others in the Arabian gulf for the Erythraean Sea,[44] whose
slipways are still visible. And these he put to use when the need arose.'
    The passage may refer to the construction of significantly more galleys than
Nekau had inherited from Psamtek I, or perhaps to an upgrading of the Egyptian

fleet. It seems unlikely that these were actually triremes, triple-tier ships, as the first mention of the word *trieres* in a Greek text occurs in the second half of the sixth century.[45] More likely they were pentaconters, biremes or simply the best available ships at that time. This type of vessel would have required a certain technical capability in its construction, and would have necessitated a major expenditure of resources, particularly with regard to the timber which would have had to be imported from the Lebanon.

It is known that Greek and particularly Phoenician expertise was employed in building up the Saite fleet as their knowledge and naval experience would have been superior to that of the Egyptians. Greek mercenaries were already employed on a large scale in Egypt, and links with merchants and their ships were extensive – Greek and Phoenician sailors would have been in demand. Traditional Egyptian vessels with no keel and little longitudinal strength would have been unsuitable for naval warfare as it was now developing. Manoeuvrable galleys and ramming tactics were the realities of conflict in the seas of the Mediterranean during the Saite Period.[46]

Nekau II would appear to have put increasing emphasis on building up naval forces following the loss of the Egyptian territories in the Levant, although there are no naval titles in the extant texts datable to his reign. His policy was now one of taking steps to protect the Mediterranean coast against possible Babylonian attacks, as well as attempting to maintain commercial relations with the sea ports of the Levant. Herodotus (II, 159) states that Nekau established a naval presence in the Red Sea, a statement which has given rise to considerable discussion.[47] It may have been that Nekau reopened commercial relations with Punt (see below) and the threats from piracy in the sea route to this part of Africa would have necessitated maintaining a naval presence to combat this menace.[48]

The Red Sea canal

Herodotus (II, 158) is the first Classical author to mention the construction by Nekau of a canal that connected the Nile to the Red Sea, a waterway which subsequently may have been completed by Darius I.[49] The Persian canal is described as running from the Nile above Bubastis via Patoumos (Tell el-Maskhuta) into the Red Sea, passing through the Wadi Tumilat and then southwards into the Gulf of Suez[50] (Figure 5.3). Herodotus narrates that Nekau II abandoned the project after 120,000 workers died during its construction, and also how an oracle had revealed to him that only foreigners would profit from his labours. Accounts of the canal by subsequent Classical authors such as Diodorus Siculus and Pliny are somewhat contradictory and may well have derived some if not all of their evidence from Herodotus.[51]

There is no firm archaeological or textual evidence from Egyptian sources to confirm that Nekau engaged in this project. Darius I, during the later Persian occupation of Egypt, mentions that he inspected a waterway at the proposed

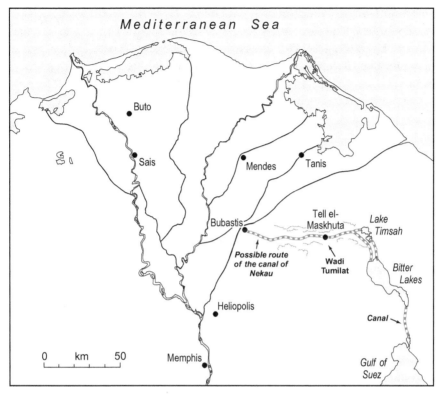

5.3 The Delta showing the possible route of the canal of Nekau.

site before commencing work on his canal which could imply Nekau's earlier scheme but could also refer to earlier irrigation canals that may have run through the Wadi Tumilat. Nekau is recorded in Herodotus (II, 158–59) as having an interest in the Red Sea, and the scheme was within the technological resources of ancient engineering.

If the historicity of the project is accepted then was the main function of the waterway intended to be defensive or commercial? If this undertaking was commenced following the Egyptian defeat at Carchemish and with the Babylonians at the borders of Egypt, then it could be construed as an attempt to strengthen the eastern border. The canal could have been used to transport troops to the Bitter Lakes for defensive purposes.[52]

An alternative purpose could have been to redirect Egyptian trade passing between the Indian Ocean and the Mediterranean.[53] Such an alternative route would have avoided the trans-shipment of goods overland from the Red Sea to the Mediterranean and would have permitted Egypt to impose taxes on such commerce.[54] The improved access to the Red Sea would also have allowed passage to the land of Punt. Punt was famous in the New Kingdom and also mentioned in 26th-Dynasty sources as a source of incense important for Egyptian religious ritual. The canal would have enabled the outward journey to be made entirely by water, an easier alternative than a combined land and sea route. The prevailing northerly winds, which would have assisted the outward journey, would, however, have prevented ships from returning the same way. Cargoes would have had to be unloaded at a port on the Red Sea coast such as Koseir or a similar location, and then the goods transported across land to Egypt.[55]

Africa

Herodotus (IV, 42) in his descriptions of the continents of the world described how Nekau II sent a fleet manned by Phoenician sailors around Africa, a voyage that took nearly three years to complete. The ships reputedly navigated down the Red Sea into the Indian Ocean, circumnavigated Africa and then sailed back to Egypt via the Straits of Gibraltar. Food was obtained by putting into shore, sowing seeds and harvesting the crops before continuing with the expedition.

Many aspects of this remarkable narrative are perplexing, such as the reasons for undertaking such a hazardous voyage, the difficulties of navigating and sailing these ancient vessels in unknown waters for an extended period of time, the significant problems in supplying such an expedition and the often-voiced scepticism about Herodotus being a reliable source. Other than Herodotus's account there is a lack of any evidence, either textual or archaeological, to support such an expedition and so it is difficult to determine whether a voyage did indeed take place.[56]

II Psamtek II

In 595 BC Nekau died and his son, Psamtek II, who was then about twenty-five, succeeded to the throne of Egypt. Of his known family, his wife, Takhuit, is named on the sarcophagus of Ankhnesneferibre,[57] their daughter. In Psamtek's first regnal year Ankhnesneferibre was adopted by the incumbent God's Wife of Amun, Nitiqret, to be her successor, as recorded on the adoption stela of Ankhnesneferibre.[58] With the death of Nitiqret in 586 BC, Ankhnesneferibre became the last God's Wife of Amun, as this role was abolished during the Persian Period.[59]

Psamtek's wife, Takhuit ('the One of the [goddess] Khuit'), was named after Khuit, who was the principal deity at Athribis during the first millennium BC.[60] The tomb of Takhuit was discovered in the main necropolis at Athribis and supports the view that she was originally from this region.[61] Takhuit is considered to be the mother of Haaibra (Apries), Psamtek II's successor and only known son, information which is also recorded on the stela of Ankhnesneferibre.

Officials, military personnel and the 'beautiful name'

The use of the monarch's name, either the nomen or prenomen, was a popular trait amongst the officials during Psamtek's reign, usually with the addition of the 'beautiful name' (*rn nfr*).[62] The 'beautiful name', although in existence since the Old Kingdom, saw a resurgence in the Saite Period and particularly during the reign of Psamtek II, and then continued through until the reign of Ahmose II. The 'beautiful name', an epithet used by the monarch to refer to a virtue, such as a celebration of royal power or a formula of good wish, was attached to the Psamtek element of the name. The officials would have adopted the personal name of Psamtek, including part of his royal titulary, to honour and show their loyalty to the ruler. This trend, probably related to archaising tendencies, can assist with dating a particular official to this period.

Both Ahmose ('beautiful name' Neferibrenakht), who was a royal messenger and general leading the Egyptian forces during the Nubian campaign, and Potasimto ('beautiful name' Neferibrenebken), who was commander of the mercenary troops during this same campaign, adopted such names, as did General Udjahorresne ('beautiful name' Neferibrenebpehty).[63] Inscriptions on monuments belonging to Neshor ('beautiful name' Psamtekmenekhib), which date to the reigns of Nekau II, Psamtek II and Haaibra, describe him as 'Overseer of the Frontier with the Foreign Lands of the Great Green' (*imy-r ʿзw ḫзswt Wзḏ-wr*).[64] Neshor's brief would have been the defence of the coast of the Mediterranean from foreign invasions. During his long career Neshor also exercised control over the southern frontier, in his role as 'Overseer of the Gates of the Southern Lands' (*imy-r ʿзw ḫзswt rswt*) (see p. 147).

Nothing is known about any naval encounters during the reign of Psamtek II, but there is evidence for naval titles, with older ones which related to the Nile river traffic being replaced by newer titles, now mentioning the Mediterranean (the Great Green).[65] The title 'Chief of the Royal Warships of the Great Green' (*imy-r ʿḥʿw nsw n ʿḥʿ m Wзḏ-wr*) was held by a certain Hor whose 'beautiful name' was Psamtek[66] (Figure 5.4). He was also 'Commander of Mercenaries' (*ḥrp ḫзstyw ḥзw-nbw*).[67] Hor would therefore have been an important official who had control of the Mediterranean high-seas fleet and was also commander of Psamtek's mercenary troops. Another high-ranking naval officer known from this reign is Ywlhen ('beautiful name' Psamtekseneb) who was 'Overseer (admiral) of the Royal Fleet' (*imy-r ʿḥʿw nsw*) and is attested from a shabti figure.[68]

Nubian campaign

Perhaps the most significant event of Psamtek's reign was the campaign to Kush in his third regnal year, evidence of which is obtained from three stelae erected at Shellal, Karnak and Tanis[69] (Figure 5.5). The Shellal stela is the most

5.4 Life-size statue of Hor, 'good name' Psamtek who was 'Commander of Royal Fighting Ships in the Great Green'. Hor is shown holding a naos shrine, containing an image of a lion-headed goddess, probably a form of Bastet. Quartzite. H. 72 cm; W. 42.5 cm; L. 90 cm (Manchester Museum, Manchester).

complete and informative of the stelae whereas the Tanis and Karnak stelae, because of their fragmentary condition, provide only some complementary and on occasions conflicting information regarding this expedition.[70] Graffiti, inscribed on the legs of the colossal seated figures of Ramesses II at Abu Simbel, relating to the participation of Greek, Carian and Phoenician mercenary forces, are a further source for this campaign.[71]

5.5 Stela of Psamtek II, one of three stelae relating to the Nubian campaign. Discovered at Shellal in 1964 by workers on the High Dam, Aswan, and now sited in front of the north side of the Mandulis temple on the island of New Kalabsha, Aswan. Red granite. H. 2.53 m; W. 1.23 m; D. 68 cm.

The inscription on the Tanis stela is the only text that provides some form of justification for this invasion. After introductory royal epithets, the king is described as being involved with the restoration of temples that had fallen into disrepair, although the location of these is not specified, when he received news that the Kushites were planning to attack him. Psamtek dispatched an army to Kush to confront this threat and accompanied his forces as far the southern frontier at Elephantine, where he then remained to await their return.[72] The Karnak and Shellal stelae record that when the Egyptian army reached the region of *Pr-nbs*[73] the Kushites rose up against the Egyptians: 'The army which your majesty sent to Kush has reached the country of *Pr-nbs*. It is a land devoid of flat areas, a place lacking horses. The Kushites of every foreign land rose up against him, their hearts filled with anger.'[74] The Kushites appeared to have offered little resistance and the Egyptians went on to achieve a resounding victory: 'it was misery for the rebels', 'one waded in their blood like water' and '4200 prisoners were taken'.[75]

The Tanis stela is more fragmentary but does provide some additional details relating to the military action that occurred in the heart of Kush, between the Third and Fourth Cataracts. Line 8 describes how the *Kwr* (the title used for the Kushite king) was burned in his residence at Iruwa. Aspelta, the King of Kush at that time, is known to have ruled until *c.* 568 BC, many years after this military action. This fact, together with the difficulty in reconstructing the Tanis stela passage, makes it uncertain what is being referred to in the stela. Archaeological evidence relating to this period indicates some destruction at Gebel Barkal and Sanam, probably caused by the Egyptian army on its journey south, while the city of Kawa seems to have been spared any damage.[76] The Egyptians may have reached Korkos near the Fourth Cataract before then returning home, passing Dendur and Buhen on route, and leaving graffiti at Buhen.[77]

Herodotus (II, 161) records this campaign but is strangely silent about the outcome. The Phoenician graffiti at Abu Simbel support a military victory, and noticeable among them is the vivid expression 'they crushed dogs' (*grs klbm*).[78] The longer Greek texts[79] at Abu Simbel provide more detail and refer to the command structure of the expedition, with Potasimto leading the mercenary troops and Ahmose, the royal messenger,[80] the Egyptian troops. The grafitti also provide details of the origin of the mercenaries, with at least three different East Greek cities represented (Teos, Ialysos, Kolophon), as well as Caria and Phoenicia. This would suggest a complex recruiting system for mercenaries, especially with the large numbers who eventually were to become part of the Egyptian military forces.[81]

The ease with which Psamtek's forces overcame the Kushite threat indicates that Kush was not the power it had been a century earlier. Psmatek may have chosen an opportune moment to attack, as the kingdom of Kush was beset with internal problems, relating to the succession of Aspelta as the new ruler. It was, therefore, a weakened Kush that faced the Egyptian invasion.[82] The overwhelming victory crushed any lingering ambition that the Kushites may have had of retaking Egypt, and Egypt now confirmed its supremacy over the Nile Valley. Although Psamtek took booty and prisoners, Aspelta continued to rule the country for another thirty years, but it is possible that, following the conflict, Egypt may have controlled the trade routes along the Nile, beyond the Third Cataract.[83]

Campaign to Khor

At the same time as Psamtek's successful campaign against Kush, an anti-Babylonian conference was being held in Jerusalem, hosting envoys from the minor kingdoms of Edom, Moab, Ammon, Tyre and Sidon. The meeting discussed the possibility of either rebelling against Babylonian control or continuing to remain subjugated to Babylon.[84] The Babylonians came to hear about this gathering and Zedekiah, the ruler of Judah, or possibly his envoy, was summoned to Babylon to explain the nature of the conference. As it is known that Zedekiah returned to Jerusalem and remained king, Nebuchadnezzar seemed to have been satisfied with his explanations.[85] There is no evidence for the Babylonians returning to the southern Levant between 597 BC and 588 BC, and so during Psamtek's short reign he was able to enter the region without fear of confrontation, as borne out by his expedition to the region in Year 4.[86]

Papyrus Rylands IX (14.16–22) refers to this excursion, noting that Psamtek II invited priests to accompany him on his journey to Khor.[87] This expedition is often characterised as being peaceful in nature, with a description of how the priests and their attendants carried bouquets of flowers. The event is portrayed as more of a triumphal march and religious procession, thanking the gods for victory in Kush and proclaiming Psamtek's military successes, rather than a show of force. There is a tendency in this same literature to perceive Psamtek as deliberately avoiding military contact with the Babylonians,[88] although it would seem likely that Psamtek would also have taken military forces with him through what was now probably hostile territory. Presumably some Babylonian troops would have been stationed in the region, and the states of the Levant would have been obligated to Babylon by treaty. Therefore, an incursion by an anti-Babylonian power would understandably carry political and military implications.

Another motive for Psamtek's visit to Palestine may well have been reassertion of his claims to Syria–Palestine and his attempt to resume commercial contact with some of the states that Egypt traditionally dominated and traded with.[89] With his victory in Kush, Psamtek was endeavouring to persuade the Levantine states to change sides once again and come under Egyptian protection. With little Babylonian presence in the region at that time, it is possible that the Babylonians were now perceived to be less of a threat. Whether the expedition was in some sense ceremonial or more military is difficult to determine but it is possible that this was not Psamtek's first Egyptian campaign to the region, and parts, if not all, of the Levantine territory may already have come under Egyptian control. Psamtek may also have visited Jerusalem, conferred with Zedekiah and entered into a treaty with him.[90] The discovery of scarabs of Psamtek II at Tell el-Safi, Tell el-Far'ah and Tell Keisan lend support to this suggestion,[91] and indeed in *c.* 592 BC, with Egypt seemingly once again a powerful force in the region and Babylon absent from the area, Judah repudiated its allegiance to Babylon and rebelled[92] – a move, presumably, indictated by its failure to render the annual tribute, which it then followed up by a request for military assistance from Egypt.[93] Of the other states in the region only Ammon and Tyre followed Judah's example and similarly rose up.[94]

On Psamtek's return from Palestine a sphinx was set up in Heliopolis or possibly Sais, of which now only part of the base survives.[95] The text celebrates his triumph in the traditional Egyptian tone,[96] mentioning both Kushites and Asiatics within the main text. Around this time Psamtek became ill and early in 589 BC died. This is attested by Petiese, who had accompanied the expedition and, after returning home to Teudjoy, attempted to petition the king. Petiese was informed that Psamtek was ill, 'they said to him, Pharaoh, *Life Prosperity, Health,* is sick and goes not forth'[97] and Petiese was later told that he had died.[98] Psamtek's death is also recorded on the Ankhnesneferibre adoption stela.

The uncertainty that usually surrounded any ancient ruler's death and the succession of a new ruler may have been one of the reasons that then prompted Babylon to strike into the Levant and particularly at Judah, following that state's betrayal. However, Babylon had been involved with quashing severe internal revolt in its heartlands until late 588 BC, and was probably not in a position to dispatch an army to the Levant until after Psamtek's death.

Damnatio memoriae

There is a suggestion that Psamtek directed a *damnatio memoriae* against his father, Nekau, because of his having lost Egypt's territories in the Levant. As a consequence, Nekau's name was hacked out in temples and from monuments, and erased from the statues of high officials.[99] It is necessary to distinguish between usurpation and the related custom of *damnatio memoriae*. Usurpation is the practice of reusing one person's monuments by another for the latter's own purposes, and in the process denying the commissioning ruler's claim to it. *Damnatio memoriae* is a Latin expression, devised in modern times, to describe the practice of attacking or erasing the memory of disgraced individuals and rulers who were considered illegitimate by their successors, often by destroying the relevant monument.[100]

Ancient Egypt had a long tradition of erasing the name of one or several of a ruler's predecessors.[101] A celebrated example is the proscription of Hatshepsut's monuments in the earlier 18th Dynasty, as her rule was later considered illegitimate, and is a clear example of *damnatio memoriae*.[102] In the early 19th Dynasty the Ramesside rulers frequently usurped their predecessors' monuments, but they were motivated not necessarily by a desire to discredit or suppress the memory of the ruler whose monuments they appropriated but rather by a desire to promote their own rule. The phenomenon of erasure of names is a frequent finding during the Saite Period.[103]

During the reign of Psamtek II the changing of royal names on monuments was a noticeable phenomenon, with a number of royal and private monuments, mainly belonging to Nekau, being modified, although their numbers are limited.[104] There are many monuments and statues from the entire country belonging to Nekau which did not suffer any erasure, including those at the capital, Sais. If any form of attack was to be undertaken against Nekau's monuments, surely Sais would have been the first place it would have been expected to take place. The funerary stelae of the third and fourth Apis bulls have the names of Nekau intact, as do a number of statues in the Louvre,[105] Philadelphia[106] and Brooklyn museums,[107] as well as a fragmentary stela from Elephantine.[108]

Although the reasons for the erasure of the monuments of Nekau by Psamtek are not completely understood, there are too many surviving objects among the corpus of Nekau II to support the idea of a *damnatio memoriae*.[109] It may be that Psamtek, because of advanced age or illness, suspected that his reign would be short, and usurped some of the monuments of his predecessors in order to promote his own reign.[110] This defacement appears to be an example not of *damnatio memoriae* but more of usurpation. Royal monuments were simply usurped for reusage, while the name of Nekau on private monuments was changed by their owners to Psamtek, in order to demonstrate their loyalty to the new ruler.[111]

The Nekau erasures contrast with the extensive desecration campaign carried out by Psamtek II against the monuments of the 25th-Dynasty rulers and their associated God's Wives of Amun. When Psamtek's army was in Kush, monuments were modified both at the capital, Napata, and at Sanam, where the names of the rulers were erased, and in many cases their names replaced by that of Psamtek II. Also, Kushite iconographic features such as the ram's head amulets on the necklaces, and one of the two uraei on rulers' foreheads, were either altered or removed, in order to conform to Egyptian iconographic style. This process was later repeated, especially at Thebes and other sites throughout Egypt, seemingly in an attempt to eliminate the memory of the Kushite rulers, and is a clear example of a *damnatio memoriae*.[112]

Monuments and artefacts

Considering the shortness of Psamtek II's reign, the number of buildings carrying his name is significant, again partly the result of the programme of usurpation of his father's monuments.[113] Examples include a granite obelisk[114] found at Karnak, which has the name of Psamtek carved over that of the original dedicator, a naos from Athribis[115] and a granite altar dedicated to Mehit from Deir el-Abiad.[116] Many cartouches of Psamtek are conspicuous at the granite quarries at Aswan, suggesting an increase in quarrying activities there. Remains of granite obelisks and sphinxes belonging to Psamtek have been found in the sea in front of the Qait Bey fort at Alexandria.[117] A pair of obelisks were erected in the temple of Heliopolis, one of which was taken to Rome in 10 BC by the Emperor Augustus.[118] A kiosk was donated on Philae, representing the earliest known monument on the island.[119] Psmatek is known to have commissioned a building at the temple of Hibis in the el-Kharga oasis, and a block found with the cartouches of Psamtek at Abydos could indicate building work there.[120]

There are a few dated inscriptions for the reign of Psamtek II, such as donation stelae known from his Years 1, 2, 3 and 4,[121] Demotic papyri dating to Years 4, 5 and 6[122] and a record of a mining expedition to the Wadi Hammamat in Year 3,[123] but they add little further information relating to his reign. A number of scarabs are inscribed with the name of Psamtek although some of these may have been carved after his death, such as those produced at Naukratis for export.[124]

Notes

1   Redford 2000: 190–91; Miller and Hayes 2006: 460–61.
2   II Kings is considered to have been written between about 560–540 BC, and II Chronicles somewhat later, around 450–425 BC.
3   Malamat 1990: 68.
4   Spalinger 1977; Sweeney 2001: 310; Schipper 2010; Kahn 2015.
5   Frost 1968: 372.
6   Frost 1968: 370–71.
7   Cline 2000: 91.
8   See for example Frost 1968; Malamat 1973; Spalinger 1977; Avioz 2007 and n. 2 for bibliography; Schipper 2010; Kahn 2015.
9   Frost 1968: 370–71; Cline 2000: 99.
10 Kahn 2015: 519.
11 Kahn 2015.
12 Chron. 2.35. 25; Malamat 1975: 124.
13 Malamat 1975: 126–27.
14 Biblical sources are II Kings 23.33; II Chronicles 36.3, and I Ezra 1.34.
15 Schipper 2010: 212–14.
16 Grayson 1975: 96, Chron. 3.66–69.
17 Lipschits 2005: 20.
18 Redford 1992: 452.
19 Grayson 1975: 98, Chron. 4.16–26; Redford 2000: 188–89; Lipschits 2005: 33–34.
20 Chron. 5 is inscribed on tablet, BM 21946 (Grayson 1975: 99), see Chron. 5, obv. ll. 1–8.
21 Redford 1992: 453–54.
22 Grayson 1975: 101, Chron. 5.6–7.
23 Eph'al 2003: 180–89; Kahn 2008: 140–43.
24 Katzenstein 1994: 43, 47; Lipschits 2005: 52, n. 54, 55; Kahn 2008: 142.

25 See Freedy and Redford 1970: 475 n. 57; Malamat 1973: 275–76; Miller and Hayes 2006: 467; Perdu 2014: 145.

26 Heidorn 1991: 206 and 2013.

27 Kaiser et al. 1975; Junge 1987: 66–67; Jansen-Winkeln 1989; Lloyd 2000: 84.

28 Lloyd 2000: 84; Redford 2000: 192–93.

29 Arnold 1999: 74–75.

30 Davoli and Kaper 2006.

31 Bothmer 1960; 49, n. 42, pl. 39; Myśliwiec 1988: 47, nos 2–3, pl. xlvii b.

32 Leahy 2009: 240.

33 Bothmer 1960: 50–51, pl. 40; Brooklyn Museum accession No. 71.11.

34 Leiden, Rijksmuseum van Oudheden, Inv. F 1988/7.1 and Petrie Museum, Inv. UC. 38081 in Schneider 1993. Also see Janes (2002: 152) for other figures.

35 Dodson and Hilton 2004: 244.

36 Statue CG 658. See el-Sayed 1974; Vittmann 1975: 378–79; Dodson and Hilton 2004: 244; Gozzoli 2017: 18.

37 *LR* 4, 88, VI.

38 Herodotus II, 169–70.

39 There is some doubt about the existence of this scarab. See comments by Petrie 1905: 337; Schneider 1993: 164–65; Barbotin 2000: 38 n. 26; Wilson 2016: 76.

40 Lloyd 2000.

41 *ANET* 296, British Museum Text K, l. 15–19.

42 Chevereau 1985: 92, doc. 117.

43 Morrison and Williams 1968: 12–42; Wallinga 1995: 43–48.

44 Erythrian Ocean refers to the Red Sea, see Lloyd 1972: 268 n. 2.

45 Morrison and Williams 1968: 120.

46 Lloyd 1972.

47 Lloyd 1977: 142–54; Perdu 2014: 144–45.

48 Lloyd 1977: 146–48.

49 See Lloyd 1977: 142–45; Redmount 1995; Agut-Labordère 2014; for a detailed discussion of the Herodotus passage see Lloyd 1988: 149–58.

50 Naville 1903: 3–7; Lloyd 1977: 142.

51 Lloyd 1977: 142–43; Redmount 1995: 127–30.

52 Redford 2000: 192.

53 For a discussion of Egyptian relations with the west coast of the Red Sea, see Desanges 1978: 217–29; Heidorn 1991: 206 n. 28.

54 Agut-Labordère 2013: 990.

55 Lloyd 1977: 142–45.

56 For discussions on the viability of such a voyage see Lloyd 1977: 148–55; Montserrat 2003: 254–55; Agut-Labordère 2013: 990; Harrison 2017.

57 PM 1964 I, II: 685–86; Strudwick 2006: 276–77; Ayad 2009: 27.

58 Cairo JdE 36907 published in Leahy 1996; Dodson and Hilton 2004: 244–45; Gozzoli 2017: 27–32, 104–7.

59 *LR* 4, 86; de Meulenaere 1968: 186; Leahy 1996: 158; Ayad 2009: 28.

60 Vernus 1978: 441.

61 Habachi 1982: 220.

62 For a discussion of the 'beautiful name' including a list of officials which include their 'beautiful names' as well as their titles see Gozzoli 2017: 32–37, 177–208

63 Gozzoli 2017: 33.

64   Chevereau 1985: 93–94, doc. 11.

65   Spalinger 1977: 235 and 1978b: 21 n. 36.

66   Manchester Museum 3570. See Petrie and Duncan 1906: 18–19, pls XV, XX;
     Chevereau 1985: 92–93, doc. 117; Agut-Labordére 2013: 990–91; Gozzoli 2017:
     179–80; Price 2017b.

67   The meaning of '*ḫꜣstyw ḥꜣw-nbw*' has been much debated. I follow Price (2017b:
     373, comment [a]) in translating as '(foreign) mercenaries'. Also see Price for
     bibliography relating to this discussion.

68   De Meulenaere 1966: surnom 3 (doc. 1); Aubert and Aubert 1974: 222; Goyon
     1969: 167; Gozzoli 2017: 182–83.

69   There is a considerable publication list relating to this campaign. See for example
     Sauneron and Yoyotte 1951; Kienitz 1953; Bakry 1967; Habachi 1974; Goedicke
     1981; Der Manuelian 1994: 337–71; Coyotte 2016.

70   Gozzoli 1995, 2017: 45–61.

71   Bernard and Masson 1957; Schmitz 2010.

72   Sauneron and Yoyotte 1952: 162–63; der Manuelian 1994: 366–67.

73   Der Manuelian (1994: 345 n. 209 and references) considers that *Pr-nbs* denotes
     a region rather than a specific settlement. Gozzoli (2017: 57) suggests that *Pr-nbs*
     should be identified as Kerma.

74   Der Manuelian 1994: 339, ll. 6–7.

75   Der Manuelian 1994: 339, ll. 8–10.

76   Kendall 2002; Gozzoli 2017: 57–61.

77   The Greek soldiers left a graffito at Buhen (Masson 1976: 310–11) and the Carian
     mercenaries left graffiti within the temple there (Masson et al. 1978: 50–54).

78   *CIS* I, 112; Schmitz 2010.

79   Bernard and Masson 1957: 1–46.

80   It is uncertain whether the Ahmose who lead the Egyptian troops was the same
     Ahmose who was later to become king (Schmitz 2010: 327). Redford (2000: 187–88)
     provides evidence for Ahmose being a son of Nesatum.

81   Iancu 2016: 20, 24.

82   Gozzoli 2017: 47 n. 7, 52–55.

83   Török 2009: 362.

84   See Jeremiah 27.1–11 and discussed in Kahn 2008.

85   Kahn 2008: 144.

86   Kahn 2008: 143.

87   The precise extent of the territory covered by the term 'Khor' as it was used by
     the ancient Egyptians is unclear. It is thought to include the ancient kingdoms of
     Judah and Israel, Philistia, Phoenicia and Syria as well as the minor kingdoms
     of Ammon, Moab and Edom (Aubin 2002: 16). Also see Spalinger 1978a: 32, 43
     and Kitchen 1996: 558.

88   Sauneron and Yoyotte 1951: 144; Freedy and Redford 1970: 479–80; Lloyd 1988:
     168; Redford 1992: 464.

89   Miller and Hayes 2006: 474; Kahn 2008.

90   Miller and Hayes 2006: 474.

91   Rowe 1936: 211 (N. 900 and 901); Sauneron and Yoyotte 1951: 142–43; Schipper
     2010: 204: Gozzoli 2017: 75; Stripling et al. 2017: 190.

92   For a discussion of when this rebellion occurred see Freedy and Redford 1970:
     480 n. 100 and Kahn 2008: 152–53.

93   II Kings 24. 20b; Ezekiel 17.15; Miller and Hayes 2006: 474.
94   Miller and Hayes 2006: 475.
95   Cairo TN 18/7/35/1. Gauthier 1934; Gozzoli 2017: 75, 129–30.
96   This type of text has often been termed propaganda, but propaganda as such did not exist in ancient Egypt as all texts had a particular function, in this case fighting against a 'vile' enemy (Gozzoli 2009: 105).
97   P. Rylands IX, 15.8–9.
98   P. Rylands IX, 15.14.
99   For a comprehensive study see Yoyotte 1951. Also comments by Spalinger 1978b: 20; Myśliwiec 2000: 119–21. For recent studies see Koch 2014 and Gozzoli 2017: 80–91.
100   Schulman 1969–70: 36–37; Eaton-Krauss 2015.
101   Björkman (1971) has compiled a number of examples.
102   Brand 2010.
103   Blöbaum 2005: 166–69; Koch 2014: 397–98.
104   For a list of monuments relating to the reign of Nekau see Habachi 1982: 216–21; Gozzoli 2000 and 2017: 81–88. Also see Leahy 2009 and 2011.
105   Louvre A 83. See Bothmer 1960: 51 n. 44; Yoyotte 1960b: fig. 609.
106   Philadelphia E. 13004. See Bothmer 1960: 50–51, figs 95–6; Yoyotte 1960b: 366, fig. 608.
107   Brooklyn 71.11. See Fazzini 1975: 116–17, figs a, b.
108   Gozzoli 2000: 77.
109   For comments relating to this see Bothmar 1960: 50–51; Grimal 1994: 362; Gozzoli 2000: 80 and 2017: 91; Perdu 2014: 145. Contra Koch 2014: 405 who considers that this erasure was more a temporary attitude of local groups rather than a systematic action with a lasting effect.
110   Koch 2014: 403–4.
111   Gozzoli 2017: 91.
112   Russmann 1974; Leahy 1992: 238; Török 2009: 362.
113   Gozzoli: 2017: 158–76.
114   Cairo JdE 17028. Legrain 1903: 226; Leahy 2009: 239.
115   Cairo JdE 88205. See Habachi 1982: 216–22; Leahy 2009: 231; Gozzoli 2017: 160.
116   Gauthier 1935: 207–12; Klotz 2010: 131; Gozzoli 2017: 165.
117   Empereur 1996: 7–10.
118   Arnold 1999: 76 n. 70.
119   Haeny 1985: 203.
120   Arnold 1999: 76–77.
121   Meeks 1979: 676–77; Gozzoli 2017: 122–25.
122   Gozzoli 2017: 126–28.
123   Couyat and Montet 1912: 71, inscription No. 100.
124   See Hall 1913; Matouk 1971: 145, 200; Gozzoli 2017: 151–54.

6

Haaibra versus Ahmose II: civil war to prosperity

I Haaibra (Apries)

Psamtek II was succeeded in 589 BC by his son, Haaibra (Greek Apries), who went on to rule Egypt for some nineteen years. Herodotus (III, 1) attributes to him a daughter, Nitetis, but other than that little is known of Haaibra's family. In Year 4, Nitiqret, the incumbent God's Wife of Amun, who had held office for over sixty years, died and was succeeded by her heiress, Ankhnesneferibre, the sister of Haaibra. Ankhnesneferibre had previously been adopted by Nitiqret as her heir apparent in Year 1 of Psamtek II.[1]

Foreign policy

On the international front Haaibra had to deal with a number of challenges. He was confronted with the aftermath of Zedekiah's rebellion against Babylon, to which Egypt had previously given its support. Nebuchadnezzar II, who had now dealt with the unrest and internal problems in his empire, marched on Jerusalem and laid siege to it for some two years.[2]

Haaibra sent an army to assist Jerusalem, but the Egyptian sources are silent as regards this incident, and we have to rely on Ezekiel and Jeremiah. According to Ezekiel (17.17), the small number of troops that Haaibra had sent resulted in them soon being defeated, forcing the Egyptians to retreat, and so they were unable to prevent the fall of Jerusalem. This reference to the numbers of Egyptian troops may be a later addition to the passage and so this account may not be a fully reliable source.[3] Another biblical account indicates that the force was sizeable enough for reports of it to alert the Babylonians sufficiently to cause at least their temporary withdrawal,[4] before then later returning and forcing the Egyptians to retreat: 'The army of the Pharaoh had come out of Egypt; and when the Babylonians who were besieging Jerusalem heard news of them, they withdrew from Jerusalem'.

Josephus, writing some centuries later, stated that the Egyptians came with a large force:[5] 'But when the Egyptian king heard of the plight of his ally Sacchias (i.e. Zedekiah) he raised a large force and came to Judea to the siege'. It is difficult to determine what sources Josephus may have been citing, and he may merely have been interpreting Jeremiah 37.5 and 11.[6] The size of the force Egypt sent to Jerusalem is therefore uncertain, but nevertheless the Egyptians were defeated, allowing the Babylonians to continue with the siege of the city.

This second attack on Jerusalem in 586 BC was far more devastating than the previous capitulation of the city to the Babylonians in 598/7 BC. The subsequent fall and devastation of the city resulted in the deportation of many Jews to Babylon, and the flight to Egypt of some of those who did survive. The Jewish exiles reached the border fortress of Tell Dafana (Daphnae) where some of them then settled, and according to Jeremiah they went on to set up communities at Tell Dafana itself and also at Memphis and Elephantine.[7]

Herodotus (II, 161) records that Haaibra sent an army against Sidon and fought a naval battle against the Tyrians. Diodorus (I, 68) complements this account by recounting that Haaibra crushed the armies of Cyprus and Phoenicia both on land and on the sea.[8] The Babylonians had no naval forces at this period to oppose them. The exact date of these campaigns is not certain, with many sources suggesting that this activity took place early in Haaibra's reign, although its exact correlation with the Babylonian siege of Jerusalem and that of Tyre is not certain.[9] This active foreign policy in the Levant was aimed not only at blocking Babylonian progress southwards but also at defending Egyptian commercial interests in the eastern Mediterranean.[10] This strategy appears to have been successful as, by the end of Haaibra's reign, the Egyptian presence in the Levant had been further consolidated.

An event that occurred during this period was a rebellion at Elephantine by the foreign mercenary forces of Haaibra. This incident is known only from the biographical inscription on the restored theophorous statue of Neshor called Psamtikmenkhib,[11] who served under the successive rulers Nekau II, Psamtek II and Haaibra. The many military titles and epithets listed on this statue reveal his role in the revolt. The only detail known is that the foreign mercenaries who were stationed at Elephantine rebelled, and planned to migrate further south to Shais-Heret.[12] Neshor as 'Overseer of the Gate of the Southern Foreign Lands' intervened, and by unknown means was able to put down the revolt:[13]

> According as you saved me from a difficulty at the hands of the Bowmen, Bedouins, Greeks, Asiatics, and the rebels who had put (plan)s into their heart(s) to go flee to Shais-Heret, being afraid of His Majesty on account of the wretched act which they had done. I paralysed their hearts with my actions, I did not allow them to go over to Kush, but I made them go before the place where His Majesty was. What His Majesty did was their. …

The date of this rebellion is not certain but it is thought to be early in the reign of Haaibra, possibly in his first regnal year.[14] As Haaibra was occupied with events in the Levant at that time, the foreign mercenaries may have taken advantage and rebelled. The causes of the revolt are uncertain, but it may have been a local small-scale affair which did not involve the native population. The mutiny appears to be an isolated event and provides little information about events in Egypt at that time.[15]

Civil war[16]

At the end of 572 BC Haaibra received an appeal for assistance from the 'Libyan' king, Adikran, to help him block the expansion of the Greek colony of Cyrene, then ruled by Battos II.[17] The possible reason for Egyptian involvement was that the continuing growth of Cyrene caused by the increasing numbers of Greek immigrants was not only encroaching on 'Libyan' territory but was also becoming an economic threat to Egypt in the eastern Mediterranean.[18] Haaibra dispatched an army west to Cyrene, composed of Egyptian troops, and purposely excluded his Greek mercenary forces, as these troops would have been unlikely to be willing to fight against their fellow Greeks. In addition, as a precaution against the ever-present threat posed by Babylon, Haaibra retained the Greek mercenaries at the border posts of Elephantine, Marea and in particular Pelusium in the east.[19]

The Egyptians were heavily defeated by the battle-hardened Greeks at Irasa, to the east of Cyrene, and suffered considerable losses. Those troops who did return home to Egypt were very disgruntled as they considered that the expedition had intended to weaken and possibly eradicate them in favour of Haaibra's preferred mercenary troops. This feeling was bolstered by the ongoing nationalistic resentment among the native forces at their constantly being displaced by Greek mercenaries within the Egyptian military establishment, with privileged positions being allotted to the foreign mercenaries. Haaibra preferred to trust mercenaries over native Egyptians to form his bodyguard.[20] The unrest gradually spread, leading to rebellion within Egypt, as according to Herodotus (II, 161) 'they thought that Haaibra had knowingly sent his men to their doom, that by their so perishing he might be the safer in his rule over the rest of the Egyptians'.

When Haaibra dispatched one of his officials, General Ahmose, in an attempt to negotiate and quell the disturbance, the native troops decided to proclaim Ahmose as their king and to no longer recognise Haaibra. Haaibra succeeded in alienating the Egyptians further, as in a fit of rage he mutilated the courtier, Patarbemis, who brought the bad news of Ahmose's defection to the rebel cause. The Greek sources indicate that, rapidly losing the support of the Egyptian elite, Haaibra had to flee from this growing opposition and had to rely on his Greek mercenary forces to support him and bolster his regime.[21]

The continuing unrest gradually led to civil war, but the exact order of events leading up to this incident is confusing as the sources vary in their narrative. The Elephantine stela of Ahmose,[22] the only extant document to describe this episode, is rather fragmentary and has been the subject of a number of studies. There are considerable discrepancies between the secondary sources, those of Herodotus and Diodorus Siculus, and the text of the Elephantine stela. One possible scenario for the events is that in 570 BC Ahmose advanced on Sais at the head of his rebellious Egyptian troops and confronted Haaibra and his mercenary forces. The encounter resulted in Haaibra retreating, with the subsequent seizure of Sais by Ahmose, who dated his reign from this point. Within a short period of time he was recognised as ruler as far south as Sharuna in Middle Egypt.[23]

The Elephantine stela makes no reference to the events leading up to Ahmose being declared king, beginning its account with Ahmose already installed at Sais. The stela consists of two sections which are dated to Year 1 and Year 4 of his reign. The first reports a counter-attack by Haaibra and his Greek mercenaries, in October/November 570 BC. This confrontation resulted in Haaibra being defeated by Ahmose at *Im3w* (Kom el-Hisn). The text makes no reference to Haaibra's fate, although it is assumed that Haaibra escaped and fled abroad, probably to Babylonian territory.[24] Diodorus and Herodotus state that Haaibra was captured by Ahmose and taken to Sais, and that later Ahmose, unwillingly, had him executed.[25]

The second part of the stela, dated to Year 4, describes the defeat of an attempted 'Asiatic' (Babylonian) invasion of Egypt that was intended to reinstall Haaibra as king. Ahmose II responded to this attack by raising forces from Cyrene and the Greek states as well as from Egypt. Haaibra, who appears to have been in league with the Babylonians, was killed in the course of the battle, and later buried with full honours by Ahmose II.[26] This respectful burial, and the fact that there is then little evidence for the widespread erasure of his monuments, suggest a desire by Ahmose II to reconcile opinion in Egypt, and unite the country behind him.[27] The account is partially supported by a Babylonian cuneiform tablet fragment,[28] which may record an attack on Egypt in Year 37 of Nebuchadnezzar (568/567 BC, corresponding to year 4 of Ahmose II).[29] Much of the remainder of the tablet is lost, the outcome of the attempted invasion is unknown and there is no mention of Haaibra being present.

There is no reference in the Classical sources to an invasion by the Babylonians; this may, however, be due to ignorance as Herodotus, particularly, is considered to have a poor understanding of Egypt's relations with the Near East.[30] As always, the Classical authors relied on the information provided by their Egyptian informants, and such information may have been withheld due to its disparaging nature, and the perceived standing of Egypt thus being presented to the Greeks.[31] There are a variety of prophetic statements in the Old Testament by Jeremiah and Ezekiel, although these are not specific as to the date and could refer to later events.[32] An important premise of many earlier biblical utterances is to apparently depict Egypt as untrustworthy using the image of a 'broken reed',[33] a powerful representation of unreliability, due to the perception that Egypt had repeatedly failed Israel.

There is a gap in the extant versions of the *Babylonian Chronicle* covering this period. Josephus (X, 9, 7), writing some six hundred years after these events, records that an invasion did occur, although again it is unknown whether he had access to any extra-biblical sources to compile his account: 'He fell upon Egypt, in order to overthrow it. And he slew the King that then reigned and set up another: and he took those Jews that were there captives, and led them away to Babylon'. Some later Egyptian texts[34] seem to preserve a tradition of a Babylonian invasion of Egypt during the reign of Haaibra, although the texts have been suggested as a conglomeration of the Babylonian with the more recent Persian invasion, resulting in a corrupted tradition in the sources.[35]

The first known inscription that lists Ahmose as king is a donation stela[36] from Sharuna, dated to early 570 BC, while another stela found in the western Delta,[37] dated to the summer of 570, suggests that by then Ahmose was gaining further control of the Delta region. A stela[38] from Pharbaithos in the eastern Delta, dated soon after the victory of Ahmose, indicates that by the end of 570 BC his control extended over Lower Egypt.[39] An abnormal hieratic papyrus from Thebes[40] recording a loan contract reveals that Haaibra was still recognised there in October 570 BC, some eight months after Ahmose had declared himself king. Perhaps Thebes, not being directly involved in the rebellions in Lower Egypt, continued to acknowledge the legitimate and better-established of the two claimants to the throne, until the defeat of Haaibra was apparent. Also, this may call into question the perception that support for Haaibra was essentially Greek, and not as strong amongst the population of Egypt, as suggested by Herodotus. Perhaps Ahmose, conscious of his position as a usurper, popularised this version throughout his long reign, an account later accepted by Herodotus when writing his *Histories*.[41]

The stela that Ahmose set up at Elephantine makes no reference to the manner in which Ahmose had become king, perhaps in order to maintain a propaganda campaign. Ahmose was also careful to record on his Elephantine stela that he buried Haaibra with full honours in the dynastic cemetery in the precinct of Neith at Sais. When eulogising him, Ahmose employs the complimentary epithet 'confidant' (*mḥ-ib*) and writes his name in a cartouche. This is unusual for an Egyptian victor when portraying a defeated enemy, but it does help to portray Ahmose as a magnanimous ruler;[42] also, not being from the royal line,

6.1 Head of a statue, thought to be Ahmose II. Siltstone. H. 25 cm; W. 28.3 cm; D. 30.5 cm (Ägyptisches Museum und Papyrussammlung der Staatlichen Museen zu Berlin).

he needed to show himself as a true heir to the Egyptian throne (Figure 6.1). As previously noted, this acknowledgement of Haaibra's legitimacy is further supported by the lack of any significant erasures of his monuments.[43]

II Ahmose II (Amasis)

The mother of Ahmose II (Greek Amasis), Tashereniset, is known from the upper section of an incomplete granodiorite statue, and a block found at Mehallet el-Kubra in the Delta, which also appears to name his grandmother, Tjenmutetj.[44] A number of wives are attested for Ahmose, with Herodotus (II, 181) stating that Ahmose married Ladice, the daughter of a leading Cyrenian citizen, although she is not known from any of the Egyptian sources. Tenkheta, the mother of the future king Psamtek III, is mentioned alongside him on a stela from the Serapeum.[45] Another wife, Nakhtsebastetru, is buried at Giza (G 9550) with her son Ahmose: a burial which includes a massive sarcophagus[46] and several shabtis. She is also recognised on a stela from the Serapeum (266)[47] which records another son, Pasenkhons. It is through Pasenkhons that her relationship to Ahmose is known, stating as he does that he is the son of Ahmose.

A daughter of Ahmose is attested, Nitiqret B, who attained the position of High Priest of Amun. Nitiqret was only the second woman to hold this position, the first being Ankhnesneferibre, the God's Wife of Amun.[48] Around 569 BC Ankhnesneferibre adopted Nitiqret B as her heiress, but Nitiqret never succeeded to the position of God's Wife of Amun owing to its abolition during the Persian Period, as no Egyptian, man or woman, was allowed to hold an office of supreme political significance under Persian rule.[49]

Greek tales associated with Ahmose depict him as a common man, fond of drinking.[50] This tradition reappears in the third-century BC tale of *Ahmose and the Skipper* which is written on the verso of the oracular *Demotic Chronicle*[51] and relates to the story of Ahmose drinking very heavily while on a boating trip with his harem, so much so that that next morning he was unable to stand up.[52] This tradition is attested in Egyptian sources where tales of royal self-indulgence are common throughout the Dynastic age. The Westcar Papyrus dated to the Middle Kingdom, but relating to tales set in the Old Kingdom, describes a bored King Sneferu being entertained on the palace lake by ladies from his harem. Similarly, in the New Kingdom tale of a King Neferkare and the military Commander Sasenet, sexual acts between the two men are implied.[53]

The concept of the king in the Late Period, preserved in popular later tradition, in which he is characterised by marked irreverence for the royal office, is therefore witnessed in other periods where the ruler is similarly represented in a light-hearted vein. The motivation behind such representations could be merely be to provide comic relief in order to counter the all-powerful image of the god-king, the overwhelming majesty of the pharaoh.[54] Ahmose, although starting his period in office as a usurper, was later to become respected amongst the population and is considered by many researchers to be a very capable leader and one of the last great pharaohs of Egypt.[55]

Foreign relations

During much of the four decades of Ahmose II's rule he was to benefit from a peaceful and stable international scene. With the death of Nebuchadnezzar II in 562 BC, Babylonian power began to decline, and it became no longer the serious threat to Egypt that it once had been. Meanwhile, the next great empire on the world scene, that of the Persians, which was established by Cyrus the Great in 559 BC, was still in its early stages of expansion.

Ahmose II continued to maintain a strong army, powerfully reinforced by Greek mercenaries. During this period a significant proportion of the army consisted of reserve soldiers, native Egyptians who supported themselves when not on campaigns. Herodotus used the Greek term 'warriors' or *machimoi* to identify these forces. Because of the origins of the Dynasty the army was largely inherited from Egyptian-'Libyan' military forces that included infantrymen, archers and a cavalry corps which was being developed, initially to patrol the extensive frontier zones, before later being used on the battlefield.[56] The need for increased military forces led the Saites to include more and more foreign mercenary soldiers, who were paid in land-holdings as well as in wages. There are records of them in administrative and legal papyri, on private stelae and in Egyptian and Assyrian royal inscriptions. In addition, they are mentioned in Classical sources, and their presence is demonstrated by graffiti such as that at Abu Simbel and Carian graffiti at Wadi el-Shatt el-Regal and Gebel el-Silsila.[57] Such evidence indicates that the mercenaries came from mainland Greece, the Aegean islands, Caria, Lydia, Libya, Kush, Phoenicia, Aram, Israel and Judah.[58]

Ahmose II had at his disposal a potent navy to protect Egyptian trade routes. He seized Cyprus,[59] already coveted by the Babylonians who had previously occupied Cilicia, the nearest mainland state. The seizure demonstrates that Egypt was now a naval power in the Mediterranean, and taking Cyprus would, in particular, have been strategically and economically advantageous as the island had a strong hold on maritime lines of communication along the Levantine coast. Also, the rich metal, particularly copper, and timber resources that Cyprus possessed, both central in shipbuilding, would have been valuable for Egypt's navy. The brief period of Egyptian domination of Cyprus left its influence on the island mainly in the arts, particularly sculpture. Cyprus was later conquered by the Persians at the end of the Saite Period in 525 BC.

Again, like his predecessors, Ahmose put great emphasis on diplomacy, forging a number of foreign alliances intended to support his country's interests. Cyrene, the state that had played a major part in the downfall of Haaibra, now became an ally of Egypt, perhaps fostered by Ahmose having chosen a Cyrenean bride in order to forge political links.[60] He formed an alliance with Croesus of Lydia who was himself allied with Sparta and Nabonidus of Babylon.[61] He had close relationships with a number of Greek states, and not only traded with them but obtained from them his mercenary forces.[62] Ahmose showed his goodwill to the Greek states by sending gifts to be dedicated in many Greek temples such as those at Cyrene, Lindos and Delphi.[63] He made an alliance with and sent gifts to Polycrates, the Greek tyrant of the rich island of Samos off the coast of Ionia, and owner of the most powerful fleet in the Aegean. By the 520s BC Polycrates had become dominant in the Aegean Sea region.[64] These gifts would not only have been intended to further relations with the specific states but would also have had economic and strategic motives. Such donations could perhaps be considered as favours intended to be later repaid by economic and military assistance.[65] All of these alliances were intended to create a strong coalition aimed at resisting Persian ambitions, and maintain the independence of Egypt, particularly later in his reign when Persia was beginning to pose a serious threat.

In Year 41, towards the end of Ahmose's reign, there is some evidence for an expedition to Nubia as attested in a number of Demotic papyrus fragments. The Demotic texts refer to the passage of a caravan under military protection, although this column could have been a military expedition. Owing to the incomplete nature of the textual evidence it has been suggested that it could relate to the earlier Nubian campaign of Psamtek II.[66]

Within Egypt

Within Egypt Ahmose paid particular attention to the Greeks, and specifically the trading post of Naukratis where he encouraged the concentration of Greek commercial activity: 'the gift of Naukratis as a commercial headquarters for any who wished to settle in the country'.[67] Rather than referring to the founding of the city, the passage points to promoting Greek presence in the city, perhaps aiming at a new phase of commercial expansion. This policy may also have been intended to restrict the Greeks to an easily controllable location not too far from Sais.[68] Ahmose also relocated his Greek mercenaries from their camp at Pelusium in the eastern Delta to Memphis, which Herodotus (II, 178) states was to ensure his security, but the motive could have been to monitor their activities and exert greater control over them. Ahmose would have been aware of Greek loyalties to the previous ruler, Haaibra, and, being a usurper to the throne, he would have wished to have the mercenaries in a location that he was able to oversee.

There was increased interest in the oases of the western desert during the reign of Ahmose, as attested by building activity and inscriptions at Dakhla, Baharia and Siwa. There are few records of Saite activity in the eastern desert, but large numbers of greywacke statues indicate that quarrying was carried out in the Wadi Hammamat. An inscription from the statue of a royal messenger (*wpwty-nsw*), unearthed in the Delta, records a voyage to Punt travelling via Coptos.[69]

III Building activities during the reigns of Haaibra and Ahmose II

Most of the 26th-Dynasty temples and monuments that exist today are in ruins. Nevertheless, what blocks and reliefs that have survived demonstrate a high standard of workmanship and a sophisticated archaising style that is typical for this period.[70] Haaibra undertook a large number of building projects, particularly at Sais where he built a Sed-festival gate in the temple complex of Neith and also a tomb for Osiris.[71] At Mendes, he commenced a new temple to Banebdjed, the Ram-god of Mendes, a building that was later usurped by Ahmose. The temple appears to have been particularly impressive with a length of 100 m and contained four 7.8-metre-high granite naoi, one of which is still standing

6.2 A 7.8 m granite naos of Haaibra on top of the partially missing foundations for the temple of the Ram-god Banebdjedet at Mendes, as it looks today.

and today dominates an open field (Figure 6.2). At Tanis, the temples to Mut and Amun were renovated and embellished. There is also evidence of building work at sites such as Hermopolis, Abydos and the Bahariya oasis.[72]

Haaibra carried out major building work at Memphis, where he modified into a palace the existing fortress at the north end of the site near the temple of Neith. The palace stood on an artificial mud-brick mound, of a type characteristic of the Late Period with a casemate construction. One of the impressive features of the palace was its main gate, constructed of limestone blocks that were decorated with temple scenes, copied from Old and Middle Kingdom models, a striking Saite example of archaism. When Flinders Petrie excavated the palace in 1909, he considered that for stylistic reasons the blocks were from an earlier structure, dating perhaps to the 12th Dynasty. A 26th-Dynasty date for this structure has since been recognised by a number of scholars.[73] Part of the monumental gateway depicts Haaibra in the regalia of the Sed-festival, but owing to its fragmentary nature the exact reconstruction of the various reliefs is still uncertain, particularly as the blocks were originally discovered in a ditch, and not in an identifiable gateway position.[74] Blocks from the Ptah temple at Memphis also indicate that Haaibra carried out work at this site.

The forty-four-year reign of Ahmose was marked by massive building projects. At Buto, Ahmose constructed a new temple dedicated to the Cobra-goddess, Wadjet. The walls and roof of this large temple were constructed of limestone blocks cased with quartzite, an exceptional and time-consuming building method. At the time of Herodotus the temple was still standing, and he commented on its exceptional nature:[75] 'I will mention the most amazing thing I saw there: it was a temple within this precinct of Wadjet, which is made out of a single block of stone (at least its sides were), with each wall forty cubits long and forty cubits high. Its roof was made out of another block of stone, with cornices measuring four cubits. So, the temple was the most amazing thing I saw.'

Again, according to Herodotus (II, 175), Ahmose continued works at the temple of Neith at Sais, building a gateway or pronaos to the sanctuary, and Herodotus (II, 169) also describes the funerary temple of Ahmose at Sais: 'In fact, although Ahmose's tomb is further from the temple than the tombs of Haaibra and his ancestors, it too is still within the courtyard of the sanctuary; his tomb is a huge stone colonnade lavishly decorated with, for instance, columns made to look like palm-trees. There are two doorways set into this colonnade and behind these doors is the actual tomb.'

Ahmose II is known to have celebrated a Sed-festival, and a block inscribed with texts and Sed-festival decoration scenes was found at Rosetta, having originated in the temple of Neith at Sais[76] (Figure 6.3). Over the years many other blocks with various inscriptions have similarly been found in surrounding villages and traced to Sais; some of these also attest to building work there by Haaibra and Ahmose.[77]

6.3 Block found at Rosetta showing the Sed-festival scene of Ahmose II, similar to scenes such as that of Thutmose III in his Festival Hall at Karnak.

At Memphis, a stela dated to Year 29 (541 BC) records a damaging Nile flood which resulted in destruction to the dykes at Memphis. Ahmose is known to have carried out work on the Ptah temple, possibly repairing damage caused by this flooding.[78] At Philae some three hundred decorated blocks of a small temple of Ahmose were found in the foundations of the later temple of Ptolemy VI.[79] Many other temples in Egypt were renovated or received additions, including those at Mendes, Behbeit el-Hagar, Arthribis, Coptos and Abydos.

The Bahariya oasis,[80] similarly to the other oases of the western desert, enjoyed a resurgence during the Saite period, particularly in the reign of Ahmose II when they became important agricultural and trade centres. Bahariya was a major exporter of wine and an important stop on the trade routes between sub-Saharan Africa, Egypt and the Mediterranean coast. The main 26th-Dynasty structures at the oasis are the temple at Ain el-Muftella and the tombs of Zedamunefankh and his son, Bannentiu.

The rock-cut shaft-tomb of Zedamunefankh, with its four internal sandstone columns and its vibrant tomb paintings, hints at the status and wealth of its owner. Although the tomb inscriptions include no official titles, the nature of the tomb point to Zedamunefankh being an influential figure in the community, possibly a landowner or merchant. The tomb has no separate burial chamber which would suggest that Zedamunefankh was interred in the main chamber. The tomb of his son, Bannentiu, is situated next to his father's and is larger and even more richly decorated with fine reliefs. The elaborate shaft-tomb leads to a large columned hall with adjoining burial chambers. Again, because of the nature of the tomb, Bannentiu is, similarly, suggested to have been an important individual in the community.

The small well-preserved Amun temple at Hibis in the el-Kharga oasis is usually attributed to Darius I, but is thought to have been commenced by Ahmose. The celebrated Ammoneion (Amun temple) of the Siwa oasis was built during the reign of Ahmose. This structure, although built in an Egyptian style, demonstrates a high degree of finish on the block edges, and has markings consistent with the use of the claw chisel, all of which suggest that Greek as well as Egyptian craftsmen worked on its construction.[81]

IV Administration in the later Saite Period

The late Saite Period witnessed a considerable number of internal reforms to the country, aimed at improving economic management and modifying existing administrative structures. From an economic viewpoint, this involved attention to the royal domain, to the assets of the king and to general taxation. A central accounting office was established, whose role included that of assessment, economic control and provisioning, and was placed under the control of the

'Manager of the Scribes of the Council' (*imy-r sš(w) ḏзḏзt*).[82] A number of holders of this office can be traced, with Pefteuawyimen, a contemporary of Psamtek II, being the oldest known bearer of the title. He is attested by an inscription on a statue from the temple of Ptah at Memphis, as well as a number of other artefacts.[83] Tjaennahebu,[84] known from his tomb at Saqqara, and Haaibrameryptah[85] were further holders of this office.

Another important administrative role, relating to management of the royal assets, was that of 'Manager of the Royal Boats' (*imy-r ḥʿw nsw*).[86] This function related to controlling freight movements within Egypt and maintaining the royal fleet.[87] The title can be traced back to reign of Psamtek I, when it is attested on two statues belonging to a certain Pakhraef.[88] At that time, the role related to Psamtek's reform of the administration in Middle Egypt. Later it is attested during the reign of Psamtek II when the title was held by Yulehen, and again during the reign of Ahmose by Psamtik-Meryptah.[89]

Increased attention was given to the administration of temples and their land-holdings during the later Saite Period. In the reign of Ahmose there appears a 'Manager of the Fields' (*mr зḥ*) who had the power to assign and reassign the right to cultivate fields. This official also ensured that land belong to the royal domain was not appropriated by a temple or by private individuals, and the produce of such lands was similarly not diverted away from the Crown. In Papyrus Rylands IX (16.1–18) a Manager of the Fields visited the temple of Teudjoi to investigate and enforce the law relating to such irregularities.[90]

The title of *Senti*, a high-level administrator, who was common in the later Persian and Greek Periods, first makes an appearance at the end of the Saite Period. The *senti* seems to have replaced the vizier, although there were different sentis responsible for various parts of the country. Among the duties of this officiant was that of being responsible for economic documentation or registration of people and objects, possibly for tax purposes. The senti was assisted by local agents throughout the country.[91] Horkheby, who held the position of senti during the reign of Ahmose II, is mentioned on the stela of Hor, his great-grandson.[92]

An administrative official and close adviser to the king during the latter part of the Saite Dynasty carried the title of Chief Physician (*wr swnw*).[93] The Chief Physician, although having had an established role in ancient Egypt since the Old Kingdom and entrusted to look after the health of the sovereign, can now be recognised as seemingly having the role of an adviser to the monarch. Psamtik Seneb was 'Chief Physician', 'Chief Dentist' (*wr ibḥ*) and also 'Commandant of the War Fleet' (*ḥrp ḵḵ(w)t*).[94] The lengthy inscription on the private statue of the Chief Physician Peftuaneith records the extensive renovation works he conducted at Abydos for both Haaibra and Ahmose.[95]

This function of Chief Physician is well illustrated in both the inscription on the celebrated statue of Udjahorresnet, originally set up in the temple of Neith at Sais during the reign of Darius I,[96] and from his shaft-tomb at Abusir (see p. 109). This high-ranking official held important titles under both Ahmose II and Psamtek III, as well as during the reigns of the Persian rulers Cambyses and Darius. He was 'Chief Physician of Upper and Lower Egypt' (*wr swnw Šmʿ Mḥw*) under all these rulers, and he occupied major military positions such as 'Leader of the Mercenary Troops' (*imy-r ḫ3swt ḥʿw nbw*) and 'Overseer (admiral) of the Royal Fleet' (*imy-r kbnwt nsw*) under Ahmose II and Psamtek III. Udjahorresnet was an important military commander but also carried the title of physician. Therefore, the holder of the title of Chief Physician in the Saite Period was a high official who had a close relationship with the monarch, and its use may relate to an archaising usage of an older title. It is quite possible that the functional 'medical' weight of the title may not reflect his duties in reality.

Taxation

The Saite Period witnessed increasing control by the state over various aspects of taxation, including custom duties on goods entering the country, reforms in taxes associated with temples and a reorganisation of the taxation of private individuals. Custom posts or 'Gates' had existed at the borders of Egypt from early times, and, with Saite Egypt being increasingly involved with the trade networks that were developing throughout the Mediterranean and the Near East, the administration associated with the collection of customs dues expanded rapidly.[97] The later stelae erected by Nectanebo I in 380 BC at Naukratis and Thonis-Heracleion, dedicated ten per cent of the harbour custom dues and local tax revenues to the temple of Neith at Sais, while the state kept the remainder (Figure 6.4). The origins of this tax can be traced back to the reign of Ahmose.[98]

The chief official controlling the customs was the 'Overseer of the Gate of Foreign Lands' (*imy-r ʿ3 ḫ3swt*), with a celebrated holder of this position during the reign of Ahmose being a certain Wahibre. Wahibre also held the position of 'Overseer of the Southern Gate' (*imy-r ʿ3 rsyw*), controlling trade with Nubia.[99] This position is attested as early as the reign of Psamtek I, being held then by the Vizier Harsiese, and later during the reign of Haaibra it was held by Neshor (see above). As can be seen from the various inscriptions of Neshor, his role not only related to customs affairs but also included security and the regulation of peoples entering the country.

The ill-defined border between Egypt and the territories to the west was controlled by the 'Overseer of the Gate of the Tjehenu Foreign Lands' (*imy-r ʿ3 ḫ3swt Ṯḥnw*). One prominent official who held this position was the cavalry

6.4 The Decree of Sais on the Thonis-Heracleion stela. The Decree issued by Nectanebo I regarding the taxation of goods passing through Thonis and Naukratis. Black granodiorite. H. 1.99 m; W. 88 cm; D. (max.) 33 cm (National Museum of Alexandria).

chief Sematawytefnakht, whose monument[100] is dated to Year 39 of the reign of Ahmose. His function would probably have involved guarding the western borders of Egypt and overseeing trade along the various caravan routes. Sematawytefnakht additionally held the title of 'Overseer of the Lands of the Setetyu-Asiatics' (*imy-r ḫꜣswt Styw*). There is also mention on his monument of the 'Land of the Tjemehu' (*ḫꜣswt Ṯmḥw*), thought to refer to Marea in the north-west Delta, and it is possible that Sematawytefnakht was stationed there and used his cavalry to guard this region.[101]

Little is known about the administration of the eastern frontier, but General Ahmose, the military officer who organised Psamtek II's expedition to Nubia, and who left graffiti at Abu Simbel, held the title 'Overseer of the Double Gate of the Northern Foreign Lands' (*imy-r ꜥꜣ.wy m ḫꜣswt mḥtw*). The Double Gate referred to Sinai and possibly the eastern part of the Mediterranean, although two holders of the position of 'Overseer of the Gate of the Great Green (Mediterranean)' (*imy-r ꜥꜣ ḫꜣswt Wꜣḏ-wr*) are also known. Neshor, mentioned above, held the position during the reign of Psamtek II, and a certain Nakhthorheb, chief of troops, was overseer during the reign of Ahmose.[102]

It was during the reign of Ahmose that, according to Herodotus (II, 177), a national census of personal income was conducted: 'Ahmose established an admirable custom, which Solon borrowed and introduced at Athens where it is still preserved; this was that every man once a year should declare before the Nomarch, or provincial governor, the source of his livelihood; failure to do this, or inability to prove that the source was an honest one, was punishable by death'. Again Diodorus (I, 95): 'Their king Amasis gave attention to the laws, who, according to their accounts, drew up the rules governing the nomarchs and the entire administration of Egypt'. Both these Classical passages refer to the administration of the nomes, suggesting that that such reforms were carried out at a local level. Herodotus did not state the purpose of the personal declarations, but they may have been used to collect taxes. No census lists have survived from the Saite Period to confirm this, nor are there any surviving papyri tax receipts relating to personal taxation.

Temple administration

As in most periods of ancient Egyptian history, a high proportion of the wealth of the country was possessed by the temples. This is illustrated by inscriptions, such as the Nitiqret Adoption Stela (see p. 63), which details the 2230 acres of cultivable land given to Nitiqret as a royal endowment. Also, Haaibra's Mit Rahina (Memphis) Stela describes a substantial tax-free perpetual endowment to the temple of Ptah at Memphis, consisting of an entire estate involving both the cultivable and marsh land, the agricultural workers tied to the land (*mrt*), cattle and produce. Another example was the Petition of Petiese which documents tax-free temple estates and herds of cattle belonging to Amun.[103]

From the time of Ahmose there is widespread evidence of 'declarations' or 'land leases' which involved the letting of temple land to individuals, some of whom then further sublet the land. In many cases the land lease was concluded orally, but in certain situations, perhaps for added security, a written lease was drawn up.[104] A number of examples of such written leases relating to the temple of Amun at Thebes have survived. They refer to arrangements between individuals, one or both of whom held a sacerdotal title. The land belonging to the temple may have been assigned as an element of his remuneration to a member of the clergy, who could then cultivate it or lease it to a tenant, thus supplementing his income.[105] Papyrus Louvre 7837, dated to 535 BC, details how the God's Father, Udjahor, leased land and an ox to a group of farmers in the district of Coptos, with the rent being one-third of the harvest and also one-sixth of two-thirds of the harvest, on account of the ox.[106]

The Saite leases, usually fixed for a term of one year only, were all share-crop arrangements. There is no evidence of fixed rental or of rental paid partially or wholly in advance, a practice that was to become common during the Ptolemaic Period.[107] Land still belonged to the temple and so was subject to 'harvest-tax' (*šmw*), and the lease would specify who had to pay this tax. Such taxes were under the control of the 'Scribe of the Account of the Corn' (*sš ḥsb it*), who supervised and administered payments, managed deliveries of corn to the granary and drew up tax-receipts.[108] Land was now being leased in this manner to 'free workers' (*nmḥw*) because of a lack of 'tied (institutional) workers' (*iḥwtyw*) such as prisoners of war, criminals, debtors or individuals born into this status.[109]

During the Saite period new forms of taxation were initiated, with, for example, temples introducing a ten per cent sales tax on property transfers.[110] Similarly, the temples began to administer and control access to the cemeteries in the neighbouring desert regions, with overall responsibility being in the hands of the 'Overseer of the Necropolis' (*mr ḫ3st*). Burial plots had now to be purchased from the temple, and taxes were then collected on burials in these cemeteries. In Stela Louvre C 101,[111] dated to Year 8 of Psamtek I (657 BC), the overseer of the necropolis states that he is satisfied with the money he received for a tomb built in the necropolis: 'Regnal Year 8, second month of Akhet under King Psamtek, may he live for ever. The overseer of the necropolis Kayrou son of Ptahhotep has said to the washerwoman Peteamunip son of Pakem: "You have satisfied my heart with the price for this tomb that is located in the mountain of Anubis".'

A group of individuals involved in the mortuary sphere who rose to prominence in the Saite Period were the 'pourers of water' (*w3ḥw-mw*). They are more usually known by their Greek form, *choachytes*, and are similar to the older title of 'soul-servants' (*ḥm-k3*) who were members of the priesthood. They usually held office on a hereditary basis, and their working activities involved helping to prepare the funeral, storage and transportation of the mummy, providing and furnishing a tomb and the arrangement of funerary offerings. After the funeral, they also performed rituals for the dead at regular intervals, being paid by the deceased relatives for these services. From the income they received, the choachytes then had to settle the various taxes that were due to the temple on whose land the tomb was located.[112]

As regards the organisation of other members of the priesthood and temple staff, no significant changes appear to have been introduced during the Saite Period. But numbers of officials, members of the priesthood and various facilities involved with animal cults would undoubtedly have increased during the Saite Period when the cult of divine animals proliferated enormously.

Landownership

Royal grants of land donated to temples are attested throughout much of the Dynastic Period and were used by the king not only as a means to provide these institutions with income to sustain their daily cultic activities but also to obtain the support of the local elite. This was particularly notable during the Saite Period when considerable donations of land were made to the temples in an attempt to persuade the local elite to integrate into the new administration, following the previous period of political instability and foreign occupation.[113] Examples of this type of land donation are detailed on the Nitiqret Adoption Stela as well as on the Mit Rahina stela.

The Crown also rewarded and honoured officials and private individuals by bestowing plots of land. Smallholdings of one to ten arourae[114] were granted to individuals of middle social class status such as soldiers, scribes and priests. Similarly, land donations were granted by the temples to individuals, but equally individuals handed over large tracts of land to the temple. This seemed to be intended not only to be an act of piety but also to help strengthen the individual's relationship with the temples and ultimately the monarch. The donor of these land-holdings could continue to receive the income from the land making up the endowment. Neshor, the high official in charge of the frontiers at Elephantine and Naukratis, made donations of land to the temples in these two cities, and to the temples at Mendes, Sais, Abydos and Hermopolis. With the wide geographical range of these gifts, Neshor was probably seeking to obtain maximum prestige and prominence by his close association with these many institutions.[115]

Private funerary endowments are attested both in donation stelae and papyri. Papyrus Turin 2121 (old 248), dated to Year 47 of Psamtek I, describes the donation of ten arourae of fields to the temple of Osiris at Abydos to create a funerary endowment for the husband of the donor. The donation was put under the control of a choachyte, with a clause that stated that the other relatives of the donor were not to question this decision. The papyrus illustrates an important element of these endowments, in that the land donations could be protected from later being contested by their owner's family.[116] Similarly, during the reign of Psamtek I, Harbes donated 60 arourae of land to the temple of Osiris at Busiris in return for funerary services to be performed for his votive statue[117] that he had had erected in the temple.[118]

Landownership thus underwent significant changes during the Saite Dynasty, with the demotic land leases indicating an increase in sales of land and private ownership. This process would have been aided by the high Nile inundations that were occurring at that time, as these brought about changes in the Nile tributaries, particular in the Delta regions. This process allowed new areas to be brought under cultivation, benefiting the landowners and increasing resources available for taxation.[119]

Judicial system

In Saite Egypt the king possessed ultimate judicial and administrative authority, and as in many periods of ancient Egyptian history his subjects could come to the royal palace and petition him to hear their complaints. On occasions the king did hear and decide judicial cases himself, as for example with the Petition of Petiese, when in Year 31 of Psamtek I, it was the king who found the priests at el-Hiba guilty of murdering Petiese I's grandson.[120]

Following the Saite reunification of Egypt various provincial governors and army generals served as local representatives of the monarch and were responsible for the administration of criminal justice in their regions. There were a number of juridical terminology changes, new types of legal documents began to appear, and the phrasing and makeup of existing document types was modified. These legal changes seem not to have been put into the shape of a single legal corpus until the Persian Period, when Darius I in Year 3 ordered a compilation of earlier Egyptian laws.[121] Persian documents relating to this period no longer exist, and it is only from the early Ptolemaic Period that there are extant copies of a Demotic version. Although only a small part of the original Demotic corpus is known to have survived, certain of these law codes are suggested to date back to the Saite Period. These surviving documents indicate that the original corpus would have been fairly comprehensive in its scope, covering such topics as leases, matrimonial property settlements and maintenance obligations, inheritance, sale of tombs, loans and related interest, and servitude.[122]

As regards Saite law in practice, the earlier regional *ḳnbt* courts, which had been staffed by local dignitaries, were now termed 'the house of judgement' (*pꜣ ꜥ.wy n wpy*), and were put under the control of boards of judges (*wpṭyw*). These courts were associated with the temples in the major provincial towns and are considered to be closer to modern courts of justice. Access to the courts was by petitioning the relevant authority by means of a written statement in order to obtain redress for an alleged wrongdoing.[123]

Exchange and redistribution

Prior to the Saite period weights of copper and occasionally grain provided the baseline for value and exchange mechanisms. Silver came to be used more and more as the standard measure of value during the 26th Dynasty, and this is reflected in various abnormal hieratic and Demotic texts where it was increasingly documented as the media of exchange, replacing various commodities that had previously been in use. Even when silver coins entered the country from the Near East and the Mediterranean regions, it would appear that their value was as bullion, being based on the weight of the coins rather than their denominations. Although coinage began to circulate amongst the foreign mercenary troops, it is unlikely that the native Egyptians considered that it had any intrinsic value. Beyond their value as metal, coins appeared to have had little role in the economy during the Saite Period.[124]

Demotic, abnormal hieratic and other languages

Demotic, which evolved from hieratic, was the most cursive of the scripts used by the ancient Egyptians. It developed in Lower Egypt, contemporary with abnormal hieratic in Upper Egypt, during the Third Intermediate Period and into the 26th Dynasty. With the unification of Egypt under Psamtek, Demotic script spread from the Delta southwards, and by the time of Ahmose II Demotic had become the recognised script for administrative and legal documents.[125] Of the varieties of Demotic documents that have survived, particularly common are those belonging to the choachytes. Their more frequent preservation is due to them being stored in the tombs, where the choachytes worked, rather than in their homes.

In the Theban area, abnormal hieratic was used throughout the Saite Period, and it was not until the reign of Ahmose II that Demotic became widely employed, and became Egypt's accepted script, the last known use of abnormal hieratic being the signature of a witness on the reverse of Papyrus Louvre E 7837, dating to 535 BC.[126] Demotic was not the sole script available in use in Egypt, as hieroglyphs were still employed for formal inscriptions, whereas hieratic continued to be employed more for literary and religious texts.[127]

Other than the use of the Egyptian language, traders from the Levant and the Greek states as well as foreign immigrants from many countries entered Egypt during the Saite period, each group possessing its own unique language. Evidence of these languages is noticeable in a number of sites throughout Egypt. A series of stelae in a cemetery in Saqqara, used by the Carians, have bilingual inscriptions which has helped with decipherment of the Carian language and yielded information about the assimilation of the Carians into Egypt.[128] Phoenician, Aramaic and Carian inscriptions have been found in a cemetery to the west of Abusir, established at the end of the Saite Period.[129] The letter of King Adon is written in Aramaic, which was used extensively during the succeeding Persian Period.

V Technology

In technology the Saite Period is notable for the quality of its faience pieces.[130] There was a gradual alteration in long-established techniques and the first appearance of those improved methods which subsequently were to give Ptolemaic faience its distinctive character. Faience became more heterogenous and technically superior to that produced in previous periods with regards both to glaze adhesion and to colour control. The faience now being manufactured was more of a glass-like material containing frit with a high proportion of alkali. Naukratis had a thriving faience industry, as attested by the scarab factory next to the temple of Aphrodite, as did Memphis, where conventional blue and green specimens, as well as some innovative examples of blended colours, are recognised. Faience, like bronze, became a particular important medium of artistic production in Egypt during the Third Intermediate and Saite Periods and the standard of artefacts produced was high.

In bronze work, lost-wax casting was a technique used to manufacture copper objects since at least the Old Kingdom, and particularly during the Third Intermediate Period, with improvements in techniques, some fine examples were being produced. There were further developments during the Saite Period such as lead now being routinely added to the copper which lowered the melting point, increased fluidity and reduced porosity. The increased fluidity allowed more complex shapes with finer detail to be cast in one piece, with some excellent examples of large and miniature bronzes being created.

There was a reinvigoration in stone-working techniques, quarries were opened up, there was increased activity in the quarries at Aswan and expeditions sent to the Wadi Hammamat for hard stone. Colossal statues such as that of Psamtek I recently discovered at Heliopolis were being fashioned and obelisks, which had been absent from the repertoire for centuries, made their reappearance. There was a marked increase in temple building and renovation work, made all the more possible by the political and economic recovery of Egypt.

One aspect of technology that the Saites were slow to embrace was the introduction of widespread iron smelting. Iron-rich Anatolia seems to have been the earliest home of large-scale iron working in the late second millennium BC,[131] and by the middle of the first millennium production was widespread throughout the Near East with the exception of Egypt. Iron was important for tools and weaponry as the blades of iron tools and weapons usually had a tougher, sharper cutting edge than their copper alloy equivalents. The lack of iron weapons in Egypt has been suggested as a factor in the conquest of Egypt by the Assyrians and then later by the Persians, although this view has not been universally accepted. It is not certain why this technology was slow to be introduced into Egypt, particularly as Saite Egypt had many innovative developments in the working of materials and manufacturing of artefacts. It may have been that iron-working was initially rejected not because it was distrusted but because there were no obvious discernible problems with the existing technologies.[132] However, wood was the industrial fuel that provided the energy for smelting iron in the ancient world and the lack of trees in Egypt would have also been an important factor in the lack of development of this technology.

VI Conclusion

The second part of the Saite Period was characterised by a number of economic and administrative reorganisations including the strengthening of the customs administration and greater tax control over the assets of the individual. These economic and commercial reforms contributed to a growing prosperity in Egypt. This is reflected by Herodotus (II, 177) when he commentated on the remarkable productivity of the land, although the occurrence of high Nile inundations would undoubtedly have assisted with these plentiful harvests: 'It is said that the reign of Ahmose was a time of unexampled material prosperity for Egypt; the river gave its riches to the earth and the earth to the people'. This wealth is also attested from the substantial documentary evidence surviving from this time, as well as the quality of the many royal works that Ahmose II undertook at temples throughout Egypt.

Another important change occurring in the later part of the Saite Dynasty was that temples now leased out considerable parcels of land, as a result in part of the shortage of tied labour. This major change resulted in the development of private enterprise, with individuals now able to lease such land and derive income it, with other groups in society such as the choachytes able to benefit from the resulting improved prosperity of the people.[133]

Notes

1   Leahy 1996: 157–60.
2   Spalinger 1977: 232–36; Miller and Hayes 2006: 474–76.
3   Greenberg 1983: 323.
4   Jeremiah 37.5.
5   Josephus X: 109–10.
6   Hoffmeier 1981: 165–66.
7   Jeremiah 43.1–7; Smoláriková 2006: 247–48.
8   Herodotus II, 161; Diodorus Siculus I, 68.1; Spalinger 1977: 236.
9   Kienitz 1953: 27ff; Freedy and Redford 1970: 481; Spalinger 1977: 234; Perdu 2014: 147.
10 Perdu 2014: 147.
11 Louvre A 90. See Vernus 1991; Heise 2007; Perdu 2011; Jansen-Winkeln 2014b: vol. 1, 408–10; Bassir 2016 (includes an extensive bibliography pp. 90–95).

12   Shais-Heret in Nubia translated as 'run in a remote place' is probably south of the Second Cataract. See Pope 2014: 87–94; Bassir 2016: 77 n. 46.

13   Louvre A 90 theophorous statue of Neshor, back pillar column 7. See Bassir 2016 for translation, commentary and bibliography.

14   Bassir 2016: 88.

15   Leahy 1988: 198.

16   The sources for the civil war are Herodotus II, 162–69; Diodorus Siculus I, 68.2–5; the Elephantine Stela of Ahmose and a fragment of a Babylonian text (BM 33041). See Leahy 1988: 183–99.

17   Herodotus II, 161.

18   See Lloyd 1988: 173–74 for a discussion on possible motives for the attack on Cyrene.

19   Spalinger 1979b: 593.

20   Murray 1980: 221; Lloyd 1988: 174.

21   Herodotus II, 162–63; Spalinger 1979b: 594.

22   Formerly Cairo 13/6/24/1, now in the Nubian Museum, Aswan. Originally published by Daressy (1900), for discussions see Edel 1978; Spalinger 1982: 18, 59, 108–9, 111; Leahy 1988; Ladynin 2006 and Jansen-Winkeln 2014a.

23   Leahy 1988: 192.

24   Leahy 1988: 190–93.

25   Herodotus II, 172; Diodorus I, 68.5; Posener 1947: 128–30; Spalinger 1979b: 594. See Ladynin (2006: 44–8) for the suggestion that the Classical authors' description of Haaibra being executed by Ahmose were fictitious accounts, deliberately introduced to present the victory of Ahmose as total.

26   Spalinger 1979b: 595–98; Leahy 1988: 191; Jansen-Winkeln 2014a.

27   Leahy 1988: 198; cf. the evidence that carrying out the burial of a predecessor was key to legitimate succession (e.g. the depiction of Ay burying Tutankhamun on the wall of the latter's burial chamber).

28   *Nbk* 329 = BM EA 33041. See Wiseman 1956: 94–95, pls XX–XXI, translated Pritchard 1969: 308; Edel 1978: 14–15; Leahy 1988: 191; Ladynin 2006: 32.

29   An earlier interpretation by Spalinger (1979b: 597) cautions that as the cuneiform tablet is a list of troop requisitions with only a few military phrases being able to be recognised, it cannot, therefore, be used as proof of a Babylonian invasion of Egypt.

30   Leahy 1988: 191. See Ladynin (2006) for alternative explanation as to why the Classical accounts are silent about the Babylonian invasion. For a discussion of Herodotus's knowledge of Egypt's relations with the Near East see Lloyd 1988: 117, 241.

31   Ladynin 2006: 36.

32   'Nebuchadnezzar ... shall come and smite the land of Egypt' (Jeremiah 43.10–13) and 'he will turn the land of Egypt into ruins of parched desolation from Migdol to Syene, to the border of Cush' (Ezekiel 29.10).

33   II Kings 18.21 – 'If you lean on Egypt, it will be like a reed that splinters beneath your weight and pierces your hand'; Isaiah 36.6 – 'you are depending on Egypt, that splintered reed of a staff'; Ezekiel 29.6 – 'And all the inhabitants of Egypt shall know that I am the Lord, because they have been a staff of reed to the house of Israel'.

34 See for example the complex Coptic story of Cambyses' invasion of Egypt (Jansen 1950) and the Chronicle of John, Bishop of Nikiu (Charles 1916) who both confuse Cambyses with Nebuchadnezzar. Also see Spalinger 1979b: 595 n. 21.

35 Spalinger 1977: 238–40 and 1979b: 595; Ladynin 2006: 46.

36 BM EA 952. For a list of all known stelae from the reign of Ahmose see Meeks 1979: 679; Leahy 1988: 186 n. 3.

37 Berlin 14998.

38 Louvre C 298.

39 Spalinger 1979b: 594.

40 P. BM 10113. See Leahy 1988; Donker van Heel 2012: 35–39.

41 Leahy 1988: 197.

42 Spalinger 1978b: 26.

43 Leahy 1988: 198.

44 Statue BM EA 775 *LR* 4, 128.

45 Louvre SIM 4034. *LR* 4, 129; Vercoutter 1962: 37–43; de Meulenaere 1968: 184.

46 St Petersburg 766. See Grajetski 2005: 94.

47 *LR* 4, 129–30; Vittmann 1975: 381; Troy 1986: 177 (26.6).

48 De Meulenaere 1968: 186; Leahy 1996: 158.

49 Ayad 2001: 7.

50 Herodotus II, 172–74.

51 Papyrus 215, Bibliothéque Nationale de Paris.

52 Ritner 2003: 450–52.

53 Posener 1957: 119ff; Meskell 1999: 94–95.

54 De Meulenaere 1951: 95; contra Spalinger 1978b: 13–14; Lloyd 1983: 288–99.

55 Arnold 1999: 83; Lloyd 1983: 285; Manning 2003: 39; Donker van Heel 2012: 2.

56 Lloyd 1983: 309–10; Agut-Labordère 2013: 986–89.

57 Ray 2001: 1190.

58 Kahn 2007a: 507.

59 Herodotus II, 182; Diodorus I, 68.6; Spalinger 1977: 243.

60 Spalinger 1979b: 597; Perdu 2014: 148.

61 Herodotus I, 77; Perdu 2014: 148.

62 Josephson 2001.

63 Herodotus II, 182.

64 Briant 2002: 52; Bresson 2005: 150–51.

65 Lloyd 1983: 330–31.

66 P. Berlin 13615 + 13606 A-B + 15824 A-B; Erichsen 1941; Heidorn 1991: 206 n. 29; Zauzich 1992; Schmitz 2010: 326.

67 Herodotus II, 178.

68 Lloyd 1988: 221.

69 Quaegebeur 1995; Klotz 2013: 904–5.

70 Zivie-Coche 2008: 6.

71 Gauthier 1922b.

72 Arnold 1999: 80–83.

73 De Wit 1958: 27; Smith 1998: 234; Kemp 1977; Kaiser 1987.

74 Petrie and Walker 1909; Kaiser 1987; Arnold 1999: 82; Lopes and Braga 2011.

75 Herodotus II, 155–56.

76 Habachi 1943: 384–85.

77   Wilson 2006: 203–30 and 2016: 76–78.

78   Cairo JdE 37494; Daressy 1923; Arnold 1999: 86.

79   Farag, Wahba and Farid 1977; Arnold 1999: 88.

80   Fakhry 1974: 14–153; Hawass 2000: 185–95.

81   Kuhlmann 1988; Arnold 1999: 83–91.

82   Perdu 1998.

83   Turin 3020; Perdu 1998: 177.

84   Bresciani et al. 1977: 30–40, pls VII–XII; Perdu 1998: 178.

85   Perdu 1998: 179; Agut-Labordère 2013: 996.

86   Goyon 1969.

87   Agut-Labordère 2013: 998–99.

88   Pernigotti 1969; Vittmann 1998: 711–13.

89   Goyon 1969: 164–65, 167.

90   Yoyotte 1989: 75; Agut-Labordère 2013: 999–1000.

91   Muhs 2016: 182–83.

92   Louvre C 317 found at the Serapeum; Yoyotte 1989: 80; Agut-Labordère 2013: 1001.

93   Agut-Labordère 2013: 972–73.

94   Ghalioungui 1983: 32; Chevereau 1985: 134–35, doc. 195.

95   Louvre A 93; Klotz 2010: 128–29.

96   This statue is now located in the Vatican (196). See Posener 1936; Lloyd 1982; Vittmann 2011; Lopez 2016.

97   Posner 1947; Somaglino 2010; Agut-Labordère 2013: 1002–6.

98   Posener 1947: 130–31; Yoyotte 2006; Bomhard 2012: 93–97.

99   Statue Cairo 34044; Gauthier 1922a: 88–89; Chevereau 1985: 107–9, 387, doc. 195.

100   Cairo 27/11/58/8; Bresciani 1967.

101   Perdu 2006: 174, n. c; Agut-Labordère 2013: 988–89, 1004–5; Klotz 2013: 904.

102   Statue Varille at Lyon; Tresson 1931: 126–44, pls VII–IX; Lichtheim 1992: 91–92.

103   Gunn 1927; Lloyd 1983: 301–9; Muhs 2016 particularly 198–202.

104   Donker van Heel 1998.

105   Agut-Labordère 2013: 1018.

106   Donker van Heel 1996: 210–15.

107   Hughes 1952: 4.

108   Donker van Heel 1996: 175 n. VIII.

109   Agut-Labordère 2013: 1019; Moreno Garcia 2013b.

110   Examples are P. Turin 2118A (246) from Thebes dated to Year 30 of Psamtek I, see Malinine 1953: 56–71; and P. British Museum 10117, also from Thebes, dated to Year 29 of Ahmose (542 BC), see Reich 1914: 9–25; Vleeming 1992: 343–50.

111   Malinine 1975: 168–74; Donker van Heel 2012: 27–28.

112   Vleeming 1995; Agut-Labordère 2013: 1020–25; Muhs 2016: 185.

113   Moreno Garcia 2013b.

114   An aroura is equivalent to 2735 sq. m. or approximately two-thirds of an acre.

115   Perdu 1990.

116   Malinine 1953: 117–24; Moreno Garcia 2013b; Muhs 2016: 200–1.

117   Black granite block statue, NY Carlsberg Glyptotek E. 78. See Iverson 1941: 18–21.

118   Ritner 2009a: 584–85.

119 Wilson 2010: 248–49.
120 P. Rylands IX, 11.17–19. See Vittmann 1998: vol. 1, 152–53.
121 Lippert 2016: 2.
122 Lippert 2004, 2015; Muhs 2016: 179.
123 Allam 1991: 116–19; Lippert 2016.
124 O'Rourke 2001; Muhs 2016: 189–93.
125 Johnson 2001.
126 Donker van Heel 2012: 26; Agut-Labordère 2013: 979–80.
127 Johnson 2001.
128 Masson et al. 1978; Ray 1982.
129 Dušek and Mynářová 2013.
130 Kaczmarczyk and Hedges 1983: 265–75.
131 Waldbaum 1978.
132 Moorey 1994: 286–87; Shaw 2012: 122–26.
133 Agut-Labordère 2013: 1027.

7

Fall of the house of Sais:
the last Saite ruler, Psamtek III

The Persian threat

Towards the end of the reign of Ahmose II, the Persian Empire, which had been increasing in size and power for a number of years, posed a serious threat to Egypt. Now it seemed only a question of time before Persia was to launch an attack on Egypt. For the events of this period, and its immediate aftermath, we have to rely primarily on Classical sources, chiefly Herodotus (III, 1–38). This particularly biased version of the ensuing Persian conquest has created an influential picture of Cambyses, the Persian ruler, as a crazed despot. Nevertheless, there is very little other evidence to set against it and, although his narrative presents structural difficulties, most scholars accept his account in broad outline.[1]

The Persian Empire evolved around a small core state in the modern province of Fars in southern Iran, referred to then as Parsa, from which is derived the modern term 'Persia'. Known also as the Achaemenid Empire, derived from the founder of the ruling dynasty, Achaemenes, whose family members were to rule the empire for two hundred years, it developed around 550 BC with the rapid conquests of Cyrus the Great (559–530 BC), who went on to defeat the Babylonians in 539 BC. The territory continued to expand under his son, Cambyses II (530–522 BC), and eventually became more powerful than the earlier Babylonian and Assyrian Empires it replaced. By 522 BC, less than thirty years from its founding, the Persian Empire extended from the First Cataract in Egypt's south to the Aegean coast and then eastwards to Central Asia. It was to become the largest 'world empire' known up to that time.[2]

Cambyses, on coming to the throne in 530 BC, inherited an immense territory from his father, Cyrus. With the lands having only recently been conquered, Persian control was quite fragile, particularly along the vulnerable coastal regions of the Levant and Aegean. Cambyses had both to maintain dominion over the conquered countries and to extend his conquest towards the only remaining power of consequence in the Near East, Egypt. The acquisition of Egypt, a potential enemy and major military force, as well as being an important source of economic power in Africa, would have been a natural objective of the imperialist policy established by his father Cyrus, which Cambyses now continued to pursue.[3]

But the Classical authors[4] narrate an alternative sequence of events, presumably a pretext, as to why Persia invaded Egypt. According to their accounts Cambyses had demanded a daughter of Ahmose II for his wife. Ahmose II was reluctant to agree to this request as he feared his daughter would become merely a concubine and not a royal wife. Instead he sent Nitetis, the daughter of the previous ruler, Haaibra, rather than his own daughter. When Cambyses found that he had been deceived, he flew into a rage and in retaliation decided to attack Egypt.

Previously, following the Persian conquest of Babylonia under Cyrus, Ahmose II had attempted to counteract this growing Persian threat by allying Egypt with a number of states, one of which was Samos. Relations between Samos and Egypt were later to break down during the reign of Cambyses. According to Herodotus (III, 40–43), Ahmose II severed links with Polycrates, the ruler of Samos, because he perceived a calamity was going to befall Polycrates, and he wished to avoid the distress that this would have caused him had Polycrates still been his friend. Polycrates, then, in an attempt to court favour with the Persians, offered the Samian fleet to the Persian king to assist him with his planned invasion of Egypt. It is likely that this shift in strategy may well have occurred after the death of Ahmose II, and that Polycrates, being informed about the preparations of Cambyses to invade Egypt, as well as seeing the Persian hold on Ionia intensifying, could well have anticipated a Persian victory and so switched his loyalty to Persia.[5] Cambyses was further aided by the Phoenician cities and Cyprus, who with their large fleets also surrendered to the Persians, resulting in Egypt becoming isolated, and its naval strength seriously depleted. Undoubtedly these states that recognised the might of the Persian Empire supported the side which they perceived to be the stronger.

For Persia to gain control of the eastern Mediterranean seaboard as well as Egypt, it required not only powerful military forces but also a strong navy which in the early stages of planning the attack on Egypt it did not possess. Herodotus (III, 19) claims that, although Cambyses was the creator and organiser of the fledgling Persian navy, naval power on the whole was dependent on the Phoenicians. It would appear that, although the Persians did build a large number of triremes and trained crews to man them, initially they may have been dependent on Phoenician expertise and experienced foreign sailors and oarsmen.[6]

Towards the end of the Saite Period, evidence would suggest that Egypt itself had a sizeable naval force which would have continued to be maintained by Ahmose II, particularly with the Persian threat looming larger all the time. Although there is no mention of the Egyptian navy in Herodotus's account of the events of 525 BC, individuals such as Udjahorresnet, Hekaemsaf[7] and Tjanehebu[8] did carry naval titles.

Death of Ahmose II and invasion

Ahmose II died in summer 526 BC and, following tradition, he was buried in the royal necropolis at Sais. He was succeeded by his son, the untried Psamtek III (526–525 BC), born of Tenkheta. Little is known of his short period on the throne as the Classical accounts emphasise the Persian attack on Egypt under Cambyses, rather than any other events of his reign. He is known to have completed a chapel to Osiris in Karnak, and his cartouches are evident on a number of artefacts such as sistrum-handles, faience plaques and a scarab.[9] He is mentioned on the statue of Udjahorresnet, but only once and then in a list of titles.

It is possible that the Persians, on hearing of the newcomer to the Egyptian throne, took advantage of the situation to launch their attack, although they had been planning such an assault for some time. Strabo (XVI, 2.25 C758) mentions that the Palestinian city of Akê (Acco) was utilised by the Persians as a base of operations against Egypt. Cambyses also made use of strategic information provided by Egyptian fugitives such as Phanes of Halicarnassus, a Carian mercenary officer serving under Ahmose II. Phanes, who fled to Persia following a disagreement with Ahmose II, provided Cambyses with intelligence relating to Egypt's defences, as well as recommendations on how to cross the Sinai desert with his army.[10] Phanes advised Cambyses to negotiate an agreement with the 'Arabs'[11], the local desert inhabitants, which was deemed crucial to the logistics of sending an army across the Sinai desert.[12] Cambyses took the advice and signed a formal treaty with the king of the 'Arabs' to enlist his help.[13] In 525 BC, with these desert-dwellers as his guides, and camels laden with waterskins, Cambyses successfully crossed the northern Sinai and entered Egypt via the Pelusiac branch of the river Nile.[14]

Psamtek had taken up positions near the coast at Pellusium with his Egyptian and mercenary army and waited for the Persian attack. Despite a vigorous resistance, Psamtek was forced to give ground and retreat to Memphis. Cambyses sent a Mytilenian ship to the city to demand the Egyptian surrender, but the Persian herald and crew were massacred by the defending Egyptians. Cambyses then marched with his army to Memphis and, following a heavy siege, the city fell to the Persians. Psamtek and his family were captured and humiliated, and

7.1 Image on a Persian seal, sixth century BC, thought to depict Cambyses II capturing Psamtek III following his conquest of Egypt, as recreated by the French painter Adrien Guignet.

a large number of the citizens of the city, including Psamtek's son, executed in retaliation for the murder of the crew of the Mytilenian ship (Figure 7.1). With the capitulation of the Egyptian forces the nearby states of Libya, Cyrenaica and Barca soon surrendered, and pre-emptively sent tribute to Cambyses as a token of their good will.[15]

Persian occupation of Egypt

Cambyses then advanced on Sais, where he disinterred the mummy of Ahmose II and abused the corpse. This action was purportedly an act of revenge against what Cambyses believed to be the earlier act of betrayal, when Ahmose II had attempted to trick him by not sending his own daughter to marry Cambyses.[16] The act of revenge is further supported by erasure of the cartouches of Ahmose II on various monuments, as well as possible targeted attacks on certain of his temples.[17] This *damnatio memoriae* appears to have been of short duration as Udjahorresnet mentions Ahmose II on his statue which was inscribed under the later Persian ruler, Darius I. Also, Udjahorresnet's son, Henat, served in Ahmose II's posthumous royal cult.[18]

Further destruction to Sais may have been halted by Udjahorresnet, who in his much-discussed statue in the Vatican recounts how he personally interceded

7.2 Black basalt statue of Udjahorresnet holding a naos bearing the image of Osiris. Udjahorresnet's life spanned the end of the 26th Dynasty and the beginning of the 27th Dynasty. Provenance unknown, thought to have come from Sais. H 58 cm; W 12.5 cm; D 27.5 cm (Museo Gregoriano Egizio, Rome).

with Cambyses during his visit to Sais (Figure 7.2). Under the left arm of his statue in eight lines is this inscription:[19]

> I made a petition to the majesty of the King of Upper and Lower Egypt, Cambyses, about all the foreigners who dwelled in the temple of Neith, in order to have them expelled from it, so as to let the temple of Neith be in all its splendour, as it had been before. His majesty commanded to expel all the foreigners [who] dwelled in the temple of Neith, to demolish all their houses and all their unclean things that were in the temple.

When they had carried [all their] personal [belongings] outside the wall of the temple, his majesty commanded to cleanse the temple of Neith and to return all its personnel to it, the [...] and the hour-priests of the temple. His majesty commanded to give divine offerings to Neith-the-Great, the mother of the god, and to the great gods of Sais, as it had been before. His majesty commanded [to perform] all their festivals and all their processions, as had been done before. His majesty did this because I had let his majesty know the greatness of Sais, that it is the city of all the gods, who dwell there on their seats forever.

Udjahorresnet is claiming, therefore, that he was able to obtain the recon-secration of the temple of Neith at Sais and also to help the people of Sais recover from the effects of the Persian invasion. The pattern of individuals presenting themselves as great restorers, following periods of destruction, is not uncommon in Pharaonic history. Earlier, Montuemhat had recorded his restoration of temples in the Mut, Montu and Amun precincts at Thebes, following the Assyrian sacking of the city in 663 BC.[20] During the later Second Persian Period, Petosiris, in his biographical texts inscribed in his tomb chapel at Tuna el-Gebel, recorded his efforts at restoring the temple at Ashmunein:[21] 'When I became controller for Thoth lord of Khmunu, I put the temple of Thoth in its former condition, I caused every rite to be as before, every priest (to serve) in his proper time'. Later, Petosiris described the renovation of a temple of Hekat, apparently damaged through Nile floods.

In the above examples, these powerful individuals are asserting that the monuments they helped to restore represented an improvement upon their previous ruined state, a claim which would enhance the individuals' profile and demonstrate active piety. It is, however, quite possible that religious motivation and true piety may have been the reason for these actions.[22]

After leaving Sais, Cambyses travelled south and invaded Nubia, probably as part of his strategic plan, but economic gain may also have been an inducement as the kingdom of Kush had traditionally been coveted for its gold and trade goods. According to Herodotus (III, 25) the overall mission ended in failure, although Cambyses did capture part of Lower Nubia and established a garrison at Elephantine. Achaemenid monuments, such as the base of the statue of Darius at Susa, list Kush as one of the subject states of the Persian Empire (Figure 7.3).[23] Cambyses also dispatched an army against the oases in the western desert with the probable aim of establishing garrisons or military colonies along the caravan routes, thus establishing control over strategic western trade routes. His forces set off probably by the desert roads linking Thebes to Kharga, but the army was lost in an unexpected sandstorm.[24]

The disappearance of this army is one of the unexplained mysteries of the ancient world, and over the years a number of different theories have been put

7.3 Statue of Darius I. On the two long sides of the base are inscribed twenty-four subject peoples of the Persian empire represented as prisoners of war with their ethnonyms written in studded cartouches representing city walls. Originally sculpted in Egypt and later transferred to the palace in Susa, capital of the Achaemenid Empire. Grey granite. H 2.46 m; Base: 105 cm (L) × 64 (W) cm × 51 (H) cm (National Museum of Iran, Tehran).

forward as to what happened to this expedition. Many Egyptologists regard this story as apocryphal, particularly as there have been a number of unsuccessful searches for the remains of this army. A suggestion by Olaf Kaper[25] proposes that the army was ambushed by an Egyptian rebel leader, Petubastis IV, who went on to reconquer a large part of Egypt and was later crowned king in

Memphis. He then assumed a titulary modelled upon those of the 26th Dynasty kings, in particular Ahmose II. That the fate of the army of Cambyses remained unclear for many years is suggested to have been due to the Persian King Darius I, Cambyses' successor. Darius ended the Egyptian revolt by Petubastis with much bloodshed fairly early in his reign, and for propaganda purposes Darius attributed the shameful rout of his predecessor to natural elements rather than his being defeated in battle by Petubastis.

Herodotus (III, 25–26) describes both the Nubian and oasis campaigns as disastrous, but an analysis of the archaeological remains at Dorginarti at the Second Cataract and evidence from the el-Kharga oasis dated to the reign of Darius I suggest that the Persians were successful in imposing their control in both areas.[26] Other Classical authors such as Strabo and Diodorus Siculus similarly associate Cambyses with a successful campaign into Nubia:[27] 'Moreover, when Cambyses conquered Egypt, he advanced with the Egyptians as far as Meroe; in fact, it is said, the name was given by him to both the island and the city, because his sister, Meroe (his wife according to some), died there'. 'There are also (in Egypt) many kinds of trees, some of which are called persea, introduced from Ethiopia by the Persians when Cambyses conquered these regions, has an unusually sweet fruit'.[28]

The archaeological evidence and these Classical accounts all contrast with the pessimistic accounts of Herodotus.[29] In addition, Cambyses is reputed to have committed atrocities and destruction in several cities and temples in Egypt, including Heliopolis, Sais, Thebes and possibly Elephantine. Herodotus (III, 29) further claims that Cambyses killed the sacred Apis bull at Memphis although this is a question that has been much debated, and it is far from certain if it is true.[30] These accusations of impiety, as well as transgressions against Egyptian culture, directed at Cambyses by Herodotus, together with the failed missions to Nubia and the oases, undoubtedly include an element of anti-Persian propaganda. Herodotus considered Cambyses unstable and mad, and the native Egyptian informants, primarily the priests whom Herodotus obtained his testimony from, would not necessarily have related the historical facts but instead distorted the events and resorted to exaggeration. They would have resented the curbing of the power of the temples introduced by Cambyses, as well as there being a foreign ruler on the throne of Egypt, and so it could well be that much of this desecration did not occur.[31] Herodotus wrote his histories about a century after Cambyses ruled Egypt, which again would have allowed time for mistruths and counter-narratives to be spread, exaggerating some facts and further besmirching his character. This negative image recorded by Herodotus, in which he openly criticises Cambyses, especially his supposed sacrilegious acts perpetrated against the shrines of Egypt, was substantially accepted in the ancient world and was to influence later writers.[32]

End of the Saite Dynasty

According to Herodotus (III, 14–15) Psamtek III's son was executed along with many other Egyptians, but Psamtek III himself was initially spared. Later when he was apprehended for fomenting rebellion among the native Egyptians, he was sentenced to death and reputedly chose to commit suicide by drinking bull's blood.[33] However, Psamtek cannot have killed himself in this fashion, as bull's blood is not poisonous, and although not pleasant it is relatively harmless to drink. Nevertheless, in the ancient world there was a belief that it was instantly poisonous, due to the observable fact that that the blood of a bull clots rapidly, becoming a congealed mass.[34] It was thus believed to produce a lethal choking, effect in the throat if swallowed.[35] Of relevance is the fact that the ancient Egyptians named materials according to different criteria from those that are in use today. An important factor was appearance; thus for example chickpea was called (ḥr-bik) 'falcon-face', because the seeds resemble the face of a falcon complete with its beak.[36] It would seem likely, therefore, that 'bull's blood' referred to some other unknown noxious substance.

With the Persian conquest of Egypt complete, and the death of Psamtek III after a reign of barely six months, the 26th Dynasty came to an end. Cambyses became Pharaoh of Egypt and Udjahorresnet claims to have undertaken the composition of his royal titulary. Egypt was now a province of the vast Persian Empire, with the Persian king head of government, and the day to day running of the country under the control of the Persian satrap Aryandes. Egypt was no longer a sovereign state and the Saite Period was over.

Notes

1 Kuhrt 2007: 104.
2 Kuhrt 2007: 135.
3 Briant 2002: 51.
4 Herodotus (III, 1–3); Athenaeus XIII, 560 d–f; Polyaenus VIII,
5 Briant 2002: 52–53.
6 Wallinga 1993: 118–29.
7 Among the titles listed on the walls of the tomb of Hekaemsaf at Saqqara are 'Prince' (rpʿ), 'Seal-bearer of the King of Lower Egypt' (sḏꜣwty bity), 'Sole-companion' (smr-wʿty) and 'Overseer of the Double Treasury of the Residence' (imy-r prwy-nbw nw ẖnw) However, 401 shabtis were found in his tomb and here the principal title was 'Overseer of Royal Ships'. See Janes 2002: 206–8 and extensive bibliography.
8 Tjanehebu's tomb lies in close proximity to that of Hekaemsaf. Again, 401 shabtis were found in his tomb and his principal title was 'Overseer of the Royal Ships' (imy-r ḥʿ.w nsw); see Janes 2002: 210–12 and extensive bibliography.
9 For chapel B at Karnak see Traunecker 2010; for a list of artefacts with bibliography see Jansen-Winkeln 2014b: vol. 1, 583–85.
10 Herodotus III, 4.

11   The term 'Arabs' was used to refer to the nomadic tribes who inhabited the desert regions between Egypt and the Euphrates. Other terms used are 'nomads' and 'desert-dwellers'.

12   Kuhrt 2007: 105.

13   Herodotus III, 7; Kahn and Tammuz 2008: 43 n. 33.

14   However, see Quack (2011), who suggests that the invasion was one year earlier in 526 BC.

15   Herodotus III, 10–13.

16   Herodotus III, 16. For a discussion on symbolic humiliation see Stolper 1997.

17   See Klotz 2015. For attacks on monuments see Bolshakov 2010 and Klotz 2010: 131–32. For attacks on temples see Coulon and Defenez 2004: 141–42 and Porten 1996: 142, 146.

18   Cruz-Uribe 2003: 39; Klotz 2015: 3.

19   Lichtheim 1980: 38, ll 17–23.

20   Leclant 1961.

21   Lichtheim 1980: 46.

22   Spencer 2010.

23   Greywacke statue, originally erected in Egypt at Heliopolis but later transferred to the gate of the king's palace at Susa. On two sides of the base are listed twenty-four subject nations of which Kush is one. See Roaf 1974: 141–43, n. 22; Morkot 1991: 324.

24   Herodotus III, 26.

25   Kaper 2015.

26   For the Kharga oasis evidence see Cruz-Uribe 1988, 2001. For Nubia see Heidorn 1991 and Morkot 1991: 326–27.

27   Strabo XVII, 1.5.

28   Diodorus Siculus I, 34.7.

29   Kuhrt 2007: 116 n. 1.

30   See Posener 1936: 30–35; Kienitz 1953: 59; Depuydt 1995; Asheri, Lloyd and Corcella 2007: 427–29; Kahn 2007b: 105–6.

31   Dillery 2005.

32   For historical sources see those cited in Jansen-Winkeln 2002. Also Kahn 2007b: 106; Klotz 2015.

33   Pétigny 2010.

34   Cambyses is suggested to have murdered his brother by forcing him to drink bull's blood (Kuhrt 2007: 114 n. 4 and 163–64). Also, Themistocles is claimed to have committed suicide by drinking bull's blood (Marr 1995). For the various modern attempts to explain the origin of the ancient belief see Touwaide 1979.

35   Marr 1995: 159.

36   Forshaw 2016: 134.

The Saite era within the history of Pharaonic civilisation

The traditional framework of dividing the history of ancient Egypt into 'kingdoms' and 'periods' is an approach developed by Egyptologists during the nineteenth century, although based to some extent on divisions in ancient sources such as the Turin Canon and Manetho's *Aegyptiaca*. The demarcations are founded on eras of political unity and stability contrasted with times of disunity, and on occasions foreign rule. Although not an arrangement the ancient Egyptians would have fully recognised, it does nevertheless today permit an overview of Pharaonic civilisation.

Was the 26th Dynasty a significant part of ancient Egyptian history or was it merely a last gasp of a once great culture, as some earlier historians have suggested? Some accounts of ancient Egypt tend to underemphasise the Saite and Late Period in general, rather highlighting the preceding more popular, comprehensible Old, Middle and New Kingdom eras. Does the Saite Period warrant such an appraisal?

This book has aimed to reveal the dynamic nature of the period, the astuteness of the Saite rulers and their considerable achievements in the political, economic, administrative and cultural spheres. The Saite Dynasty was a time of no mean achievement, with Egypt preserving its independence as a sovereign state against powerful foreign adversaries. Significantly, the Saite Period was the last noteworthy and relatively enduring period of native Egyptian rule, and, other than the short-lived 30th Dynasty, was the last major resurgence of indigenous rulers on the throne of Egypt for some two and a half millennia. It was not until AD 1952 following the Egyptian Revolution that native-born Egyptians once again fully controlled the country.

From its early 'Libyan' roots the Kingdom of the West expanded the territory under its control, and then Psamtek I, the first ruler of the 26th Dynasty, went on to reunify Egypt, a process which he seemingly achieved largely through diplomatic means. Indeed, an important aspect of the Saite Period in general was to favour diplomacy over the use of military force. Psamtek re-established central government, which in time achieved stability for the country, after the previous periods of political fragmentation and foreign rule. The administration that Psamtek put in place relied on the established elite, for both central and local control, which would have been particularly important in more distant regions such as the Thebaid. Hereditary claims to office were still important as they had been in previous periods.

Later in the Dynasty there were marked changes in organisational structures to better control state finances and to reform the taxation system. With the expansion of trade, into the western Mediterranean and beyond, customs duties were increasingly being levied, necessitating the expansion of existing administrative structures. Such changes were aided by the introduction of Demotic, a simplified and standardised cursive script which became widespread within a generation. Demotic marked the imposition of a new uniform administration across Egypt and by the reign of Ahmose II it had become Egypt's accepted script for executive, legal and economic documents.

There was a widespread temple-building programme, particularly during the reign of Ahmose II, which would have been aided by the political and economic recovery of Egypt. The Saite kings also sought closer union with the temples, and considerable endowments of land were granted to them for this end, with officials related to the ruling dynasty being appointed to positions within the temple hierarchy. Major changes occurred in ownership and tenancy of land, with Crown and temple land-holdings being less regulated than in previous periods. Land was progressively being sold and private ownership of land-holdings increased which now allowed many individuals, including such groups as foreign mercenaries, to farm their own land. Agriculture would have been aided by the high Nile inundations recorded at that time, which not only facilitated irrigation but would have enabled further land to be brought under cultivation.

Owing to the shortage of tied labour, temples were now leasing land on a large scale which permitted entrepreneurial activities to develop. Private businesses began to develop around the temples including minor workshops that manufactured, and sold to visitors, items such as amulets and figures of deities. Mortuary enterprises expanded in which choachytes provided funerary services that included the regular performance of rites and the supply of provisions for the deceased. Animal cults which underwent a considerable degree of development and proliferation during the Saite era flourished. They now required additional staff and mummification facilities to meet the increased demand, suggesting that the cults were now available to greater numbers of people. The changes in landownership associated with the increase in commercial activity and agricultural output helped to boost the economy and enlarge the tax base, and brought increasing prosperity to Saite Egypt.

In trade, Egypt traditionally looked to the states of the eastern Mediterranean, but during the Saite Period trade achieved a new impetus when Psamtek I began to promote commerce within the wider Mediterranean region and actively encouraged Greek and Phoenician merchants to come into the country. The main trading route into Egypt was now via the Canopic branch of the Nile, with the cities of Naukratis and Thonis-Heracleion being important commercial centres. By concentrating trade at emporia such as Naukratis, trade could be regulated, customs dues collected and goods more readily distributed to the Egyptian hinterland. Imports to Egypt comprised commodities such as metals, wood, wine and oil, while exports included grain, natron and manufactured goods, such as amulets, scarabs and perfume flasks (Figure 8.1). Some of these goods were produced in local workshops at Naukratis, and their finds in territories as far afield as the Levant, Cyprus, Italy, Spain and countries to the west of Egypt chart the wide range of trading networks that linked Egypt with the Mediterranean world.

The Phoenicians were the first Mediterranean trading superpower, and their early dominance in commerce had facilitated Egyptian foreign trade since at least the New Kingdom. There is evidence of Phoenicians settling in Egypt at cities such as Memphis and Tell Dafana, and Phoenician mercenaries are known to have participated in the Nubian campaign of Psamtek II, as attested by graffiti at Abu Simbel. But it is perhaps with the Greek city states that Egypt formed the strongest international relationship, and indeed Egypt can be viewed as being a major participant in the Greek world at that time. By the mid-seventh century BC, with Greek trading contacts established within the wider Mediterranean area and the founding of Greek colonies, there was a growing interconnectivity between the Greek world and the broader economic, political and cultural systems of the eastern Mediterranean and particularly with Egypt.

Contacts between Egypt and the Greek states developed through various interrelated media of exchange and communication such as commerce, mercenaries, letters and gift exchange. On the cultural level, there was a favourable picture of Egypt in early Greek literature, and Egypt appears to have been elevated above other foreign lands as a source of Greek practice and ideals. Herodotus, Solon, Plato, Pythagoras are all reputed, with varying plausibility, to have visited Egypt and been influenced by the culture and perceived 'wisdom' of the country. Greek architecture, sculpture and bronze hollow-cast statuary were inspired by Egyptian contacts.

Long-distance trade and exchange, still a royal monopoly, also continued with Nubia as it had throughout much of Pharaonic history, although specific

8.1 Aryballos (oil flask) in the form of a hedgehog. Hedgehogs are among the most common forms of faience oil flasks. Production of these vases has traditionally been identified as Naukratis. H. as restored 5.7 cm (Metropolitan Museum of Art, New York).

evidence for the Saite Period is not strong. Traditional luxury items such as gold, ebony and ivory would have continued to be in demand and the Nubians were the traditional agents for procurement of such items.

Mercenary soldiers were recruited from Caria and Ionia from early in the reign of Psamtek I and camps were established in Egypt for them to inhabit. The Carians and Ionians as well as mercenary groups from many other countries are attested throughout the 26th Dynasty and formed an essential element of the growing Saite military power. Changes to the navy and modifications in naval architecture helped Egypt secure control of its sea coast and achieve an effective Mediterranean naval presence.

On the international front, for the first time in centuries Egypt was able to occupy territory in Syria–Palestine. For a brief period, Egypt was once again a major power, although much of the Saite Period was a struggle against its more powerful neighbours to the east, firstly the Assyrian, then the Babylonian and finally the Persian Empires. Initially, the kings of the 26th Dynasty may have had expansionist designs, perhaps attempting to emulate the glories of the New Kingdom and establish a foothold in Palestine. However, following King Nekau II's military defeat at Carchemish in 605 BC, the policy towards the formidable Asiatic powers to the east became essentially defensive in character, and more one of containment.

Throughout the 26th Dynasty, the Saites were forced to manage a complex foreign relations programme with peoples of the Levant and other nations in the Near East. Gift-giving remained part of the diplomatic process, while inter-state marriage continued to cement diplomatic relations. Later during the reign of Ahmose II, Egypt occupied Cyprus and allied itself with states in the Mediterranean world to counteract the growing Persian threat. Until the Persian Empire invaded, a territory with vastly superior power and resources, the Saite Dynasty was successful in safeguarding the integrity of Egypt as a nation-state for nearly 140 years.

Although the introduction of foreign peoples and new ideas from abroad had been common throughout Pharaonic history, the Saite Period witnessed a marked increase in immigration. Foreign enclaves were established, such as the trading city of Naukratis which played a crucial role in channelling the flow of trade, people and ideas between Egypt and the Greek world. Memphis, an important political and administrative centre during the Saite Period, became a thriving cosmopolitan city and Elephantine a centre for Aramean troops with their own temple.

As in previous periods foreigners could become Egyptian merely by living within the borders of Egypt and adopting Egyptian culture, with the notion of being an Egyptian not being defined along racial lines. Multilingualism, intercultural marriages and evidence of business and legal transactions are attested from many sources, such as the graffiti at Abu Simbel, bilingual inscriptions on bronze statuettes in Egyptian sanctuaries and contracts involving the sale of land to foreigners.[1] Carian immigrants and their descendants embraced Egyptian names and Egyptian religion.[2] Foreign peoples were absorbed into Egyptian culture as they had been through the long history of Pharaonic civilisation. The Egyptian afterlife was open to all, and anyone who could afford could be mummified and be depicted with the Egyptian gods of the afterlife and yet still retain their own visual identity and name.

Egyptian culture and religion were to inspire other nations, as attested by the numerous bronze statuettes found in the sanctuary of Hera on Samos and in the development of Greek monumental architecture. Egyptian motifs were picked up in Phoenician art, such as jewellery, ivory carving, glyptic and repoussé work on metal.[3] Equally many areas of life became affected by foreign influence which the Egyptians seemed to accept from a world that was increasingly opening up to them. Amphorae from Chios, Samos, Lesbos, Miletus and Cyprus have been found in Elephantine, Memphis and Delta cities such as Sais, Mendes and Maskhuta, suggesting widespread access to products from the Mediterranean world. This may also relate to the consumption of new types of foodstuff and may have resulted in changes in food preparation techniques. Greek pottery was used by resident Greeks at their feasts and rituals and for everyday purposes, suggesting the preservation and enhancement of certain elements of their Greek identity in a foreign country. Aramaic was increasingly being used by the end of the 26th Dynasty, reflecting the increasingly multicultural nature of society.

Neither was there any diminution in cultural life, as Egyptian culture drew on the traditions of previous eras now combining them with considerable invention and originality in both materials and iconography. The archaising trends first observed at the end of the Third Intermediate Period continued throughout the 26th Dynasty. There was now an increased awareness and deployment of Egypt's past, ancient monuments were more actively investigated and scenes copied. Saite Period artisans did not aim at exact imitation of old styles, but more of a revival and reinterpretation. Not only in sculpture and architecture is there a conscious return to past styles and older models but also in literature, writing and the use of titles and names. The standard of artistic production was high and is most visibly demonstrated by the extraordinary quality achieved in some of the hard-stone statues, sarcophagi and reliefs characteristic of this period (see the image of Sasobek on the cover). Technological improvements in faience and bronze permitted the fabrication of high-quality works and these were an important medium of artistic production during this period. Saite Egypt was a resonant society intermingled with the patterns of past iconographies.

Religious ideology witnessed a number of theological developments. The ancient Egyptians now believed their progress to the afterlife depended less on grave-goods or mortuary cults but upon the personal favour of the deity to whom they were devoted. They therefore sought to be buried and to have a memorial as close as possible to the god, as attested by the many burials within hallowed ancient landscapes such as at Giza, Saqqara, Heliopolis, Thebes and Abydos.[4] Personal piety, a notable feature of the Saite Period, was characterised by direct appeals from individuals to gods in times of sickness, uncertainty, trouble and anguish, and animal cults seem to have been suited to such a direct approach on the part of the worshipper.

During the 26th dynasty, a new version of the Book of the Dead came into widespread use, a revision today known as the 'Saite recension'.[5] Spells were consistently ordered and numbered and there was a more uniform style in the drawing of the vignettes which was based more closely on the texts. The Saite recension not only reworked the text but supplemented it with compositions of Theban origin (spells 162–65). It seems that Thebes was the source of this comprehensive revision and this work probably commenced in the preceding 25th Dynasty and may have been influenced by earlier 18th-Dynasty examples.[6] The edition established a consecutive numbering of the spells, which became the standardised order in manuscripts of the Late and Ptolemaic Periods.

To return to the question, was the Saite Dynasty *a last gasp of a once great culture?* In certain ways perhaps, it could be considered so since the traditional Pharaonic culture that had survived for millennia was now rapidly changing. But the period could also be perceived as the beginning of Egypt's realignment in the Mediterranean world, heralding the Hellenistic age; a time of transformation from the Bronze Age to the Classical era. Indeed, the powerful flow of continuity associated with the dynamism of the age provided the basis for the considerable achievement of the Ptolemaic age that was to follow later. However, the period is very different from the earlier dynasties and stands apart from that neat chronological system; this may explain why those with an interest in the traditional 'kingdoms' of ancient Egyptian history find it difficult to place the Saite era within the conventional study of ancient Egypt.

The undoubted successes of the Saite era need to be emphasised. Importantly, Psamtek I successfully re-established the ideology of the Two Lands, and the subsequent Saite Period was marked by rulers who were overall both militarily and politically adept. It was a time of immense change and development on the political, social, economic, religious and cultural fronts. Egyptian society was altering and it was a time of a revival of national values; in the succeeding periods of Persian occupation, the Saite Period may well have been looked back to as a symbol of the glory that was once Egypt. Indeed, the later kings of the 30th Dynasty are known to have looked back with admiration beyond the Persian interludes to the Saite era, which to them may have appeared a golden age.[7]

Notes

1 Kaplan 2010.
2 Lloyd 1983: 317.
3 Bietak 2007: 448.
4 Davies and Smith 1997: 122.
5 Quack 2009; Munro 2010a: 58.
6 Munro 2010b.
7 Bothmer et al. 2004: 152.

References

Adams, W. Y. (1977), *Nubia: Corridor to Africa* (London: Allen Lane).

Addah, S. F. (2011), *The Scourge of God: The Umman-manda and Its Significance in the First Millennium BC* (State Archives of Assyria Studies, v. 20; Publications of the Foundation for Finnish Assyriological Research, No. 3. Helsinki: Neo-Assyrian Text Corpus Project).

Agut-Labordère, D. (2013), 'The Saite Period: The emergence of a Mediterranean power', in J. C. M. García (ed.), *Ancient Egyptian Administration* (Leiden: Brill), 965–1027.

— (2014), 'Créer la route: le canal des pharaons entre la mer Rouge et la Méditerranée de Néchao II à Darius Ier', *Égypte, Afrique & Orient*, 75, 61–66.

Allam, S. (1991), 'Egyptian law courts in Pharaonic and Hellenistic times', *JEA*, 77, 109–27.

Anthes, R. (1937), 'Der Berliner Hocker des Petamenophis', *ZÄS*, 73, 25–35.

— (1953), 'Ägypten', in F. Kern (ed.), *Historia Mundi: ein Handbuch der Weltgeschichte in zehn Bänden, Vol. 2 Grundlagen und Entfaltung der Ältesten Hochkulturen* (Bern: Franke Verlag), 130–223.

Arnold, D. (1999), *Temples of the Last Pharaohs* (New York, Oxford: Oxford University Press).

Asheri, D., Lloyd, A. B., and Corcella, A. (2007), *A Commentary on Herodotus I–IV* ed. O. Murray and A. Moreno (Oxford: Oxford University Press).

Ashmawy, A., and Raue, D. (2017a), 'Ägyptisch-deutsche Ausgrabungen in Heliopolis im Frühjahr', *Sokar*, 34, 64–65.

— (2017b), 'Héliopolis en 2017: les fouilles égypto-allemandes dans le temple du soleil à Matariya/Le Caire', *BSFÉ*, 197, 29–45.

Aston, D. A. (1996), *Egyptian Pottery of the Late New Kingdom and Third Intermediate Period (Twelfth – Seventh Centuries BC): Tentative Footsteps in a Forbidding Terrain* (Heidelberg: Heidelberger Orientverlag).

— (1999), *Elephantine XIX, Pottery from the Late New Kingdom to the Early Ptolemaic Period* (Mainz am Rhein: Philipp von Zabern).

— (2003), 'The Theban West Bank from the Twenty-Fifth Dynasty to the Ptolemaic Period', in N. Strudwick and J. H. Taylor (ed.), *The Theban Necropolis: Past, Present and Future* (London: British Museum Press), 138–66.

— (2009), 'Takeloth II, a king of the Herakleopolitan/Theban Twenty-Third Dynasty revisited: The chronology of Dynasties 22 and 23', in G. P. E. Broekman, R. J. Demarée and O. E. Kaper (ed.), *The Libyan Period in Egypt. Historical and Cultural Studies into the 21st–24th Dynasties: Proceedings of a Conference at Leiden University 25–27 October 2007* (Leuven: Peeters), 1–28.

— (2009), *Burial Assemblages of Dynasty 21–25: Chronology – Typology – Developments* (Denkschriften der Gesamtakademie / Österreichische Akademie der Wissenschaften, Band 54. Contributions to the chronology of the Eastern Mediterranean, vol. 21, Vienna: Verlag der Österreichischen Akademie der Wissenschaften).

Atherton-Woolham, S., and McKnight, L. (2015), 'Animals as votive offerings in ancient Egypt', in L. McKnight and S. Atherton-Woolham (ed.), *Gifts for the Gods: Ancient Egyptian Animal Mummies and the British* (Liverpool: Liverpool University Press), 23–24.

Aubert, J.-F., and Aubert, L. (1974), *Statuettes égyptiennes: chaouabtis, ouchebtis* (Paris: Librairie d'Amérique et d'Orient).

Aubin, H. T. (2002), *The Rescue of Jerusalem: The Alliance between Hebrews and Africans in 701 BC* (New York: Soho Press).

Austin, M. (1970), *Greece and Egypt in the Archaic Age* (Cambridge: Cambridge Philosophical Society).

Avioz, M. (2007), 'Josiah's death in the Book of Kings: A new solution to an old theological conundrum', *Ephemerides Theologicae Lovanienses*, 83 (4), 359–66.

Ayad, M. F. (2001), 'Some thoughts on the disappearance of the God's Wife of Amun', *JSSEA*, 28, 1–14.

— (2009), *God's Wife, God's Servant. The God's Wife of Amun (c. 740–525 BC)* (London: Routledge).

Baer, K. (1973), 'The Libyan and Nubian kings of Egypt: Notes on the chronology of Dynasties XXII to XXVI', *JNES*, 32, 4–25.

Baines, J., and Riggs, C. (2001), ' "Archaism and Kingship": A late royal statue and its early dynastic model', *JEA*, 87, 103–18.

Bakry, H. S. K. (1967), 'Psamettichus II and the newly-found stela at Shellal', *Oriens Antiquus*, 6, 225–44.

Bányai, M. (2013), 'Ein Vorschlag zur Chronologie der 25. Dynastie in Ägypten', *JEgH*, 6, 46–129.

Baragwanath, W., and de Bakker, M. (2010), *Herodotus: Oxford Bibliographies Online Research Guide* (Oxford University Press, USA).

Barbotin, C. (2000), 'Un bas-relief au nom de Psammétique II (595–589 av. J.-C), une récente acquisition du Louvre', *La Revue du Louvre et des Musées de France*, 5, 33–8.

Bareš, L. (1999), *Abusir IV, The Shaft Tomb of Udjahorresnet at Abusir* (Prague: The Karolinum Press).

— (2000), 'The destruction of the monuments at the necropolis of Abusir', in M. Barta and J. Krejci (ed.), *Abusir and Saqqara in the Year 2000* (Prague: Academy of Sciences of the Czech Republic, Oriental Institute).

Barguet, P., Goneim, Z., and Leclant, J. (1951), 'Les tables d'offrandes de la grande cour de la tombe de Montouemhăt', *ASAE*, 51, 491–507.

Bassir, H. (2013), 'The self-presentation of Payeftjauemawyneith on naphorous statue BM EA 83', in E. Frood and A. McDonald (ed.), *Decorum and Experience. Essays in Ancient Culture for John Baines* (Oxford: Griffith Institute), 6–13.

— (2016), 'Neshor at Elephantine in Late Saite Egypt', *JEgH* 9, 66–95.

Basta, M. (1968), 'Excavations in the desert road at Dashur', *ASAE*, 60, 57–63, pls I–X.

Bennet, C. (1999), 'Karimala, daughter of Osochor?' *GM*, 173, 7–8.

Benson, M., and Gourlay, J. A. (1899), *The Temple of Mut in Asher* (London: Murray).

Bernard, A., and Masson, O. (1957), 'Les inscriptions grecques d'Abou-Simbel', *Revue des Études Grecques*, 70, 1–46.

Beylage, P. (2002), *Aufbau der königlichen Stelentexte vom Beginn der 18. Dynastie bis zur Amarnazeit* (Agypten und Altes Testament 54; Wiesbaden: Harrassowitz).

Bickel, S., and Tallet, P. (1997), 'La nécropole saite d'Héliopolis. Étude préliminaire', *BIFAO*, 97, 67–90.

Bierbrier, M. L. (1975), *The Late New Kingdom in Egypt (c. 1300–664 B.C.)* (Warminster: Aris & Phillips Ltd).

— (1979), 'More light on the family of Montemhat', in J. Ruffle, G. A. Gabella and K. A. Kitchen (ed.), *Glimpses of Ancient Egypt: Studies in Honour of H. W. Fairman* (Warminster: Aris & Phillips Ltd), 116–18.

Bietak, M. (ed.) (2001), *Archaische griechische Tempel und Altägypten* (Vienna: Verlag der Österreichischen Akademie der Wissenschaften).

— (2007), 'Egypt and the Levant', in T. Wilkinson (ed.), *The Egyptian World* (Abingdon: Routledge), 417–48.

Binder, M. (2011), 'The 10th–9th century BC: New evidence from Cemetery C of Amara West', *Sudan and Nubia*, 15, 39–53.

Björkman, G. (1971), *Kings at Karnak. A Study of the Treatment of the Monuments of the Royal Predecessors in the Early New Kingdom* (Boreas, Uppsala Studies in Ancient Mediterranean and Near Eastern Civilizations 2; Uppsala: Tryck).

Bleiberg, E. (2013), 'Animal mummies: The souls of the gods', in E. Bleiberg, Y. Barbash and L. Bruno (ed.), *Soulful Creatures: Animal Mummies in Ancient Egypt* (Brooklyn, NY: Brooklyn Museum in association with D Giles Ltd), 64–105.

Blöbaum, A. (2005), *Denn ich bin ein König, der die Maat liebt: Herrscherlegitimation im spätzeitlichen Ägypten: Eine vergleichende Untersuchung der Phraseologie in den offiziellen Königsinschriften vom Beginn der 25. Dynastie bis zum Ende der makedonischen Herrschaft* (Aegyptiaca Monasteriensia 4; Münster: Shaker).

Blouin, K. (2014), *Triangular Landscapes* (Oxford: Oxford University Press).

Boardman, J. (1999), *The Greeks Overseas* (London: Thames and Hudson).

Boast, J. (2007), 'Egypt's foreign policy during the Saite Period', *School of Historical Studies* (Unpublished dissertation, Birmingham: University of Birmingham).

Bolshakov, A. O. (2010), 'Persians and Egyptians: Cooperation in vandalism', in S. H. D'Auria (ed.), *Offerings to the Discerning Eye: An Egyptological Medley in Honor of Jack A. Josephson* (Leiden: Brill), 45–54.

von Bomhard, A.-S. (2012), *The Decree of Sais, The Stelae of Thonis-Heracleion and Naukratis* (Monograph 7; Oxford: Oxford Centre for Maritime Archaeology).

Bonnet, C., and Valbelle, D. (2006), *The Nubian Pharaohs: Black Kings on the Nile* (Cairo: American University in Cairo Press).

Borger, R. (1956), *Die Inschriften Asarhaddons, Königs von Assyrien* (Archiv für Orientforschung, Beiheft 9, Graz: E. Weidner).

— (1996), *Beitrage zum Inschriftenwerk Assurbanipals: Die Prismenklassen A, B, C = K, D, E, F, G, H, J und T sowie andere Inschriften* (Wiesbaden: Otto Harrassowitz).

Bothmer, B. V. (1960), *Egyptian Sculpture of the Late Period 700 B.C. to A.D. 100* (Brooklyn, NY: Brooklyn Museum).

Bothmer, B. V., Cody, M. E., Stanwick, P. E., and Hill, M. (2004), *Egyptian Art: Selected Writings of Bernard V. Bothmer* (Oxford: Oxford University Press).

Brand, P. (2010), 'Usurpation of monuments', in W. Wendrich (ed.), *UCLA Encyclopedia of Egyptology*, Los Angeles, <http://digital2.library.ucla.edu/viewItem.do?ark=21198/zz0025h6fh>, accessed 10 August 2017.

Breasted, J. H. (1906 (this edition 2001)), *Ancient Records of Egypt*, 5 vols (Champaign, IL: University of Illinois Press).

Bresciani, E. (1964), *Der Kamf um den Panzer des Inaros (Papyrus Krall)* (Mitteilungen aus der Papyrussammlung der Oesterreichischen Nationalbibliothek Erzherzog Rainer N.S. 8, Vienna: George Prachner).

— (1967), 'Una statua della XXVI dinastia con il cosidetto'abito persiamo', *Studi Classici e Orientali*, 16, 273–84, pls I–V.

Bresciani, E., Betrò, M. C., Giammarusti, A., and La Torre, C. (1988), *Tomba di Bakenrenef (L. 24). Attività del cantiere scuola 1985–1987* (Pisa: Giardini).

Bresciani, E., Pernigotti, S., and Giangeri Silvis, M. P. (1977), *La tomba di Ciennehebu capo della flotta del re* (Biblioteca degli studi classici e orientali, 7; Serie egittologica, 1: Tombe d'età saitica a Saqqara, Pisa: Giardini).

Bresson, A. (2005), 'Naucratis: de l'emporion à la cité', *Topoi*, 12–13, 133–55.

Briant, P. (2002), *From Cyrus to Alexander* (Winona Lake, IN: Eisenbrauns).

Brinkman, J. A. (1977), 'Mespotamian chronology of the historical period', in A. L. Oppenheim (ed.), *Ancient Mesopotamia: Portrait of a Dead Civilisation* (2nd edn, Chicago: University of Chicago Press), 335–48.

Broekman, G. P. F. (2009), 'Takeloth III and the end of the 23rd Dynasty', in G. P. F. Broekman, R. J. Demarée and O. E. Kaper (ed.), *The Libyan Period in Egypt. Historical and Cultural Studies into the 21st–24th Dynasties: Proceedings of a Conference at Leiden University 25–27 October 2007* (Leuven: Peeters), 91–101.

— (2010), 'Libyan rule over Egypt', *SAK*, 39, 85–97.

— (2011), 'The Egyptian chronology from the start of the Twenty-Second until the end of the Twenty-Fifth Dynasty: Facts, suppositions and arguments', *JEgH*, 4, 40–80.

— (2012a), 'The Theban high-priestly succession', *JEA*, 98, 195–209.

— (2012b), 'The administration of the Thebaid in the 26th Dynasty', *SAK*, 41, 113–35.

— (2015), 'The order of succession between Shabaka and Shabataka. A different view on the chronology of the Twenty-Fifth Dynasty', *GM*, 245, 17–31.

— (2017), 'Genealogical considerations regarding the kings of the Twenty-Fifth Dynasty in Egypt', *GM*, 251, 13–20.

Brunner, H. (1975), 'Archaismus', *LÄ I*, cols 386–95.

Budge, E. A. Wallis (1912), *Annals of Nubian Kings: With a Sketch of the History of the Nubian Kingdom of Napata* (London: Kegan Paul, Trench, Trübner).

Buhl, M.-L. (1959), *The Late Egyptian Anthropoid Stone Sarcophagi* (Nationalmuseets Skrifter, Arkæologisk-Historisk Række, VI, Copenhagen: Nationalmuseet).

Buikstra, J. E., and Charles, D. (1999), 'Centering the ancestors: cemeteries, mounds and sacred landscapes of the ancient North American Midcontinent', in W. Ashmore and B. A. Knapp (ed.), *Archaeologies of Landscape* (Oxford: Blackwell), 201–28.

Burstein, S. M. (1984), 'Psamtek I and the end of Nubian domination of Egypt', *JSSEA*, 14, 31–34.

Buzon, M. R., Smith, S. T., and Simonetti, A. (2016), 'Entanglement and the formation of the ancient Nubian Napatan state', *American Anthropologist*, 118 (2), 284–300.

Caminos, R. A. (1964), 'The Nitocris Adoption Stela', *JEA*, 50, 71–101, pls VIII–X.

— (1994), 'Notes on Queen Katimala's inscribed panel in the Temple of Semna', *Hommages à Jean Leclant. vol. 2* (Bibliothèque d'étude 106/2; Cairo: IFAO), 73–80.

Chappaz, J.-L. (1982), 'Une stèle de donation de l'An 21 de Ioupout II au Musée d'art et d'histoire', *Genava*, 30, 71–81.

— (1916), *The Chronicle of John, Bishop of Nikiu, Translated from Zotenberg's Ethiopic Text* (London and Oxford: Williams and Northgate).

Chauveau, P. (2011), 'Le saut dans le temps d'un document historique: des Ptolémées aux Saïtes', in D. Devauchelle (ed.), *La XXVIe dynastie: continuités et ruptures. Promenade saïte avec Jean Yoyotte. Actes du Colloque international organisé les 26 et 27 novembre 2004 à l'Université Charles-de-Gaulle, Lille 3* (Paris: Cybele Éditions), 39–45.

Chevereau, P.-M. (1985), *Prosopographie des cadres militaires égyptiens de la Basse Époque: Carrieres militaires et carrières sacerdotales en Egypte du XIe au IIe siècle avant J.C.* (Paris: Antony).

Chugunov, K. V., Rjabkova, T. V., and Simpson St J. (2017), 'Mounted warriors', in St J. Simpson and S. Pankova (ed.), *Scythians: Warriors of Ancient Siberia* (London: Thames & Hudson, British Museum), 194–201.

Cline, E. H. (2000), *The Battles of Armageddon: Megiddo and the Jezreel Valley from the Bronze Age to the Nuclear Age* (Ann Arbor: University of Michigan Press).

Cline, E. H., and O'Connor, D. (2012), *Ramesses III: The Life and Times of Egypt's Last Hero* (Ann Arbor: University of Michigan Press).

Cogan, M. (1971), *Imperialism and Religion: Assyria, Judah, and Israel in the Eighth and Seventh Centuries B.C.E.* (Missoula, MT: Society of Biblical Literature: distributed by Scholars Press).

Corsi, A. (2017), 'A preliminary report on the identification of the texts in the pillared hall of the Tomb of Pabasa', *GM*, 29–40.

Coldstream, J. N. (1968), *Greek Geometric Pottery: A Survey of Ten Local Styles and Their Chronology* (London: Methuen & Co. Ltd).

Coulon, L., and Defernez, C. (2004), 'La chapelle d'Osiris Ounnefer Neb-Djefaou à Karnak. Rapport préliminaire des fouilles et travaux 2000–2004', *BIFAO*, 104, 135–90.

Coulson, W. D. E., and Leonard, A. (1981), *Cities of the Delta, Part I: Naukratis* (American Research Center in Egypt, Report 4, Malibu, CA: Undena).

Couyat, J. and Montet, P. (1912), *Les inscriptions hiéroglyphiques et hiératiques du quâdi Hammâmât* (Cairo: IFAO).

Coyotte, A. (2016), 'De la Nubie à Qadech: la guerre dans l'Égypte ancienne', in C. Karlshausen and C. Obsomer (ed.), *De la Nubie à Qadech: la guerre dans l'Égypte ancienne* (Brussels: Safran), 275–94.

Cruz-Uribe, E. (1988), *Hibis Temple Project I: Translations, Commentary, Discussions and Sign Lists* (San Antonio, TX: Van Siclen).

— (2001), 'The Persian presence at Qasr el-Ghuieta', <http://jan.ucc.nau.edu/~gdc/ghu/ghuieta.htm>, accessed 4 June 2017.

— (2003), 'The invasion of Egypt by Cambyses', *Transeuphraténe*, 25, 9–60.

Dalley, S. M. (1985), 'Chariotry and cavalry in the armies of Tiglath-Pileser III and Sargon II', *Iraq*, 47, 31–48.

Dalley, S. M., and Postgate, J. N. (1984), *The Tablets from Fort Shalmaneser (Cuneiform Texts from Nimrud 3)* (London: British School of Archaeology in Iraq).

D'Angelo, I. (2006), 'Imported Greek pottery in archaic Cyrene: the excavations in the Casa del Propileo', in A. Villing and U. Schlotzhauer (ed.), *Naukratis: Greek Diversity in Egypt: Studies on East Greek Pottery and Exchange in the Eastern Mediterranean* (London: British Museum Press), 181–86.

Daressy, G. (1894), 'Notes et remarques', *RecTrav*, 16, 42–60.

— (1900), 'Stèle de l'an III d'Amasis', *RecTrav*, 22, 1–9.

— (1919), 'Samtauï-Tafnekht', *ASAE*, 18, 29–33.

— (1923), 'La crue du nil de l'an XXIX d'Amasis', *ASAE*, 23, 47–48.

Darnell, J. C. (2006), *The Inscription of Queen Katimala at Semna: Textual Evidence for the Origins of the Napatan State* (Yale Egyptological Studies 7, New Haven: Yale Egyptological Institute).

Davies, N. de Garis (1902), *The Rock Tombs of Deir el Gebrâwi*, 2 vols (1; London: Egypt Exploration Fund).

Davies, S., and Smith, H. S. (1997), 'Sacred animal temples at Saqqara', in S. Quirke (ed.), *The Temple in Ancient Egypt* (London: British Museum Press), 112–31.

Davoli, P., and Kaper, O. (2006), 'A new temple for Thoth at the Dakhleh Oasis', *EA*, 28, 12–14.

De Meulenaere, H. (1951), *Herodotus over de 26ste dynastie* (Leiden: Nederlands Instituut voor het Nabije Oosten).

— (1956), 'Trois personages saites', *CdÉE*, 31, 249–56.

— (1964), 'De vestiging van de Saitische Dynastie', *Orientalia Gadensia*, 1, 95–103.

— (1965), 'La statue du general Djed-ptah-iouf-ankh, Cairo JdE 36949', *BIFAO*, 63, 19–32.

— (1966), *Le surnom égyptien à la Basse Époque* (Istanbul: Uitgaven van het Nederlands Historisch-Archaeologisch Instituut in het Nabije Oosten).

— (1968), 'La famille du roi Amasis', *JEA*, 54, 183–87.

— (1982), 'La statue d'un vizir thébain Philadelphia, University Museum E. 16025', *JEA*, 687, 139–44.

— (1989), 'Notes de prosopographie thébaine. Quatrième série', *CdÉ*, 64, 55–73.

De Meulenaere, H., Mackay, P., Swan Hall, E., and Bothmer, B. V. (1976), *Mendes II* (Warminster: Aris & Phillips Ltd).

De Witt, C. (1958), 'Une représentation rare au Musée du Cinquantenaire: La fête de l'hippopotame blanc', *Chronique d'Egypte*, 33, 24–28.

Del Francia, P. R. (2000), 'Di una statuette dedicate ad Amon-Ra dal grande capo dei Ma Tefnakht nel Museo Egizio di Firenze', in S. Russo (ed.), *Atti Del V Convegno Nazionale di Egittologia e Papirologia, Firenze, 10–12 dicembre 1999* (Florence: Istituto papirologico 'G. Vitelli'), 63–112.

Demetriou, D. (2012), *Negotiating Identity in the Ancient Mediterranean* (Cambridge: Cambridge University Press).

Depudyt, L. (1995), 'Murder in Memphis: The story of Cambyses's mortal wounding of the Apis Bull (ca. 523 B.C.E.)', *JNES*, 54, 119–26.

— (2006a), 'Saite and Persian Egypt', in E. Hornung, R. Krauss and D. A. Warburton (ed.), *Ancient Egyptian Chronology* (HdO; Leiden: Brill), 265–83.

— (2006b), 'Foundations of day-exact chronology: 690 BC–332 BC', in E. Hornung, R. Krauss and D. A. Warburton (ed.), *Ancient Egyptian Chronology* (HdO; Leiden: Brill), 458–70.

Der Manuelian, P. (1994), *Living in the Past: Studies in Archaism of the Egyptian Twenty-Sixth Dynasty* (London: Kegan Paul).

Desanges, J. (1978), *Recherches sur l'activité des Méditerranéens aux confins de l'Afrique* (Publications de l'École Française de Rome, 38, Rome: École Française de Rome).

Devauchelle, D. (1994), 'Les stèles du Sérapéum de Memphis conservées au musée du Louvre', *Egitto e Vicino Oriente*, 17, 95–114.

Dillery, J. (2005), 'Cambyses and the Egyptian chaosbeschreibung tradition', *Classical Quarterly*, New Series, 55 (2), 387–406.

Diodorus Siculus (1933), translated and edited by C. H. Oldfather, 12 vols (Cambridge, MA: Harvard University Press).

Dodson, A. (2001), 'Third Intermediate Period', in B. Redford (ed.), *Oxford Encyclopedia of Ancient Egypt*, 3 vols (3; Oxford: Oxford University Press), 388–94.

— (2002), 'The problem of Amenirdis II and the heirs to the office of God's Wife of Amun during the Twenty-Sixth Dynasty', *JEA*, 88, 179–86.

— (2012), *Afterglow of Empire* (Cairo, New York: American University in Cairo Press).

Dodson, A., and Hilton, D. (2004), *The Complete Royal Families of Ancient Egypt* (London: Thames and Hudson).

Dodson, A., and Ikram, S. (2008), *The Tomb in Ancient Egypt* (London: Thames and Hudson).

Donker van Heel, K. (1996), 'Abnormal hieratic and early demotic texts collected by the Theban choachytes in the reign of Amasis: Papyri from the Louvre Eisenlohr lot' (PhD thesis, Leiden University).

— (1998), 'Use of land in the Kushite and Saite Periods (Egypt, 747–656 and 664–525 BC)', in B. Haring and R. de Maaijer (ed.), *Landless and Hungry?* (Leiden: Research School CNWS), 90–102.

— (2012), *Djekhy and Son: Doing Business in Ancient Egypt* (Cairo, New York: American University in Cairo Press).

Dothan, M. (1971), *Ashdod, II–III, The Second and Third Seasons of Excavations 1963, 1965, 2 volumes: Text and Figures and Plates ('Atiqot, English Series, Volume IX–X)* (Jerusalem: Dept of Antiquities and Museums, Israel).

Dothan, M., and Freedman, D. N. (1967), *Ashdod I: The First Season of Excavations, 1962 ('Atiqot, Volume VII)* (Jerusalem: Dept of Antiquities and Museums, Israel).

Dunham, D. (1950), *Royal Cemeteries of Kush, I, El Kurru* (Cambridge, MA: Harvard University Press).

Dunand, F., and Lichtenberg, R. (2006), *Mummies and Death in Egypt* (Ithaca: Cornell University Press).

Dupuy, R. E., and Dupuy, T. N. (ed.) (1993), *The Harper Encyclopedia of Military History: From 3500 BC to the Present* (4th edn, New York: HarperCollins Publishers).

Dušek, J. and Mynářová, J. (2013), 'Phoenician and Aramaic Inscriptions from Abusir', in A. F. Botta (ed.), *In the Shadow of Bezalel. Aramaic, Biblical, and Ancient Near Eastern Studies in Honor of Bezalel Porten* (Leiden, Boston: Brill), 53-69.

Eaton-Krauss, M. (2015), 'Usurpation', in R. Jasnow and K. M. Cooney (ed.), *Joyful in Thebes: Egyptological Studies in Honor of Betsy M. Bryan* (Atlanta, GA: Lockwood Press), 97–104.

Ebbinghaus, S. (2006), 'Begegnungen mit Ägypten und Vorderasien im archaischen Heraheiligtum von Samos', in A. Naso (ed.), *Stranieri e non cittadini nei santuari Greci: Atti del convegno internazionale, Udine 20 al 22 novembre 2003* (Florence: Le Monnier Università), 187–229.

Edel, E. (1978), 'Amasis und Nebukadrezar II', *GM*, 29, 13–20.

Edwards, D. N. (2004), *The Nubian Past: An Archaeology of the Sudan* (London, New York: Routledge).

Eide, T., Hägg, T., Pierce, R. H., and Török, L. (1994), *Fontes Historiae Nubiorum: Textual Sources for the History of the Middle Nile Region between the Eighth Century BC and the Sixth Century AD. Vol I: From the Eighth to the Mid-Fifth Century BC* (Bergen: University of Bergen).

Eigner, D. (1984), *Die monumentalen Grabbauten der Spätzeit in der thebanischen Nekropole* (Untersuchungen der Zweigstelle Kairo des Österreichischen Archäologischen Institutes 6, Vienna: Verlag der Österreichischen Akademie der Wissenschaften).

— (2017), 'Remarks on the architecture of the *Lichthof* in TT 223, Karakhamun', in E. Pischikova (ed.), *Tombs of the South Asasif Necropolis: New Discoveries and Research 2012–14* (Cairo, New York: American University in Cairo Press), 73–88.

Einaudi, S. (2014), 'Between south and north Asasif: The tomb of Harwa (TT 37) as a "Transitional Monument" ', in E. Pischikova, J. Budka and K. Griffin (ed.), *Thebes in the First Millennium BC* (Newcastle upon Tyne: Cambridge Scholars Publishing), 323–41.

El Naggar, S. (1986), 'Etude préliminaire d'un ciel voûté de l'hypogée de Bakenrenef (L.24) à Saqqara', *Egitto e Vicino Oriente*, 9, 15–38.

Elias, J. P. (1993), 'Coffin inscriptions in Egypt after the New Kingdom: a study of text production and use in elite mortuary preparation' (PhD thesis, University of Chicago).

El-Sawi, A. and Gomaà, F. (1993), *Das Grab des Panhesi, Gottesvaters von Heliopolis in Matariya* (Wiesbaden: Harrassowitz).

El-Sayed, R. (1974), 'Quelques éclaircissements sur l'histoire de la XXVIe dynastie, d'après la statue du Caire CG. 658 [avec 2 planches]', *BIFAO*, 74, 29–44.

— (1975), *Documents relatifs à Sais et ses divinités* (Cairo: IFAO).

Empereur, J.-Y. (1996), 'Alexandria: the underwater site near Qaitbay fort', *EA*, 8, 7–10.

Eph'al, I. (1983), 'On warfare and military control in the ancient Near Eastern empires: a research outline', in H. Tadmor and M. Weinfield (ed.), *History, Historiography, and Interpretation: Studies in Biblical and Cuneiform Literatures* (The Hebrew University, Jerusalem: The Magnes Press), 88–106.

— (2003), ' Nebuchadnezzar the warrior: Remarks on his military achievements', *Israel Exploration Journal*, 53 (2), 178–91.

Erichsen, W. (1941), 'Erwähnung eines Zuges nach Nubien unter Amasis in einem demotischen Text', *Klio*, 34, 56–61.

— (1956), *Eine neue demotische Erzählung* (Akademie der Wissenschaften und der Literatur. Abhandlungen der Geistes- und sozialwissenschaftlichen Klasse, Jahrgang Nr. 2, Wiesbaden: F. Steiner).

Erman, A. (1934), *Die Religion der Ägypter* (Berlin, Leipzig: Walter de Gruyter & Co.).

Eyre, C. (1980), 'An accounts papyrus from Thebes', *JEA*, 66, 108–19.

— (2012), 'Society, economy, and administrative process', in E. H. Cline and D. O'Connor (ed.), *Ramesses III: The Life and Times of Egypt's Last Hero* (Ann Arbor: University of Michigan Press).

Fakhry, A. (1974), *The Oases of Egypt. Vol II: Bahriyah and Farafra Oases* (Cairo: American University in Cairo Press).

Fantalkin, A. (2001), 'Low chronology and Greek Protogeometric and Geometric pottery in the Southern Levant', *Tel Aviv*, 33, 117–25.

Farag, S., Wahba, G., and Farid, A. (1977), 'Reused blocks from a temple of Amasis at Philae', *Oriens Antiquus*, 16, 315–24.

Fazzini, R. A. (1972), 'Some Egyptian reliefs in Brooklyn', in Brooklyn Museum (ed.), *Miscellanea Wilbouriana* I (Brooklyn, NY: Brooklyn Museum), 34–70.

— (1975), *Images for Eternity: Egyptian Art from Berkeley and Brooklyn* (Brooklyn, NY: Brooklyn Museum).

Fecht, G. (1958), 'Zu den Namen ägyptischer Fürsten und Städte in den Annalen des Assurbanipal und der Chronik des Asarhaddon', *MDAIK*, 16, 112–19.

Fitzmyer, J. A. (1965), 'The Aramaic letter of King Adon to the Egyptian pharaoh', *Biblica*, 46 (1), 41–55.

Forshaw, R. (2016), 'Trauma care, surgery and remedies in ancient Egypt: A reassessment', in C. Price, R. Forshaw, A. Chamberlain and P. T. Nicholson (ed.), *Mummies, Magic and Medicine in Ancient Egypt* (Manchester: Manchester University Press), 124–41.

Frame, G. (1999), 'The inscription of Sargon II at Tang i-Var', *Or*, 68 (1), 31–57.

Freed, R. (1997), 'Relief styles of the Nebhepetre Montuhotep funerary temple complex', in E. Goring, N. Reeves and J. Ruffle (ed.), *Chief of Seers: Egyptian Studies in Memory of Cyril Aldred* (London: Kegan Paul International), 148–63.

Freedy, K. S., and Redford, D. B. (1970), 'The dates in Ezekiel in relation to biblical, Babylonian and Egyptian sources', *JAOS*, 90 (3), 462–85.

Frumkin, A., Shimron, A., and Rosenbaum, J. (2003), 'Radiometric dating of the Siloam Tunnel', *Nature*, 425, 169–71.

Frost, S. B. (1968), 'The death of Josiah: A conspiracy of silence', *Journal of Biblical Literature*, 87 (4), 369–82.

Fuchs, A. (1994), *Die Inschriften Sargons II aus Khorsabad* (Göttingen: Cuvillier Verlag).

Gardiner, A. H. (1932), *Late Egyptian Stories* (Bibliotheca Aegyptiaca, 1, Brussels: Fondation Égyptologique Reine Élisabeth).

— (1948), *The Wilbour Papyrus II: Commentary* (Oxford: Oxford University Press).

Gauthier, H. (1914), *Le livre des rois d'Égypte III* (Cairo: IFAO).

— (1921a), 'A travers la basse-Égypte', *ASAE*, 21, 17–39.

— (1921b), 'A travers la basse-Égypte. VII: Tombeau d'un certain Rames à Mataria', *ASAE*, 21, 197–203.

— (1922a), 'A travers la basse-Égypte', *ASAE*, 22, 81–107.

— (1922b), 'Un édifice hathorique à Sais', *ASAE*, 22, 199–202.

— (1927), 'Une tombe d'Époque Saite à Héliopolis', *ASAE*, 27, 1–18.

— (1933), 'Découvertes récentes dans la Nécropole Saite d'Héliopolis', *ASAE*, 33, 27–53.

— (1934), 'Un monument nouveau du roi Psamtik II', *ASAE*, 34, 129–34.

— (1935), 'Un autel consacré à la déesse Mehlt', *ASAE*, 35, 207–12.

Gestermann, L. (1994), ' "Neue" texte in späzeitlichen Graubanlagen von Saqqara und Heliopolis' in M. Minas and J. Zeidler (ed.), *Aspekte Spätägyptischer Kultur* (Mainz: Verlag Phillip von Zabern), 89–95.

Gestermann, L., and Gomaà, F. (2014), 'The tomb of Montuemhat (TT 34) in the Theban Necropolis: A new approach', in E. Pischikova, J. Budka and K. Griffin (ed.), *Thebes in the First Millennium BC* (Newcastle upon Tyne: Cambridge Scholars Publishing), 201–3.

Ghalioungui, P. (1983), *The Physicians of Pharaonic Egypt* (Cairo: Al-Ahram Center for Scientific Translations).

Gill, D., and Vickers, M. (1996), 'Bocchoris the wise and absolute chronology', *Römische Mitteilungen*, 103, 1–9.

Gitin, S. (1998), 'Philistia in transition: the tenth century BCE and beyond', in S. Gitin, S. Mazar and A. Stern (ed.), *Mediterranean Peoples in Transition. Thirteenth to Early Tenth Centuries BCE. In Honor of Trude Dothan* (Jerusalem: Israel Exploration society), 162–83.

Goedicke, H. (1962), 'Psammetik I. und die Libyer', *MDAIK*, 18, 26–49.

— (1981), 'The campaign of Psammetik II against Nubia', *MDAIK*, 37, 187–98.

Goelet, O. (1996), 'A new "Robbery" papyrus: Rochester MAG 51.346.1', *JEA*, 82, 102–27.

Gomaà, F. (2006), 'Die Arbeiten im Grab des Monthemhet', *Sokar*, 12, 62–64.

Gorton, A. F. (1996), *Egyptian and Egyptianizing Scarabs: A Typology of Steatite, Faience and Paste Scarabs from Punic and Other Mediterranean Sites* (Oxford University Committee for Archaeology, Monographs 44, Oxford: Oxford University School of Archaeology).

Goyon, J.-C. (1969), 'La statuette funéraire I.E. 84 de Lyon et le titre saïte *mr ꜥḥw nsw*', *BIFAO*, 67, 159–71.

Gozzoli, R. B. (1995), 'The Nubian war texts of Psammetichus II: An essay of explication', *JSSEA*, 25, 46–49.

— (2000), 'The statue BM EA 37891 and the erasure of Necho II's names', *JEA*, 86, 67–80.

— (2006), *The Writing of History in Ancient Egypt during the First Millennium BC (ca. 1070–180 BC). Trends and Perspectives* (GHP Egyptology 5, London: Golden House Publications).

— (2009), 'History and stories in Ancient Egypt: theoretical issues and the myth of the eternal return', in M. Fitzenreiter (ed.), *Das Ereignis: Geschichtsschreibung zwischen Vorfall und Befund: Workshop vom 03.10. bis 05.10.08* (Internet-Beiträge zur Ägyptologie und Sudanarchäologie; London: Golden House Publications), 103–15.

— (2017), *Psammetichus II. Reign, Documents and Officials* (London: Golden House Publications).

Graefe, E. (1981), *Untersuchungen zur Verwaltung und Geshichte der Institution der Gottesgemahlin des Amun vom Beginn des Neuen Reiches bis zur Spätzeit: Band I* (Ägyptologische Abhandlungen, Band 37, Wiesbaden: Otto Harrassowitz).

— (1990), *Das Grab des Ibi, Obervermögenverwalters der Gottesgemahlin des Amun (Thebanisches Grab Nr. 36)* (Brussels: Fondation Égyptologique Reine Élisabeth).

— (1998), 'Der autobiographische Text des Ibi, Obervermögensverwalter der Gottesgemahlin Nitokris, auf Kairo JE 36158', *MDAIK*, 50, 85–99 and pls 10–14.

— (2003), *Das Grab des Padihorresnet, Obervermögensverwalter der Gottesgemahlin des Amun (Thebanisches Grab Nr. 196)*, 2 vols (Monumenta Aegyptiaca 9; Brussels: Fondation Égyptologique Reine Élisabeth).

Grajetzki, W. (2005), *Ancient Egyptian Queens: A Hieroglyphic Dictionary* (London: Golden House Publications).

Grandet, P. (1994), *Le Papyrus Harris I (BM 9999)*, 2 vols (Bibliothèque d'Étude 109/1–2, Cairo: IFAO).

Grantovskii, E. A. (1994), 'About the chronology of the stay of the Cimmerians and the Scythians in the Near East', *RosA*, 3, 23–48.

Grayson, A. K. (1975), *Assyrian and Babylonian Chronicles* (Texts from Cuneiform Sources; Locust Valley, NY: J. J. Augustin).

Greenberg, M. (1983), *Ezekiel 21–37: A New Translation with Introduction and Commentary* (New York: Doubleday).

Gregory, S. R. W. (2014), *Herihor in Art and Iconography: Kingship and the Gods in the Ritual Landscape of Late New Kingdom Thebes* (London: Golden House Publications).

Griffin, K. (2017), 'Toward a better understanding of the Ritual of the Hours of the Night', in E. Piscikova (ed.), *Tombs of the South Asasif Necropolis* (Cairo: American University in Cairo Press), 97–134.

Griffith, F. Ll. (1909), *Catalogue of the Demotic Papyri in the John Rylands Library, Manchester*, 3 vols (London: B. Quaritch).

Grimal, N.-C. (1981), *Quatre stèles Napatéenes au Musée du Caire: JE 48863–48866, MIFAO*, 106 (Cairo: IFAO).

Grimal, N. (1994), *A History of Ancient Egypt* (Malden, MA, Oxford: Blackwell Publishing).

Gunn, B. (1927), 'The Stela of Apries at Mîtrahîna', *ASAE*, 27, 211–37.

— (1934), 'The Berlin statue of Harwa and some notes on other Harwa statues (with 1 plate)', *BIFAO*, 34, 135–42.

Gunn, B., and Engelbach, R. (1931), 'The statues of Harwa (with 7 plates)', *BIFAO*, 30, 791–815.

Habachi, L. (1943), 'Saïs and its monuments', *ASAE*, 42, 369–407.

— (1974), 'Psammetique II dans la region la première Cataracte', *Oriens Antiquus*, 13, 317–26.

— (1977), 'Mentuhotep, the vizier and son-in-law of Taharqa', in E. Endesfelder, K.-Heinz Priese, W.-Friedrich Reineke and S. Wenig (ed.), *Ägypten und Kusch* (Berlin: Adademie-Verlag), 165–70.

— (1982), 'Athribis in XXVI Dynasty [avec 7 planches]', *BIFAO*, 82, 213–35.

Haeny, G. (1985), 'A short architectural history of Philae', *BIFAO*, 85, 197–233.

Hall, H. R. (1913), *Catalogue of Egyptian Scarabs, Etc., in the British Museum* (1; London: Trustees of the British Museum).

Harrison, K. (2017), 'A Saite story of glory', *Ancient Egypt*, 18 (1), 12–17.

Hawass, Z. (2000), *Valley of the Golden Mummies: The Greatest Egyptian Discovery since Tutankhamen* (London: Virgin Books).

Heidorn, L. A. (1991), 'The Saite and Persian Period forts at Dorginarti', in W. V. Davies (ed.), *Egypt and Africa. Nubia from Prehistory to Islam* (London: British Museum Press), 205–19.

— (1997), 'The horses of Kush', *JNES*, 56 (2), 105–14.

— (2013), 'Dorginarti: Fortress at the mouth of the rapids', in F. Jesse and C. Vogel (ed.), *The Power of Walls: Fortifications in Ancient Northeastern Africa: Proceedings of the International Workshop Held at the University of Cologne 4th – 7th August 2011* (Colloquium Africanum 5, Cologne: Heinrich-Barth-Institut), 293–307.

Heise, J. (2007), *Erinnern und Gedenken. Aspekte der biographischen Inschriften der ägyptischen Spätzeit* (Fribourg: Academic Press; Göttingen: Vandenhoek & Ruprecht), 193–98.

Helck, W. (1986), *Politische Genensäze im alten Ägypten: ein Versuch* (Hildesheimer ägyptologische Beiträge, 23, Hildesheim: Gerstenberg Verlag).

Henk, M. (2012), 'Shabtis', in W. Wendrich (ed.), *UCLA Encyclopedia of Egyptology, Los Angeles*. <http://digital2.library.ucla.edu/viewItem.do?ark=21198/zz002bwv0z>, accessed 7 December 2017.

Herodotus (1996), *Herodotus: The Histories*, trans. A. de Sélincourt (Harmondsworth: Penguin Books).

Höckmann, U. (2005), 'Archaische Löwenstatuen aus Südionien in ägyptischer Haltung', *Ägypten Griechenland Rom: Abwehr und Berührung: Katalog zur Ausstellung im Städelschen Kunstinstitut Frankfurt, 26.11.2005–26.02.2006* (Tübingen: E. Wasmuth Verlag), 83–89.

Höckmann, U., and Möller, A. (2006), 'The Hellenion at Naukratis: Questions and observations', in A. Villing and U. Schlotzhauer (ed.), *Naukratis: Greek Diversity in Egypt* (London: British Museum Press), 11–22.

Hoffmeier, J. K. (1981), 'A new insight on pharaoh Apries from Herodotus, Diodorus and Jeremiah 46: 17', *JSSEA*, 11 (3), 165–70.

— (2003), 'Egypt's role in the events of 701 B.C. in Jerusalem', in A. G. Vaughn and E. Killebrew (ed.), *Jerusalem in Bible and Archaeology: The First Temple Period* (SBL Symposium Series 18, Atlanta: Society of Biblical Literature), 219–234.

Hofmann, B. (2004), *Die Konigsnovelle: Strukturanalyse am Einzelwerk* (Agypten und Altes Testament 62; Wiesbaden: Harrassowitz).

Hölscher, U. (1939), *The Excavation of Medinet Habu – Volume II. The Temples of the Eighteenth Dynasty* (Oriental Institute Publications 41, Chicago: University of Chicago Press).

— (1954), *The Excavation of Medinet Habu – Volume V: Post-Ramessid Remains* (OIP, 66, Chicago: University of Chicago Press).

Hölscher, W. (1937), *Libyer und Ägypter* (Augustin: Glückstadt).

Hooker, P. K. (1993), 'The location of the Brook of Egypt', in M. P. Graham, W. P. Brown and J. K. Kuan (ed.), *History and Interpretation: Essays in Honour of John H. Hayes* (Sheffield: Sheffield Academic Press), 203–14.

Hornung, E., Krauss, R., and Warburton D. A. (ed.) (2006), *Ancient Egyptian Chronology* (Handbuch der Orientalistik, Abt. 1, Der Nahe und der Mittlere Osten, 83, Leiden, Boston: Brill).

Hughes, G. R. (1952), *Saite Demotic Land Leases* (The Oriental Institute of the University of Chicago, Studies in Ancient Oriental Civilisation, 28, Chicago: University of Chicago Press).

Hulin, L. (1987), 'Marsa Matruh 1987, preliminary ceramic report', *JARCE*, 26, 115–26.

Iancu, L. M. (2016), 'Greek and other Aegean mercenaries in the Archaic Age: Aristocrats, common people or both?', *Studia Hercynia*, 20 (2), 9–29.

Ikram, S. (2005), 'Divine creatures', in S. Ikram (ed.), *Divine Creatures: Animal Mummies in Ancient Egypt* (Cairo, New York: American University in Cairo Press), 1–16.

Ikram, S., and Dodson, A. (1998), *The Mummy in Ancient Egypt* (London: Thames and Hudson Ltd).

Ivantchik, A. (1999), 'The Scythian "Rule Over Asia": The classical tradition and the historical reality', in G. R. Tsetskhladze (ed.), *Ancient Greeks West and East* (Leiden: E. J. Brill), 497–520.

Iverson, E. (1941), *Two Inscriptions Concerning Private Donations to Temples* (Det Kgl. Danske Videnskabernes Selskab, Historisk-filosofiske Meddelelser, 27, 5; Copenhagen: Munksgaard).

Jacquet-Gordon, H. K. (1960), 'The inscriptions on the Philadelphia-Cairo Statue of Osorkon II', *JEA*, 46, 12–23.

James, P. (2003), 'Naukratis revisited', *Hyperboreus: Studia Classica*, 9 (2), 235–64.

Janes, G. (2002), *Shabtis: A Private View* (Paris: Cybèle).

Jansen, H. L. (1950), *The Coptic Story of Cambyses' Invasion of Egypt. A Critical Analysis of its Literary Form and its Historical Purpose*, translated from the Norwegian by John J. Lund (Oslo: J. Dybwad).

Jansen-Winkeln, K. (1985), *Ägyptische Biographien der 22. und 23. Dynastie* (Ägypten und Altes Testament 8, Wiesbaden: Otto Harrassowitz).

— (1989), 'Zur Schiffsliste aus Elephantine', *GM*, 109, 31.

— (1992), 'Das Ende des Neuen Reiches', *ZÄS*, 119, 22–37.

— (1994), 'Der Beginn der libyschen Herrschaft in Ägypten', *Biblische Notizen*, 71, 78–97.

— (1998), 'Die ägyptische "Konigsnovelle" als Texttyp', *Wiener Zeitschrift für die Kunde des Morgenlandes*, 83, 101–16.

— (2002), 'Die Quellen zur Eroberung Ägyptens durch Kambyses', in T. A. Bács (ed.), *A Tribute to Excellence: Studies Offered in Honor of Ernő Gaál, Ulrich Luft and László Török* (Studia Aegyptiaca, 17, Budapest: Université Eötvös Lorand de Budapest), 309–19.

— (2006), 'Third Intermediate Period', in R. Krauss, E. Hornung, and D. A. Warburton (ed.), *Ancient Egyptian Chronology* (Handbuch der Orientalistik., Abt. 1, Der Nahe und der Mittlere Osten, 83, Leiden, Oxford: Brill), 234–65.

— (2007a), *Inschriften der Spätzeit. Teil I. Die 21. Dynastie* (Wiesbaden: Harrassowitz).

— (2007b), *Inschriften der Spätzeit. Teil II. Die 22–24. Dynastie* (Wiesbaden: Harrassowitz).

— (2009), *Inschriften der Spätzeit. Teil III. Die 25. Dynastie* (Wiesbaden: Harrassowitz).

— (2014a), 'Die Siegesstela des Amasis', *ZÄS*, 141 (2), 132–53.

— (2014b), *Inschriften der Spätzeit. Teil IV. Die 26. Dynastie*, 2 vols (1; Wiesbaden: Harrassowitz).

— (2017), 'Beiträge zur Geschichte der Dritten Zwischenzeit', *JEgH*, 10 (1), 23–42.

Japhet, S. (1993), *I & II Chronicles: A Commentry* (London: SCM Press).

Johnson, J. H. (2001), 'Demotic', in D. B. Redford (ed.), *Oxford Encyclopedia of Ancient Egypt*, 3 vols (3; Oxford: Oxford University Press), 210–14.

Jones, H. L. (1982), *Strabo: Geography, Volume VIII: Book 17. General Index* (Loeb Classical Library, 267, Cambridge, MA: Harvard University Press).

Josephson, J. A. (1997), 'Egyptian sculpture of the Late Period revisited', *JARCE*, 34, 1–20.

— (2001), 'Amasis', in D. B. Redford (ed.), *The Oxford Encyclopedia of Ancient Egypt*, 3 vols (1; Oxford: Oxford University Press), 66–67.

Josephson, J. A., and el-Dalmaty, M. M. (1999), *Catalogue General of Egyptian Antiquities in the Cairo Museum. Nrs. 48601–48649. Statues of the XXVth and XXVIth Dynasties* (Catalogue général des antiquités égyptiennes du Musée du Caire, Cairo: The Supreme Council of Antiquities).

Josephus, Flavius (1937), *Jewish Antiquities: Books 9–11*, trans. R. Marcus (Loeb Classical Library, 326; Cambridge, MA: Harvard University Press).

Junge, F. (1987), *Elephantine XI: Funde und Bauteile. 1–7. Kampagne, 1969–1976* (Archäologische Veröffentlichungen. Deutsches Archäologischen Institut Abteilung Kairo 49, Mainz am Rhein: Verlag Philipp von Zabern).

Jurman, C. (2010), 'The trappings of kingship. Remarks about archaism, rituals and cultural polyglossia in Saite Egypt', *Aegyptus et Pannonia*, 4, 73–118.

Kaczmarczyk, A., and Hedges, R. E. M. (1983), *Ancient Egyptian Faience* (Warminster: Aris & Phillips Ltd).

Kahl, J. (2010), 'Archaism', in W. Wendrich (ed.), *UCLA Encyclopedia of Egyptology*, Los Angeles, <http://digital2.library.ucla.edu/viewItem.do?ark=21198/zz0025qh2v>, accessed 12 December 2017.

Kahn, D. (2001), 'The inscription of Sargon II at Tang-i Var and the chronology of Dynasty 25', *Or*, 70 (1), 1–18.

— (2004), 'Taharqa, King of Kush and the Assyrians', *JSSEA*, 31, 109–28.

— (2006a), 'The Assyrian invasions of Egypt (673–663 BC) and the final expulsion of the Kushites', *SAK*, 34, 251–67.

— (2006b), 'Tefnakht's "Letter of Submission" to Piankhy', *Beiträge zur Sudanforschung*, 9, 45–61.

— (2006c), 'Was there a coregency in the 25th Dynasty', *Mitteilungen der Sudanarchaeologischen Gesellschaft*, 17, 135–41.

— (2007a), 'Judean auxiliaries in Egypt's wars against Kush', *JAOS*, 127 (4), 507–16.

— (2007b), 'Note on the time-factor in Cambyses' deeds in Egypt as told by Herodotus', *Transeuphraténe*, 34, 103–12.

— (2008), 'Some remarks on the foreign policy of Psammetichus II in the Levant (595–589 B.C.)', *JEgH*, 1, 139–55.

— (2009), 'The transition from Libyan to Nubian rule in Egypt: Revisiting the reign of Tefnakht', in G. P. F. Broekman, R. J. Demarée and O. E. Kaper (ed.), *The Libyan Period in Egypt. Historical and Cultural Studies into the 21st–24th Dynasties: Proceedings of a Conference at Leiden University 25–27 October 2007* (Leiden: Peeters), 139–48.

— (2015), 'Why did Necho II kill Josiah', in J. Mynářová, P. Onderka and P. Pavúk (ed.), *There and Back Again – the Crossroads II: Proceedings of an International Conference Held in Prague, September 15–18, 2014* (Prague: Charles University in Prague), 511–28.

Kahn, D. and Tammuz, O. (2008), 'Egypt is difficult to enter: Invading Egypt – A game plan (seventh – fourth centuries BCE)', *JSSEA*, 35, 37–66.

Kaiser, W. (1987), 'Die ältere Torfassade des spätzeitlichen Palastbezirkes von Memphis', *MDAIK*, 43, 123–44.

Kaiser, W., Dreyer, G., Grimm, G., Haeny, G., Jaritz, H., and Müller, G. (1975), 'Stadt und Tempel von Elephantine: Fünfter Grabungsbericht', *MDAIK*, 31, 39–84.

Kaper, O. E. (2015), 'Petubastis IV in the Dakhla Oasis: New evidence about an early rebellion against Persian rule and its suppression in political memory', in J. M. Silverman and C. Waerzeggers (ed.), *Political Memory in and after the Persian Empire* (Ancient Near East monographs, 13, Atlanta: SBS Press), 125–49.

Kaplan, P. (2010), 'Cross-cultural contacts among mercenary communities in Saite and Persian Egypt', *Mediterranean Historical Review*, 18 (1), 1–31.

Katzenstein, H. J. (1994), 'Gaza in the Neo-Babylonian Period 626–539 B.C.E.', *Transeuphraténe*, 7, 35–49.

Kemp, B. J. (1977), 'The palace of Apries at Memphis', *MDAIK*, 33, 101–8.

— (2006), *Ancient Egypt: Anatomy of a Civilisation* (2nd edn; New York: Routledge).

Kendall, T. (1999), 'The origin of the Napatan state: El Kurru and the evidence for the royal ancestors', *Meroitica*, 15, 3–17.

— (2002), 'Napatan temples: A case study from Gebel Barkal (paper delivered at the 10th International Conference for Nubian Studies, Rome)', <http://rmcisadu.let.uniroma1.it/nubiaconference/kendall.doc>, accessed 23 March 2017.

Kessler, D. (1989), *Die heiligen Tiere und der König* (Ägypten und Altes Testament 16, Wiesbaden: Harrassowitz).

Kessler, D., and Nur el-Din, A. H. (2015), 'Tuna al-Gebel: Millions of ibises and other animals', in S. Ikram (ed.), *Divine Creatures: Animal Mummies in Ancient Egypt* (Cairo, New York: American University in Cairo), 120–63.

Kienitz, F. K. (1953), *Die politische Geschichte Ägyptens vom 7. bis zum 4. Jahrhundert vor der Zeitwende* (Berlin: Akademie-Verlag).

Kinnier Wilson, J. V. (1972), *The Nimrud Wine Lists: A Study of Men and Administration at the Assyrian Capital in the Eighth Century, B.C. (Cuneiform Texts from Nimrud)* (London: British School of Archaeology in Iraq).

Kitchen, K. A. (1982), 'The Twentieth Dynasty revisited', *JEA*, 68, 116–25.

— (1983), 'Egypt, the Levant and Assyria in 701 BC', in H. Brunner and M. Görg (ed.), *Fontes Atque Pontes: Eine Festgabe für Hellmut Brunner* (ÄAT 5. Wiesbaden: Harassowitz), 243–53.

— (1990), 'The arrival of the Libyans in Late New Kingdom Egypt', in A. Leahy (ed.), *Libya and Egypt c 1300–750 BC* (London: Society for Libyan Studies), 15–27.

— (1996), *The Third Intermediate Period in Egypt (1100–650 BC)* (2nd edn; Oxford: Aris & Phillips Ltd).

— (2009), 'The Third Intermediate Period in Egypt: An overview of fact and fiction', in G. P. F. Broekman, R. J. Demarée and O. E. Kaper (ed.), *The Libyan Period in Egypt* (Leuven: Peeters), 161–202.

— (2012), 'Ramesses III and the Ramesside Period', in E. H. Cline and D. O'Connor (ed.), *Ramesses III: The Life and Times of Egypt's Last Hero* (Ann Arbor: University of Michigan Press), 1–26.

Kloth, N. (2002), *Die (auto-)biographischen Inschriften des ägyptischen Alten Reiches: Untersuchungen zu Phraseologie und Entwicklung* (Studien zur altägyptischen Kultur Beiheft 8, Hamburg: Buske).

Klotz, D. (2010), 'Two studies on the Late Period temples at Abydos', *BIFAO*, 110, 127–63.

— (2013), 'Administration of the deserts and oases: First millennium B.C.E.' in J.-C. Moreno Garcia (ed.), *Ancient Egyptian Administration* (Leiden, Boston: Brill), 901–9.

— (2015), 'Persian Period', in W. Grajetzki and W. Wendrich (ed.), *UCLA Encyclopedia of Egyptology*, Los Angeles, <http://digital2.library.ucla.edu/viewItem.do?ark=21198zz002k45rq>, accessed 20 October 2017.

Knudtzon, J. A. (1893), *Assyrische Gebete an den Sonnengott für State und königliches Haus aus der Zeit Asarhaddons und Asurbanipals I–II* (Leipzig: E. Pfeiffer).

Koch, C. (2014), 'Usurpation and the erasure of names during the Twenty-Sixth Dynasty', in E. Pishchikova, J. Budka and K. Griffin (ed.), *Thebes in the First Millennium BC* (Newcastle upon Tyne: Cambridge Scholars Publishing).

— (2017), 'The sarcophagus of Nitocris (Inv. Cairo TN 6/2/21/1): Further considerations about the God's Wives' burial places', in A. Amenta and H. Guichard (ed.), *Proceedings First Vatican Coffin Conference 19–22 June 2013*, 2 vols (1; Vatican City: Edizioni Musei Vaticani), 231–48.

Kouriou, N. (2004), 'Inscribed imports, visitors and pilgrims in the Archaic sanctuaries of Camiros', in A. Giannikoure et al. (ed.), *Χάρις Χαῖρε: Μελέτες στη μνήμη της Χάρης Κάντζια* (2; Athens), 11–30.

Krahmalkov, C. R. (1981), 'The historical setting of the Adon Letter', *BA*, 44, 197–98.

Kritsky, G. (2015), *The Tears of Re: Beekeeping in Ancient Egypt* (Oxford: Oxford University Press).

Kuhlmann, K. P. (1988), *Das Ammoneion: Archäologie, Geschichte und Kultpraxis des Orakels von Siwa* (Mainz am Rhein: Philipp von Zabern).

Kuhlmann, K. P., and Schenkel, W. (1983), *Das Grab des Ibi: Theben Nr. 36 I Beschreibung der unterirdischen Kult- und Bestattungsanlage* (AV 15, Mainz am Rhein: Verlag Philipp von Zabern).

Kuhrt, A. (1995), *The Ancient Near East c. 3000–330 BC*, 2 vols (London, New York: Routledge).

— (2007), *The Persian Empire: A Corpus of Sources from the Achaemenid Period* (London, New York: Routledge).

Ladynin, I. A. (2006), 'The Elephantine Stela of Amasis: Some problems and prospects of study', *GM*, 211, 31–56.

Lauer, J.-Ph. (1972), *Les Pyramides de Sakkarah* (Bibliothèque générale 3, Cairo: IFAO).

Lawson Younger, K. Jr, (2000), ' "Tiglath-pileser" and "Sargon II"', in W. W. Hallo (ed.), *The Context of Scripture, Volume Two: Monumental Inscriptions from the Biblical World* (Leiden, Boston: Brill), 284–300.

Leahy, A. (1980), 'Harwa and Harbes', *CdÉ*, 55, 43–63.

— (1984a), 'Tanutamon, son of Shabako?' *GM*, 83, 43–45.

— (1984b), 'The name *P3-wrm*', *GM*, 76, 67–79.

— (1984c), 'Death by fire in ancient Egypt', *Journal of the Economic and Social History of the Orient*, 27, Part II, 199–206.

— (1984d), 'Saite royal sculpture: A review', *GM*, 80, 59–76.

— (1985), 'The Libyan Period: An essay in interpretation', *Libyan Studies*, 16, 51–65.

— (1988), 'The earliest dated monument of Amasis and the end of the reign of Apries', *JEA*, 74, 183–99.

— (1992), 'Royal iconography and dynastic change, 750–525 BC: The Blue and Cap crowns', *JEA*, 78, 223–40.

— (1996), 'The adoption of Ankhnesneferibre', *JEA*, 82, 145–65.

— (2000), 'Libya', in D. B. Redford (ed.), *The Encylopedia of Ancient Egypt*, 3 vols (2; Oxford: Oxford University Press), 290–93.

— (2009), 'A mysterious fragment and a monumental hinge: Necho II and Psammetichus II once again', in I. Régen and F. Servajean (ed.), *Verba manent: Recueil d'études dédiées à Dimitri Meeks par ses collègues et amis* (CENiM 2, Montpellier: Université Paul Valéry), 227–40.

— (2011), 'Somtutefnakht of Herakleopolis: The art and politics of self-commemoration in the seventh century BC', in D. Devauchelle (ed.), *La XXVIe dynastie: continuités et ruptures: promenade saïte avec Jean Yoyotte: actes du colloque international organisé les 26 et 27 novembre 2004 à l'Université Charles de Gaulle, Lille 3* (Paris: Cybèle), 197–224.

Leclant, J. (1961), *Montouemhat: Quatrième Prophète D'Amon Prince de la Ville* (Cairo: IFAO).

— (1963), 'Kashta, Pharon, en Egypte', *ZÄS*, 90 (1), 74–81.

— (1980), 'La "famille libyenne" au temple haut de Pépi I', in J. Vercoutter (ed.), *Livre du centenaire, 1880–1980, Mémoires publiés par les membres de l'institut français d'archéologie du Caire* 104 (Cairo: IFAO), 49–54.

— (2001), 'Montuemhet', in D. B. Redford (ed.), *Oxford Encyclopedia of Ancient Egypt*, 3 vols (2; Oxford: Oxford University Press), 436.

Leclère, F. (2008), *Les villes de basse Égypte au Ier millénaire av. J.-C.* (Cairo: IFAO).

Leclère, F., and Spencer, J. (2014), *Tell Dafana Reconsidered: The Archaeology of an Egyptian Frontier Town* (British Museum Research Publication no. 199, London: British Museum Press).

Lefebvre, G. (1925), 'Le grand prêtre d'Amon, Harmakhis, et deux reines de la XXVe dynastie', *ASAE*, 25, 25–33.

— (1929), *Inscriptions concernant les grands prêtres d'Amon, Romê-Roÿ et Amenhotep* (Paris: P. Geuthner).

Legrain, G. (1897), 'Deux stèles trouvées à Karnak en février 1897', *ZÄS*, 35, 12–19.

— (1903), 'Notes d'inspection. III–X', *ASAE*, 4, 193–226.

— (1906), 'Deux stèles inédites', *ASAE*, 7, 226–27.

— (1914), *Statues et statuettes de rois et de pariculars, III* (Catalogue Général des Antiquités Égyptiennes du Musée du Caire, Nos 42192–42250, Cairo: IFAO).

Lehmann, G. (1998), 'Trends in the local pottery development of the Late Iron Age and Persian Period in Syria and Lebanon, ca. 700 to 300 B.C.' *BASOR*, 311, 7–37.

Leonard, A. Jr, (1997), *Ancient Naukratis: Excavations at a Greek Emporium in Egypt. Part I: The Excavations at Kom Ge'if* (Atlanta, GA: American Schools of Oriental Research).

Levin, K. (1964), 'The male figure in Egyptian and Greek sculpture of the seventh and sixth centuries B.C.' *American Journal of Archaeology*, 68 (1), 13–28.

Lichtheim, M. (1975), *Ancient Egyptian Literature: A Book of Readings. Volume I: The Old and Middle Kingdom* (Berkeley, Los Angeles, London: University of California Press).

— (1976), *Ancient Egyptian Literature: A Book of Readings. Volume II: The New Kingdom* (Berkley, Los Angeles, London: University of California Press).

— (1980), *Ancient Egyptian Literature: A Book of Readings. Volume III: The Late Period* (Berkley, Los Angeles, London: University of California Press).

— (1992), *Maat in Egyptian Autobiographies and Related Studies* (Orbis Biblicus et Orientalis: Universitätsverlag Freiburg Schweiz, Göttingen: Vandenhoek & Ruprecht).

Lindblad, I. (1984), *Royal Sculpture of the Early Eighteenth Dynasty in Egypt* (Medelhavsmuseet Memoir 5; Stockholm: Museum of Mediterranean and Near Eastern Antiquities).

Lippert, S. L. (2004), *Ein demotisches juristisches Lehrbuch: Untersuchungen zu P. Berlin 23757 rto* (Ägyptologische Abhandlungen 66, Wiesbaden: Harrassowitz), 155–57.

— (2016), *Egyptian Law, Saite to Roman Period* (Oxford Handbooks Online).

Lipschits, O. (2005), *The Fall and Rise of Jerusalem* (Winona Lake, IN: Eisenbrauns).

Lloyd, A. B. (1972), 'Triremes and the Saite navy', *JEA*, 58, 268–79.

— (1975), *Herodotus Book II, Introduction* (Leiden: E. J. Brill).

— (1976), *Herodotus Book II, Commentaries 1–98* (Leiden: E. J. Brill).

— (1977), 'Necho and the Red Sea: Some considerations', *JEA*, 63, 142–55.

— (1982), 'The inscription of Udjahorresnet. A collaborator's testament', *JEA*, 68, 166–90.

— (1983), 'The Late Period, 664 BC – 323 BC', in B. G. Trigger, B. J. Kemp, D. O'Connor and A. B. Lloyd (ed.), *Ancient Egypt: A Social History* (Cambridge: Cambridge University Press), 279–348.

— (1988), *Herodotus Book II, Commentaries 99–182* (Leiden: E. J. Brill).

— (2000), 'Saite navy', in J. G. Oliver, R. Brock, T. J. Cornell and S. Hodkinson (ed.), *The Sea in Antiquity* (Oxford: Archaeopress), 81–91.

Logan, T. (2000), 'The Imyt-pr document: Form, function and significance', *JARCE*, 37, 49–73.

Lopes, M. H. T., and Braga, S. F. (2011), 'The Apries Palace, Memphis/Kôm Tumân: The first Portuguese mission in Egypt', *JARCE*, 47, 247–58

Lopez, F. (2016), *Democede di Crotone e Udjahorresnet di Sais* (Pisa: Pisa University Press).

Loprieno, A. (1996), 'The "King's Novel" ', in A. Loprieno (ed.), *Ancient Egyptian Literature: History and Forms* (Probleme der Agyptologie 10 Leiden: Brill), 277–95.

Luckenbill, D. D. (1927), *Ancient Records of Assyria and Babylonia*, 2 vols (2; Chicago: Chicago University Press).

Macadam, M. F. Laming (1949), *The Temples of Kawa: The Inscriptions, Text, Plates*, 2 vols (London: Griffith Institute).

Malamat, A. (1973), 'Josiah's bid for Armageddon: The background of the Judean–Egyptian encounter in 609 BC', *JANES*, 5, 267–79.

— (1974), 'Megiddo, 609 BC: The conflict re-examined', *Acta Antiqua Academiae Scientiarum Hungaricae*, 22, 445–49.

— (1975), 'The twilight of Judah: In the Egyptian–Babylonian maelstrom', *Vetus Testamentus Supplement*, 28, 123–45.

— (1990), 'The kingdom of Judah between Egypt and Babylon', *Studia Theologica, Nordic Journal of Theology*, 44 (4), 65–77.

Malinine, M. (1953), *Choix de textes juridiques en hiératique 'anormal' et en démotique (XXVe–XXVIIe Dynasties)*, 2 vols (Bibliothèque de l'Ecole des hautes études. Fasc. 300, 1, Paris: Librairie Ancienne Honore Champion).

— (1975), 'Vente de tombes à l'Epoque Saite', *RdÉ*, 27, 164–74.

Malinine, M., Posener, G., and Vercoutter, J. (1968), *Catalogue des Stèles du Sérapéum de Memphis* (Paris: Imprimerie Nationale).

Malouta, M. (2015), 'Naucratis', *Oxford Handbooks Online*, https://dx.doi.org/10.1093/oxfordhb/9780199935390.013.114 (accessed 16 October 2017).

Manessa, C. (2003), *The Great Karnak Inscription of Merneptah: Grand Strategy in the 13th Century B.C.* (Yale Egyptological studies 5, New Haven, CT: Yale Egyptological Seminar, Yale University).

Manley, B. (1996), *The Penguin Historical Atlas of Ancient Egypt* (London: Penguin Group).

Manning, J. G. (2003), *Land and Power in Ptolemaic Egypt* (Cambridge: Cambridge University Press).

Marković, N. (2015), 'The cult of the sacred Bull Apis: History of study', in M. Tomorod (ed.), *A History of Research into Ancient Egyptian Cultures Conducted in Southeast Europe* (Oxford; Archaeopress), 135–46.

Marr, J. (1995), 'The death of Themistocles', *Greece & Rome*, 42 (2), 159–67.

Maspero, G. (1884), 'Notes sur quelques points de grammaire et d'histoire', *ZÄS*, 22, 78–93.

— (1904), 'Deux monuments de la princesse Ankhnasnofiribrî', *ASAE*, 5, 84–92.

Masson, O. (1976), 'Nouveax graffites grecs d'Abydos et de Bouhen', *CdÉ*, 51, 305–13.

Masson, O., Martin, G. T., and Nicholls, R. (1978), *Carian Inscriptions from North Saqqara and Buhen* (Excavations at North Saqqara Documentary Series 3, London: Egypt Exploration Society).

Masson, O., and Yoyotte, J. (1988), 'Une inscription ionienne mentionnant Psammetique Ier', *Epigraphica Anatolica*, 11, 171–80.

Matouk, F. (1971), *Corpus du scarabée egyptien: Vol. 1 Les scarabées royaux* (Beyrouth, Liban: Imprimerie Catholique).

McDowell, A. G. (1990), *Jurisdiction in the Workmen's Community of Dier el-Medina* (Egyptologische Uitgaven, 5, Leiden: Nederlands Instituut voor het Nabije Oosten).

— (1999), *Village Life in Ancient Egypt* (Oxford: Oxford University Press).

McKnight, L. M., Bibb, R., Mazza, R., and Chamberlain, A. T. (2018), 'Appearance and reality in ancient Egyptian votive animal mummies', *Journal of Ancient Egyptian Interconnections*, 20, 52–57.

Meeks, D. (1979), 'Les donations aux temples dans l'Égypte du Ier millénaire avant J.-C.', in E. Lipinski (ed.), *State and Temple Economy in the Ancient Near East* Vol. 2 (Leuven: Peeters), 605–87.

Melville, S. C. (2006), 'Sennacherib', in M. W. Chavalas (ed.), *The Ancient Near East: Historical Sources in Translation* (Oxford: Blackwell Publishing), 342–50.

Mendoza, B. (2015), 'Egyptian connections with the larger world: Greece and Rome', in M. Hartwig (ed.), *A Companion to Ancient Egyptian Art* (Chichester: Wiley-Blackwell), 399–422.

Meskell, L. (1999), *Archaeologies of Social Life* (Oxford: Blackwell Publishers Ltd).

Milde, H. (2012), 'Shabtis', in W. Wendrich (ed.), *UCLA Encyclopedia of Egyptology*, Los Angeles. http://digital2.library.ucla.edu/viewItem.do?ark=21198/zz002bwvoz, accessed 10 August 2017.

Milgrom, J. (1955), 'The date of Jeremiah, chapter 2', *JNES*, 14 (2), 65–69.

Miller, J. M., and Hayes, J. H. (2006), *A History of Ancient Israel and Judah* (2nd edn; London: SCM Press).

Mokhtar, M. G. E. (1983), *Ihnâsya el-Medina (Herakleopolis Magna): Its Importance and its Role in Pharaonic History* (Cairo: IFAO).

Möller, A. (2000), *Naukratis: Trade in Archaic Greece* (Oxford: Oxford University Press).

— (2001), 'Naukratis: Griechisches Emporion und ägyptischer "Port of Trade" ', in U. Höckmann and D. Kreikenbom (ed.), *Naukratis: Die Beziehungun zu Ostriechenland, Ägypten und Zypern in archaischer Zeit; Akten der Table Ronde in Mainz, 25.-27. November 1999* (Möhnesee, Paderborn: Bibliopolis).

Montet, P. (1966), *Le lac sacré de Tanis* (Mémoires de l'Académie. Offprint, Vol. 44, Paris: Imprimerie Nationale).

Montserrat, D. (2003), 'Did Necho send a fleet around Africa?', in B. Manley (ed.), *The Seventy Great Mysteries of Ancient Egypt* (London: Thames and Hudson), 244–45.

Moorey, P. R. S. (1994), *Ancient Mesopotamian Materials and Industries: The Archaeological Evidence* (Oxford: Clarendon Press).

Moran, W. L. (1992), *The Amarna Letters* (Baltimore, London: Johns Hopkins University Press).

Moreno Garcia, J.-C. (2013a), 'The study of ancient Egyptian administration', in J.-C. Moreno Garcia (ed.), *Ancient Egyptian Administration* (Leiden: Brill), 1–17.

— (2013b), 'Land donations', in E. Frood and W. Wendrich (ed.), *UCLA Encylcopedia of Egyptology*, Los Angeles, <http://digital2.library.ucla.edu/viewItem.do?ark=21198/zz002hgp07>, accessed 15 December 2017.

— (2014), 'Invaders or just herders? Libyans in Egypt in the third and second millennia BCE', *World Archaeology*, 46 (4), 610–23.

Morkot, R. G. (1991), 'Nubia and Achaemenid Persia: Sources and problems', in H. Sancisi-Weerdenburg and A. Kuhrt (ed.), *Achaemenid History VI: Asia Minor and Egypt: Old Cultures in a New Empire* (Leiden: Nederlands Instituut voor het Nabije Oosten), 321–36.

— (1999), 'Kingship and kinship in the empire of Kush', in S. Wenig (ed.), *Studien zum Antiken Sudan: Akten der 7. Internationalen Tagung für meroitische Forschungen vom 14. bis 19. September 1992 in Gosen/bei Berlin* (Meriotica 15, Wiesbaden: Harrassowitz), 179–229.

— (2000), *The Black Pharaohs* (London: The Rubicon Press).

— (2003a), 'On the priestly origin of the Napatan kings: The adaptation, demise and resurrection of ideas in writing Nubian history', in A. Reid and D. O'Connor (ed.), *Ancient Egypt in Africa* (Encounters with Ancient Egypt, London: UCL Press), 151–68.

— (2003b), 'Archaism and innovation in art from the New Kingdom to the Twenty-sixth Dynasty', in J. Tait (ed.), *'Never Had the Like Occurred': Egypt's View of Its Past* (Encounters with Ancient Egypt, London: UCL Press), 79–99.

— (2014), 'Thebes under the Kushites', in E. Pischikova (ed.), *Tombs of the South Asasif Necropolis* (Cairo, New York: American University in Cairo Press), 5–22.

Morkot, R. G., and James, P. (2009), 'Peftjauawybast, King of Nen-nesut: genealogy, art history, and the chronology of late Libyan Egypt', *Antiguo Oriente*, 7, 13–55.

Morrison, J. S., and Williams, R. T. (1968), *Greek Oared Ships 900–322 B.C.* (Cambridge: Cambridge University Press).

Moussa, M. A. (1981), 'A stela of Taharqa from the desert road at Dashur', *MDAIK*, 37, 331–37.

Muhs, B. (2016), *The Ancient Egyptian Economy: 3000–30 BCE* (Cambridge: Cambridge University Press).

Müller, M. (1979), 'Zum Bildnistypus Thutmosis I', *GM*, 32, 27–32.

Munro, I. (2010a), 'The evolution of the Book of the Dead', in J. Taylor (ed.), *Journey Through the Afterlife: Ancient Egyptian Book of the Dead* (London: British Museum Press), 54–77.

— (2010b), 'Evidence of a master copy transferred from Thebes to the Memphite area in the 26th Dynasty', in J. Taylor (ed.), *BMSAES*, 15, 201–24.

Murray, O. (1980), *Early Greece* (Cambridge, MA: Harvard University Press).

Myśliwiec, K. (1988), *Royal Portraiture of the Dynasties XXI–XXX* (Mainz: P. von Zabern).

— (2000), *The Twilight of Ancient Egypt: First Millennium B.C.E.* (Ithaca and London: Cornell University Press).

Na'aman, N. (1979), 'Sennacherib's campaign to Judah and the date of the *LMLK* stamps', *VT*, 29, 61–86.

— (1991), 'The Kingdom of Judah under Josiah', *Tel Aviv*, 18, 3–71.

Naunton, C. (2011), 'Regime change and the administration of Thebes during the Twenty-fifth Dynasty' (Unpublished thesis, Swansea University).

Naveh, J. (1962), 'The excavations at Mesad Hashavyahu: Preliminary report', *Israel Exploration Journal*, 12, 89–113.

Naville, E. (1903), *The Store City of Pithom and the Route of the Exodus* (London: Egypt Exploration Fund).

Neureiter, S. (1994), 'Eine neue Interpretation des Archaismus', *SAK*, 21, 219–54.

Nicholson, P. T. (2005), 'The sacred animal necropolis at Saqqara', in S. Ikram (ed.), *Divine Creatures: Animal Mummies in Ancient Egypt* (Cairo, New York: American University Press in Cairo), 44–71.

O'Connor, D. (1983), 'New Kingdom and Third Intermediate Period', in B. G. Trigger, B. J. Kemp, D. O'Connor and A. B. Lloyd (ed.), *Ancient Egypt: A Social History* (Cambridge: Cambridge University Press), 183–278.

— (1986), 'The location of Yam and Kush and their historical implications', *JARCE*, 23, 27–50.

— (1990), 'The nature of Tjemhu (Libyan) society in later New Kingdom Egypt', in A. Leahy (ed.), *Libya and Egypt c. 1300–750 BC* (London: Society for Libyan Studies), 29–113.

— (2003), 'Egypt's view of others', in J. Tait (ed.), *'Never Had the Like Occurred': Egypt's View of Its Past* (Encounters with Ancient Egypt; London: UCL Press), 155–85.

O'Connor, D., and Quirke, S. (2003), 'Introduction: Mapping the unknown in ancient Egypt', in D. O'Connor and S. Quirke (ed.), *Mysterious Lands* (Encounters with Ancient Egypt, London: UCL Press), 1–21.

Onash, H.-U. (1994), *Die Assyrischen Eroberungen Ägyptens*, 2 vols (Egypt and Old Testament studies on history, culture and religion of Egypt and the Old Testament, 27, Wiesbaden: Otto Harrassowitz).

Oren, E. D. (1984), 'Migdol: A new fortress on the edge of the Eastern Nile Delta', *BASOR*, 256, 7–44.

— (1993), 'Ethnicity and regional archaeology: The western Negev under Assyrian rule', in A. Biran and J. Aviram (ed.), *Biblical Archaeology Today (1990): Proceedings of the Second International Conference on Biblical Archaeology* (Jerusalem: Brill), 102–5.

— (ed.) (2000), *The Sea Peoples and Their World: A Reassessment* (University Museum Monograph 108. University Museum Symposium Series 11, Philadelphia: University Museum, University of Pennsylvania).

Orlinsky, H. M. (1972), *Understanding the Bible through History and Archaeology* (New York: KTAV Publishing House).

O'Rourke, P. F. (2001), 'Coinage', in D. B. Redford (ed.), *Oxford Encyclopedia of Ancient Egypt*, 3 vols (1; Oxford: Oxford University Press), 288–90.

Osing, J. (1980), 'Libyen, Libyer', in W. Helck, E. Otto and W. Westendorf (ed.), *Lexikon der Ägyptologie* (3; Wiesbaden: Harrassowitz), 1015–33.

Otto, E. (1969), 'Das "Goldene Zeitalter" in einem ägyptischen Text', in *Religions en Égypte hellénistique et romaine*, Colloque de Strasbourg, 16–18 mai, 1967. (Paris: Bibliothèque des centrés d'Études supérieurs spécialisées), 92–108.

Parker, R. A. (1962), *A Saite Oracle Papyrus from Thebes in the Brooklyn Museum (Papyrus Brooklyn 47.218.3)* (Brown Egyptological Studies 4, Providence: Brown University Press).

Parkinson, R. B. (1997), *The Tale of Sinuhe and Other Ancient Egyptian Poems 1940–1640 BC* (Oxford: Oxford University Press).

Parpola, S. (ed.) (1993), *Letters from Assyrian and Babylonian Scholars* (State Archives of Assyria, 10, Helsinki: Helsinki University Press).

— (2004), 'National and ethnic identity in the Neo-Assyrian Empire and Assyrian identity in Post-Empire times', *Journal of Assyrian Academic Studies*, 18 (2), 5–22.

Payraudeau, F. (2014), 'Retour sur la succession Shabaqo-Shabataqo', *NeHet: Revue Numérique d'Égyptologie*, 1, 115–27.

Peet, T. E. (1920), *The Mayer Papyri A & B* (London: Egypt Exploration Society).

— (1930), *The Great Tomb Robberies of the Twentieth Egyptian Dynasty* (Oxford: Clarendon Press).

Perdu, O. (1990), 'Neshor à Mendès sous Apriès', *BSFÉ*, 118, 38–49.

— (1998), 'Le directeur des scribes de conseil', *RdÉ*, 49, 175–94.

— (2002a), 'De Stéphinatès à Néchao ou les débuts de la XXVIe dynastie', *CRAIBL*, 1215–44.

— (2002b), *Recueil des inscriptions royales saïtes. Volume 1, Psammétique Ier* (Paris: Cybèle).

— (2004), 'La chefferie de Sébennytos de Piankhy à Psammétique I', *RdÉ*, 55, 95–111.

— (2006), 'Documents relatifs aux gouverneurs du Delta au début de la XXVIe dynastie', *RdÉ*, 57, 151–98.

— (2011), 'Neshor brisé, reconstitué et restauré (Statue Louvre A 90)', in D. Valbelle and J.-M. Yoyotte (ed.), *Statues égyptiennes et kouchites démembrées et reconstituées: Hommage à Charles Bonnet* (Paris: Presses de l'Université Paris-Sorbonne).

— (2014), 'Saites and Persians (664–332)', in A. B. Lloyd (ed.), *A Companion to Ancient Egypt* (Chichester: Wiley Blackwell), 140–58.

Pernigotti, S. (1969), 'Una statua du Pakhraf (Cairo JE. 37171)', *Rivista degli Studi Orientali*, 44, 259–71.

Peterson, B. J. (1967), 'Hatshepsut and Nebhepetre Mentuhotep', *CdÉ*, 42, 266–68.

Pétigny, A. (2010), 'Le châtiment des rois rebelles à Memphis dans la seconde moitié du Ier millénaire av. J.-C.', in L. Bareš, F. Coppens and K. Smoláriková (ed.), *Egypt in Transition: Social and Religious Development of Egypt in the First Millennium BCE* (Prague: Charles University), 343–53.

Petrie, W. M. Flinders (1888), *Tanis. Part II. Nebesheh (Am) and Defenneh (Tahpanhes) 2* (Excavation Memoirs, Exploration Fund; London: Trübner & Co.).

— (1901), *Royal Tombs of the Earliest Dynasties II* (London: Egypt Exploration Fund).

— (1905), *A History of Egypt from the XIXth to the XXXth Dynasties* (A History of Egypt 3, London: Methuen).

— (1917), *Scarabs and Cylinders with Names: Illustrated by the Egyptian Collection in University College, London* (London: School of Archaeology in Egypt).

— (1935), *Shabtis: Illustrated by the Egyptian Collection in University College, London, with catalogue of figures from many other sources* (London: British School of Egyptian Archaeology).

Petrie, W. M. Flinders, and Duncan, J. G. (1906), *Hyksos and the Israelite Cities* (London: Office of School of Archaeology).

Petrie, W. M. Flinders, and Walker, J. H. (1909), *The Palace of Apries (Memphis II)* (Egyptian Research Account 17, London: London School of Archaeology in Egypt and B. Quaritch).

Pischikova, E. (1998), 'Reliefs from the tomb of the vizier Nespakashuty: reconstruction, iconography, and style', *Metropolitan Museum Journal*, 33, 57–90.

— (2014), *Tombs of the South Asasif Necropolis* (Cairo, New York: The American University in Cairo Press).

Plutarch (1970), *Plutarch's De Iside et Osiride*, ed. J. G. Griffiths (Cardiff: University of Wales).

Polyaenus (1974), *Polyænus's Stratagems of War: Translated from the Original Greek, by Dr. Shepherd, F.R.S.* (Chicago: Ares Publishers).

Polz, D. (1998), 'The Ramsesnakht dynasty and the fall of the New Kingdom: A new monument at Thebes', *SAK*, 25, 257–93.

Pope, J. (2014), *The Double Kingdom under Taharqo* (Leiden, Boston: Brill).

Porten, B. (1981), 'The identity of king Adon', *BA*, 44 (1), 36–52.

— (1996), *The Elephantine Papyri in English. Three Millennia of Cross-Cultural Continuity and Change* (Leiden: E. J. Brill).

Posener, G. (1936), *La première domination Perse en Égypte: Recueil d'inscriptions hiéroglyphiques* (Bibliothèque d'étude Vol. 11, Cairo: IFAO).

— (1947), 'Les douanes de la Méditerranée dans l'Égypte saïte', *Revue de Philologie de Littérature et d'Histoire Anciennes*, 21, 117–31.

— (1957), 'Le conte de Néferkarê et du général Siséné (Recherhes littéraires VI)', *RdÉ*, 11, 119–37.

Prada, L. (2017), 'Dreams, rising stars and falling geckos: divination in ancient Egypt', *EA*, 51, 4–9.

Pressl, D. A. (1998), *Beamte und Soldaten: Die Verwaltung in der 26. Dynastie in Ägypten (664–525 v. Chr.)* (Frankfurt am Main: Peter Lang).

Price, C. (2017a), ' "His image as perfect as the ancestors" – On the transmission of forms in non-royal sculpture during the first millennium B.C.', in T. Gillen (ed.) *(Re)productive Traditions in Ancient Egypt: Proceedings of the Conference Held at the University of Liège, 6th–8th February 2013* (Aegyptiaca Leodiensia 10, Liège: Presses Universitaires de Liège), 395–410.

— (2017b), 'The "admiral" Hor and his naphorous statue (Manchester Museum acc. no, 3570)', in C. Jurman, D. Aston and B. Bader (ed.), *A True Scribe of Abydos. Essays on First Millennium BC in Honour of Anthony M. Leahy* (Leuven: Peeters), 369–83.

Priese, K.-H. (1972), 'Der Beginn der kuschitischen Herrschaft Ägypten', *ZÄS*, 98, 16–32.

— (1973), 'Zur Entstehung der meroitischen Schrift', *Meroitica*, 1, 273–306.

Quack, J. F. (2009), 'Redaktion und Kodifiziung im spätzeitlichen Ägypten', in J. Schaper (ed.), *Die Textualisierung der Religion* (Tübingen: Mohr Siebeck), 11–34.

— (2010), 'How unapproachable is a pharaoh?', in G. B. Lanfranchi and R. Rollinger (ed.), *Concepts of Kingship in Antiquity. Proceedings of the European Science Foundation Exploratory Workshop. Held in Padova, November 28th – December 1st, 2007* (History of the Ancient Near East Monographs XI, Padua: S.A.R.G.O.N. Editrice e Libreria), 1–14.

— (2011), 'Zum Datum der persischen Eroberung Ägyptens unter Kambyses', *JEgH*, 4 (2), 228–46.

Quaegebeur, J. (1995), 'À propos de l'identification de la "Kadytis" d'Hérodote avec la ville de Gaza', in A. Schoors and K. van Lerberghe (ed.), *Immigration and Emigration within the Ancient Near East. Festschrift E. Lipinski* (Leuven: Peeters), 245–70.

Quirke, S. (2015), *Exploring Religion in Ancient Egypt* (Chichester: Wiley Blackwell).

Radner, K. (2008), 'Esarhaddon's expedition from Palestine to Egypt in 671 BCE: A trek through Negev and Sinai', in D. Bonatz, R. M. Czichon and F. J. Kreppner (ed.), *Fundstellen: Gesammelte Schriften zur Archäologie und Geschichte Altvorderasiens ad honorem Hartmut Kühne* (Wiesbaden: Harrassowitz Verlag), 305–14.

— (2012), 'After Eltekeh: Royal hostages from Egypt at the Assyrian court', in H. D. Baker, K. Kaniuth and A. Otto (ed.), *Stories of Long Ago: Festschrift für Michael D. Roaf* (Münster: Ugarit Verlag), 471–79.

Ranke, H. (1907–8), 'Statue eines hohen Beamten unter Psammetich I', *ZÄS*, 44, 42–54.

Ray, J. D. (1976), *The Archive of Hor* (London: Egypt Exploration Society).

— (1982), 'The Carian inscriptions from Egypt', *JEA*, 68, 181–98.

— (2001), 'Soldiers to Pharaoh: The Carians of southwest Anatolia', in J. M. Sasson (ed.), *Civilizations of the Ancient Near East*, 2 vols (2; reprint edition, New York: Hendrikson Pub.), 1185–94.

Reade, J. (2002), 'Early monuments in Gulf stone at the British Museum, with observations on some Gudea statues and the location of Agade', *ZA*, 92 (2), 258–95.

Redford, D. B. (1985), 'Sais and the Kushite invasions of the Eighth Century BC', *JARCE*, 22, 5–15.

— (1992), *Egypt, Canaan, and Israel in Ancient Times* (Princeton, NJ: Princeton University Press).

— (1994), 'Taharqa in Western Asia and Libya', *Eretz Israel*, 24, 188–91.

— (1999), 'A note on the chronology of Dynasty 25 and the inscription of Sargon II at Tang-i Var', *Or*, 68 (1), 58–60.

— (2000), 'New light on Egypt's stance towards Asia, 610–586 BCE', in S. L. Mackenzie and T. Römer (ed.), *Rethinking the Foundations. Historiography in the Ancient World and in the Bible in Honour of John Van Seters* (Berlin: Walter de Gruyter), 183–95.

— (2004), *From Slave to Pharaoh: The Black Experience of Ancient Egypt* (Baltimore, London: Johns Hopkins University Press).

Redmount, C. A. (1995), 'The Wadi Tumilat and the "Canal of the Pharaohs" ', *JNES*, 54 (2), 127–35.

Redon, B. (2012), 'L'identité grecque de Naucratis. Enquête sur la fabrication de la mémoire d'une cite grecque d'Égypte aux époques hellénistiques et romaine', *Revue des Études Grecques*, 125, 55–93.

Redon, B., and Dhennin, S. (2013), 'Plinthine on Lake Mareotis', *EA*, 43, 36–38.

Régan, I. (2014), 'The Amduat and the Book of the Gates in the tomb of Padiamenope (TT33): A work in progress', in E. Pischikova, J. Budka and K. Griffin (ed.), *Thebes in the First Millennium BC* (Newcastle upon Tyne: Cambridge Scholars Publishing), 307–20.

Reich, N. J. (1914), *Papyri juristischen Inhalts in hieratischer und demotischer Schrift aus dem British Museum* (Denkschriften der Kaiserlichen Akademie der Wissenschaften. Philosophisch-Historische Klasse 55, 3, Vienna: A. Holder).

Reiger, A. K., Vetter, T., and Möller, H. (2012), 'The desert dwellers of Marmarica, Western Desert: Second millennium BC to first millennium BC', in H. Barnard and K. Duistermaat (ed.), *The History of the Peoples of the Eastern Desert* (Los Angeles: Cotsen Institute of Archaeology Press), 156–73.

Reisner, G. A. (1931), 'Inscribed monuments from Gebel Barkal', *ZÄS*, 66, 76–100.

Revez, J. (2004), 'Un stèle inédite de la Troisième Période Intermédiare à Karnak: Une guerre civile en Thébaïde?', *CdK*, 11, 535–65.

Revillout, E. (1892), 'Un papyrus bilingue du temps de Philopator, Part III', *PSBA*, 14, 229–55.

Ridgeway, D. (1999), 'The rehabilitation of Bocchoris: Notes and queries from Italy', *JEA*, 85, 143–52.

Ritner, R. K. (1990), 'The end of the Libyan anarchy in Egypt: P. Rylands IX. cols. 11–12', *Enchoria*, 17, 101–8.

— (2003), 'The tale of Amasis and the skipper', in W. K. Simpson (ed.), *The Literature of Ancient Egypt* (New Haven and London: Yale University Press), 450–52.

— (2009a), *The Libyan Anarchy: Inscriptions from Egypt's Third Intermediate Period*, ed. E. Wente (Writings from the Ancient World, Atlanta: Society of Biblical Literature).

— (2009b), 'Egypt and the vanishing Libyan: institutional responses to a nomad people', in J. Szuchman (ed.), *Nomads, Tribes, and the State in the Ancient Near East: Cross-Disciplinary Perspectives* (Chicago: Oriental Institute), 43–56.

— (2009c), 'Fragmentation and reintegration in the Third Intermediate Period', in G. P. F. Broekman, R. J. Demarée and O. E. Kaper (ed.), *The Libyan Period in Egypt: Historical and Cultural Studies into the 21st–24th Dynasties: Proceedings of a Conference at Leiden University 25–27 October 2007* (Leiden: Peeters), 327–40.

Roaf, M. (1974), 'The subject peoples on the base of the statue of Darius', *Cahiers de la Délégation archéologique française en Iran*, 4, 73–160.

Robins, G. (1993), *Women in Ancient Egypt* (London: British Museum Press).

— (1997), *The Art of Ancient Egypt* (London: British Museum Press).

Robins, S., and Fowler, A. S. (1994), *Proportion and Style in Ancient Egyptian Art* (London: Thames and Hudson).

Roebuck, C. (1959), *Ionian Trade and Colonization* (New York: Archaeological Institute of America).

Rowe, A. (1936), *A Catalogue of Egyptian Scarabs, Scaraboids, Seals and Amulets in the Palestine Archaeological Museum* (Cairo: IFAO).

Russmann, E. R. (1971), *An Index to Egyptian Sculpture of the Late Period (700 B.C. to A.D. 100)* (Brussels: Fondation Égyptologique Reine Élisabeth).

— (1974), *The Representation of the King in the XXVth Dynasty* (Monographies Reine Élizabeth, 3, Brussels: Fondation Égyptologique Reine Élisabeth).

— (1994), 'Relief decoration in the tomb of Mentuemhet (TT 34)', *JARCE*, 31, 1–19.

— (1997), 'Mentuemhat's Kushite wife (further remarks on the decoration of the Tomb of Mentuemhat, 2)', *JARCE*, 34, 21–39.

— (2001), 'Archaism', in E. R. Russmann (ed.), *Eternal Egypt: Masterpieces of Ancient Art from the British Museum* (London: British Museum Press), 40–45.

Russmann, E. R., and Finn, D. (1989), *Egyptian Sculpture: Cairo and Luxor* (London: British Museum Publications).

Ryholt, K. S. B. (2004), 'The Assyrian invasion of Egypt in Egyptian literary tradition', in J. G. Dercksen (ed.), *Assyria and Beyond: Studies Presented to Mogens Trolle Larsen* (Leiden: Nederlands Instituut voor het Nabije Oosten), 483–510.

— (2011a), 'King Necho I son of king Tefnakhte II', in S. Feder, L. Morenz and G. Vittmann (ed.), *Von Theben nach Giza: Festmiscellan für Stefan Grunert zum 65. Geburtstag*, Göttinger Miszellen Beihefte 10, 123–27.

— (2011b), 'New light on the legendary king Nechepsos of Egypt', *JEA*, 97, 61–72.

Saad, Z. (1947), 'Preliminary report on the excavations at Saqqara and Helwan 1941–1942', *ASAE*, 41, 381–93.

Saggs, H. W. F. (1955), 'The Nimrud Letters, 1952: Part II', *Iraq*, 17 (2), 126–60.

Sagrillo, T. L. (2013), 'Libya and the Libyans', in R. S. Bagnall, K. Brodersen, C. B. Champion, A. Erskine and S. R. Huebner (ed.), *The Encyclopedia of Ancient History* (Oxford: Blackwell Publishing Ltd), 4071–75.

Sandars, N. K. (1985), *The Sea Peoples: Warriors of the Ancient Mediterranean 1250–1150 BC* (rev. edn; Ancient Peoples and Places, London: Thames & Hudson).

Sauneron, S., and Yoyotte, J. (1951), 'Sur le voyage asiatique de Psammetique II', *VT*, 1, 140–44.

— (1952), 'La campange nubienne de Psammétique II et sa signification historique', *BIFAO*, 50, 157–207.

Schauss, G. (2006), 'Naukratis and Archaic pottery finds from Cyrene's extramural sanctuary of Demeter', in A. Villing and U. Schlotzhauer (ed.), *Naukratis: Greek Diversity in Egypt. Studies on East Greek Pottery and Exchange in the Eastern Mediterranean* (London: British Museum), 175–81.

Schipper, B. U. (2010), 'Egypt and the kingdom of Judah under Josiah and Jehoiakim', *Tel Aviv*, 37 (2), 200–26.

Schmitz, P. C. (2010), 'The Phoenician contingent in the campaign of Psammetichus II against Kush', *JEgH*, 3 (2), 321–37.

Schneider, H. D. (1977), *Shabtis: An Introduction to the History of Ancient Egyptian Funerary Statuettes with a Catalogue of the Collection of Shabtis in the National Museum of Antiquities at Leiden*, 3 vols (Leiden: Rijksmuseum van Oudheden te Leiden).

Schneider, H. D. (1993), 'Disparate events of one time: two shabtis of Necho II, with a repertory of royal funerary statuettes of the Late Period (Dynasties 26, 29, 30)', in L. Limme and J. Strybol (ed.), *Aegyptus museis rediviva: miscellanea in honorem Hermanni de Meulenaere* (Brussels: Musées Royaux d'Art et d'Histoire), 153–68.

Schneider, H. D., Martin, G. T., Aston, B. G., Van Dijk, J., Perizonius, R. and Strouhal, E. (1990–91), 'The Tomb of Maya and Meryt: Preliminary report on the Saqqara excavations', *JEA*, 77, 7–21.

Schulman, A. R. (1969–70), 'Some remarks on the alleged "fall" of Senmūt', *JARCE*, 8, 29–48.

— (1979), 'Diplomatic marriage in the Egyptian New Kingdom', *JNES*, 38 (3), 177–93.

Shaw, I. (2012), *Ancient Egyptian Technology and Innovation: Transformations in Pharaonic Material Culture* (Bloomsbury Egyptology, London: Bloomsbury).

Smith, M. (1991), 'Did Psammetichus I die abroad?', *OLP*, 22, 101–9.

Smith, S. T. (2013), 'Revenge of the Kushites: Assimilation and resistance in Egypt's New Kingdom Empire and Nubian ascendancy over Egypt', in G. Areshian (ed.), *Empires and Complexity: On the Crossroads of Archaeology* (Los Angeles: Cotsen Institute of Archaeology at UCLA), 84–107.

Smith, W. S. (1998), *The Art and Architecture of Ancient Egypt* (3rd edn; New Haven and London: Yale University Press, Pelican History of Art).

Smolárikova, K. (2006), 'The mercenary troops – an essential element of the Late Period's military power', in K. Daoud and S. Abd el-Fatah (ed.), *The World of Ancient Egypt. Essays in Honour of Ahmed Abd el-Qader el-Sawi* (Supplement aux Annales Du

Service Des Antiquités De L'Egypte, 35, Cairo: Publications du Conseil Suprême des Antiquités de l'Égypte), 245–48.

— (2008), *Saite Forts in Egypt: Political-Military History of the Saite Dynasty* (Prague: Czech Institute of Egyptology, Faculty of Arts, Charles University in Prague).

— (2010), 'The phenomenon of archaism in the Saite Period funerary architecture', in L. Bareš, F. Coppens and K. Smoláriková (ed.), *Egypt in Transition: Social and Religious Development of Egypt in the First Millennium BCE: Proceedings of an International Conference: Prague, September 1–4, 2009* (Prague: Czech Institute of Egyptology, Faculty of Arts, Charles University in Prague), 431–40.

Snape, S. R. (2003), 'The emergence of Libya on the horizon of Egypt', in D. O'Connor and S. Quirke (ed.), *Mysterious Lands* (Encounters with Ancient Egypt, London: UCL Press), 93–106.

— (2012), 'The legacy of Ramesses III and the Libyan ascendancy', in E. H. Cline and D. O'Connor (ed.), *Ramesses III* (Ann Arbor: University of Michigan Press), 404–41.

Somaglino, C. (2010), 'Les "portes" de l'Égypte de l'Ancien Empire à l'époque saïte', *Égypte, Afrique & Orient*, 59, 3–16.

Spalinger, A. J. (1974a), 'Esarhaddon and Egypt: An analysis of the first invasion of Egypt', *Or*, 43, 295–326.

— (1974b), 'Assurbanipal and Egypt: A source study', *JAOS*, 94 (3), 316–28.

— (1976), 'Psammetichus, King of Egypt: I', *JARCE*, 13, 133–47.

— (1977), 'Egypt and Babylonia: A survey (c. 620 B.C. – 550 B.C.)', *SAK*, 5, 221–44.

— (1978a), 'The foreign policy of Egypt preceding the Assyrian conquest', *CdÉ*, 53, 22–47.

— (1978b), 'The concept of the monarchy during the Saite Epoch: an essay in synthesis', *Or*, 47 (1), 12–36.

— (1978c), 'Psammetichus, King of Egypt: II', *JARCE*, 15, 49–57.

— (1979a), 'The military background of the campaign of Piye (Piankhy)', *SAK*, 7, 273–301.

— (1979b), 'The civil war between Amasis and Apries and the Babylonian attack against Egypt', in W. F. Reineke (ed.), *Acts / First International Congress of Egyptology Cairo, October 2 – 10, 1976* (Berlin: Akademie-Verlag), 593–604.

— (1979c), 'Some notes on the Libyans of the Old Kingdom and later historical reflexes', *JSSEA*, 9, 125–60.

— (1982), *Aspects of the Military Documents of the Ancient Egyptians* (New Haven and London: Yale University Press).

Spencer, A. J. (1996), *Excavations at Tell El-Balamun, 1991–1994* (London: British Museum Press).

— (1999), *Excavations at Tell El-Balamun, 1995–1998* (London: British Museum Press).

— (2003), *Excavations at Tell El-Balamun, 1999–2001* (London: British Museum Press).

— (2011), 'The Egyptian temple and settlement at Naukratis', *BMSAES*, 17, 31–39.

Spencer, N. (2010), 'Sustaining Egyptian culture? Non-royal initiatives in Late Period temple building', in L. Bareš, F. Coppens and K. Smoláriková (ed.), *Egypt in Transition: Social and Religious Development of Egypt in the First Millennium BCE: Proceedings of an International Conference: Prague, September 1–4, 2009* (Prague: Czech Institute of Egyptology, Faculty of Arts, Charles University), 441–90.

— (2014), 'Amara West: considerations on urban life in colonial Kush', in D. Welsby and J. R. Anderson (ed.), *Proceedings of the 12th International Conference for Nubian Studies*

1–6 August 2012 (London: British Museum Publications on Egypt and Sudan), 1, 457–85.

Spiegelberg, W. (1903), 'Die Tefnachtosstele des Museums von Athen', *RecTrav*, 25, 190–98.

— (1911), 'Beiträge zu den demotischen Rylands Papyri', *RecTrav*, 33, 175–79.

— (1915), 'Ein Denkmaldes Admirals Semtu-tef-nakhte', *ZÄS*, 52, 112.

Stager, L. E. (1996), 'Ashkelon and the archaeology of destruction', *Eretz Israel*, 25, 61–74.

Stammers, M. (2016), *The Elite Late Period Egyptian Tombs of Memphis* (BAR International Series 1903, Oxford: BAR Publishing).

Starr, I. (ed.) (1990), *Queries to the Sungod: Divination and Politics in Sargonid Assyria* (Helsinki: Helsinki University Press).

Steindorff, G. (1939), 'The statuette of an Egyptian commissioner in Syria', *JEA*, 25 (1), 30–33.

Stolper, M. W. (1997), 'Flogging and plucking', *Topoi*, Suppl. 1, 347–50.

Stripling, S., Brandl, B., Peterson, B., and Seevers, B. (2017), 'A scarab of Psamtek I from Kh. el-Maqatir', *Palestinian Exploration Quarterly*, 149 (3), 186–200.

Strudwick, N. (2006), *Masterpieces of the British Museum* (London: British Museum Press).

Sullivan, R. D. (1996), 'Psammetichus I and the Foundation of Naukratis', in W. D. E. Coulsen (ed.), *Ancient Naukratis, Volume II: Survey at Naukratis and Environs Part 1, The Survey at Naukratis* (Oxford: Oxbow Books), 177–95.

Sweeney, M. (2001), *King Josiah of Judah: The Lost Messiah of Israel* (Oxford: Oxford University Press).

Tadmor, H. (1958), 'The campaigns of Sargon II of Assur: A chronological-historical study', *Journal of Cuneiform Studies*, 12 (3), 77–100.

— (1966), 'Philistia under Assyrian Rule', *BA*, 29 (3), 86–102.

— (1994), *The Inscriptions of Tiglath-Pileser III, King of Assyria: Critical Edition, with Introductions, Translations and Commentary* (Jerusalem: Israel Academy of Sciences and Humanities).

— (1999), 'World dominion: The expanding horizon of the Assyrian empire', in L. Milano, S. de Martino, F. M. Fales and G. B. Lanfranchi (ed.), *Landscapes: Territories, Frontiers and Horizons in the Ancient Near East* (Padua: Sargon srl).

Tanner, J. (2003), 'Finding the Egyptian in early Greek art', in C. R. Matthews and C. Roemer (ed.), *Ancient Perspectives on Egypt.* (London: UCL Press), 114–43.

Taylor, J. H. (1987), 'A note on the family of Montemhat', *JEA*, 73, 229–30.

— (2000), 'The Third Intermediate Period', in I. Shaw (ed.), *Oxford History of Ancient Egypt* (Oxford: Oxford University Press), 330–68.

— (2001), *Death and the Afterlife in Ancient Egypt* (London: British Museum Press).

Thijs, A. (2003), 'The troubled careers of Amenhotep and Panehsy: The High Priest of Amun and the Viceroy of Kush under the last Ramessides', *SAK*, 31, 289–306.

— (2005), 'In search of King Herihor and the penultimate ruler of the 20th Dynasty', *ZÄS*, 132, 73–91.

— (2014), 'Once more, the length of the Ramesside Renaissance', *GM*, 240, 69–81.

Thomas, N. (2000), 'Petamenophis', in D. B. Redford (ed.), *Oxford Encyclopedia of Ancient Egypt*, 3 vols (3; Oxford: Oxford University Press), 37–38.

Thomas, R. I., and Villing, A. (2013), 'Naukratis revisited 2012: Integrating new fieldwork and old research', *BMSAES*, 20, 81–125.

Thomas, R., Villing, A., Pennington, B., Strutt, K., Masson, A., and Lindenlauf, A. (2014), 'The harbour of Naukratis, "Mistress of Ships" ', *British Museum Naukratis Project Fieldwork Report 2014*, <www.britishmuseum.org/pdf/Thomas_Naukratis_2014.pdf>, accessed 10 October 2016.

Tiradritti, F. (1998), 'Three years of research in the tomb of Harwa', *EA*, 13, 3–6.

Török, L. (1995), 'The emergence of the Kingdom of Kush and her myth of the state in the first millennium BC', *CRIPEL*, 17, 243–63.

— (1997), *The Kingdom of Kush: Handbook of the Napatan–Meroitic Civilisation* (Leiden, New York, Cologne: Brill).

— (2009), *Between Two Worlds. The Frontier Region between Ancient Nubia and Egypt 3700 BC – AD 500* (Probleme der Ägyptologie, 29, Leiden, Boston: Brill).

Touwaide, A. (1979), 'Le sang de toureau', *L'Antiquité Classique*, 48, Fasc. I, 5–14.

Traunecker, C. (2010), 'La chapelle d'Osiris "seigneur de l'éternité-neheh" à Karnak', in L. Coulon (ed.), *Le culte d'Osiris au Ier millénaire av. J.-C.: Découvertes et travaux récents. Actes de la table ronde internationale tenue à Lyon Maison de l'Orient et de la Méditerranée (université Lumière-Lyon 2) les 8 et 9 juillet 2005, BdÉ*, 153, 155–94.

— (2014), 'The "Funeral Palace" of Padiamenope: Tombs, place of pilgrimage and library. Current research', in E. Pischikova, J. Budka and K. Griffin (ed.), *Thebes in the First Millennium BC* (Newcastle upon Tyne: Cambridge Scholars Publishing), 205–34.

Tresson, Abbé P. (1931), 'Sur deux monuments égyptiens inédits de l'époque d'Amasis et de Nectanébo Ier', *Kémi*, 4, 126–50.

Trigger, B. G. (1976), *Nubia under the Pharaohs* (London: Thames and Hudson Ltd).

Troy, L. (1986), *Patterns of Queenship in Ancient Egyptian Myth and History* (Uppsala: Uppsala University (Acta Universitatis Upsaliensis)).

Van De Mieroop, M. (2004), *A History of the Ancient Near East* (Malden, MA, Oxford: Blackwell Publishing).

— (2011), *History of Ancient Egypt* (Malden, MA: Wiley-Blackwell).

Van der Wilt, E. (2010), 'Lead weights and ingots from Heracleion-Thonis: an illustration of Egyptian trade relations with the Aegean', in A. Hudecz and M. Petrik (ed.), *Commerce and Economy in Ancient Egypt* (Bar International Series 2131, Oxford: Archaeopress), 157–64.

Van Dijk, J. (2000), 'The Amarna Period and the later New Kingdom', in I. Shaw (ed.), *The Oxford History of Ancient Egypt* (Oxford: Oxford University Press), 272–313.

Van Pelt, W. (2013), 'Revising Egypto-Nubian relations in New Kingdom Lower Nubia: From Egyptianization to cultural entanglement', *Cambridge Archaeological Journal*, 23 (3), 523–50.

Vercoutter, J. (1962), *Textes biographiques du Serapeum de Memphis* (Paris: Champion).

Verner, M. (2002), *Abusir-Realm of Osiris* (Cairo: American University in Cairo Press).

Vernus, P. (1975), 'Inscriptions de la Troisième période intermédiaire (I)', *BIFAO*, 75, 1–66.

— (1978), *Athribis, textes et documents relatifs à la géographie aux cultes, et à l'histoire d'une ville du delta égyptien à l'epoque pharaonique* (BdÉ 74, Cairo: IFAO).

— (1991), 'Une statue de Neshor surnommé Psamétik-Menkhib', *RdÉ*, 42, 241–49.

— (1999), 'Le discours politique de l'Enseignement de Ptahhotep', in J. Assmann and E. Blumenthal (ed.), *Literatur und Politik im pharaonischen und ptolemäischen Ägypten*,

Vorträge der Tagung zum Gedenken an Georges Posener 5.-10. September 1996 in Leipzig (BdE 127, Cairo: IFAO), 139–52.

Verreth, H. (1999), 'The Egyptian eastern border region in Assyrian sources', *JAOS*, 119 (2), 234–47.

Villing, A. and Schlotzhauer, U. (2006), 'Naukratis and the Eastern Mediterranean: Past, Present and Future', in A. Villing and U. Schlotzhauer (ed.), *Naukratis: Greek Diversity in Egypt: Studies on East Greek Pottery and Exchange in the Eastern Mediterranean* (London: British Museum), 1–10.

Villing, A. (2017), 'Naukratis: the Greeks in Egypt', <www.britishmuseum.org/research/research_projects/all_current_projects/naukratis_the_greeks_in_egypt.aspx>, accessed 10 December 2017.

Vittmann, G. (1975), 'Die Familie der satischen Könige', *Or*, 44, 375–87.

— (1978), *Priester und Beamte im Theben der Spätzeit: Genealogische und prosopographische Untersuchungen zum thebanischen Priester- und Beamtentum der 25. und der 26. Dynastie* (Vienna: Afro-Pub.).

— (1998), *Der demotische Papyrus Rylands 9*, 2 vols (Wiesbaden: Harrassowitz).

— (2001a), 'Zwei Priestereinführungsinschriften der 25. Dynastie aus Luxor (Berlin 2096 und 2097)', *SAK*, 29, 357–70.

— (2001b), 'Ägyptisch-Karisches', *Kadmos*, 40, 39–59.

— (2003), *Ägypten und die Fremden im ersten vorchristlichen Jahrtausend* (Mainz am Rhein: Verlag Philipp von Zabern).

— (2009), 'Rupture and continuity: On priests and officials in Egypt during the Persian Period', in P. Briant and M. Chauveau (ed.), *Organisation des pouvoirs et contacts culturels dans les pays de l'empire Achéménide* (Persika 14, Paris: De Boccard), 89–121.

— (2011), 'Ägypten zur Zeit der Perserherrschaft', in R. Rollinger, B. Truschnegg and R. Bichler (ed.), *Herodot und das Perische Weltreich* (Wiesbaden: Harrassowitz Verlag).

Vleeming, S. P. (1992), 'The tithe of the scribes (and) representatives', in J. H. Johnson (ed.), *Life in a Multi-Cultural Society: Egypt from Cambyses to Constantine and Beyond* (SAOC 51, Chicago: Oriental Institute), 343–50.

— (1995), 'The office of a choachyte in the Theban area', in S. P. Vleeming (ed.), *Hundred-Gated Thebes: Acts of a Colloquium on Thebes and the Theban Area in the Graeco-Roman Period* (Leiden: Brill), 241–55.

Von Beckerath, J. (1997), *Chronologie des pharaonischen Ägypten: Die Zeitbestimmung der gypotischen Geschichte von der Vorzeit bis 332 v. Chr.* (MÄS 46, Mainz: von Zabern).

Waldbaum, J. C. (1978), *From Bronze to Iron: The Transition from the Bronze Age to the Iron Age in the Eastern Mediterranean* (Studies in Mediterranean Archaeology Vol. LIV, Göteborg: Paul Astroms).

Wallinga, H. T. (1993), *Ships and Sea-Power before the Great Persian War* (Leiden, New York, Cologne: E. J. Brill).

— (1995), 'The ancestry of the trireme 1200–525 BC', in R. Gardiner (ed.), *The Age of the Galley: Mediterranean Oared Vessels since Pre-Classical Times* (London: Conway Maritime Press), 36–48.

Wall-Romana, C. (1990), 'An aerial location for Agade', *JNES*, 49 (3), 205–45.

Webb, V. (1978), *Archaic Greek Faience: Miniature Scent Bottles and Related Objects from East Greece, 650–500 B.C.* (Warminster: Aris & Phillips Ltd).

Weidemann, A. (1886), 'Inschriften aus der satischen Periode', *RT*, 8, 63–69.

Wenning, R. (2001), 'Griechische Söldner in Palästina', in U. Höckmann and D. Kreikenbom (ed.), *Naukratis: Die Beziehungen zu Ostgriechenland, Ägypten und Zypern in archaischer Zeit: Akten der Table Ronde in Mainz, 25.-27. November 1999* (Möhnesee: Bibliopolis), 257–68.

Wente, E. F. (1966), 'On the suppression of the High-Priest Amenhotep', *JNES*, 25, 73–87.

— (2003), 'The Israel Stela', in W. K. Simpson (ed.), *The Literature of Ancient Egypt* (New Haven, London: Yale University Press), 356–60.

Wessetzky, W. (1963), 'Die Familiengeschichte des Peteêse als historische Quelle für die Innenpolitik Psametiks I', *ZÄS*, 88, 69–73.

West, S. (2002), 'Scythians', in E. J. Bakker, I. J. F. De Jong and H. van Wees (ed.), *Brill's Companion to Herodotus* (Leiden: Brill), 437–56.

White, D. (1994a), 'Before the Greeks came: A survey of the current archaeological evidence for the Pre-Greek Libyans', *Libyan Studies*, 25, 31–44.

— (1994b), 'Excavations on Bates's Island, Marsa Matruh: Second preliminary report', *JARCE*, 26, 87–114.

Wilson, P. (2002), 'Recent work at Sa al-Hagar', in Z. Hawass (ed.), *Egyptology at the Dawn of the Twenty-First Century*, 3 vols (1; Cairo, New York: American University Press in Cairo), 568–73.

— (2006), *The Survey of Sais (Sa el-Hager) 1997–2002* (London: Egypt Exploration Society).

— (2010), 'Consolidation, innovation and renaissance', in W. Wendrich (ed.), *Egyptian Archaeology* (Maldon, MA: Wiley Blackwell), 241–58.

— (2016), 'A Psamtek ushabti and a granite block from Sais (Sa el-Hager)', in C. Price, R. Forshaw, A. Chamberlain and P. T. Nicholson (ed.), *Mummies, Magic and Medicine in Ancient Egypt* (Manchester: Manchester University Press), 75–92.

Wilson, P. and Gilbert, G. (2007), 'Sais and its trading relations with the eastern Mediterranean', in P. Kousoulis and K. D. Magliveras (ed.), *Moving across Borders: Foreign Relations, Religion, and Cultural Interactions in the Ancient Mediterranean* (Orientalia Lovaniensia Analecta, 159, Leuven: Peeters), 251–66.

Wiseman, D. J. (1956), *Chronicles of Chaldaean Kings (626–556 B.C.) in the British Museum* (London: The Trustees of the British Museum).

Younis, S. A. (2002), 'Psamtik I and Gyges: A secret alliance', in Z. Hawass (ed.), *Egyptology at the Dawn of the Twenty-First Century*, 3 vols. (2; Cairo, New York: American University Press in Cairo), 582–86.

Yoyotte, J. (1951), 'Le martelage des noms royaux éthiopiens par Psammétique II', *RdÉ*, 8, 215–39.

— (1960a), 'La talisman de victoire d'Osorkon', *BSFÉ*, 31, 13–22.

— (1960b), 'Nechao', *Dictionnaire de la Bible, Supplement, VI* (Paris: Letouzey et Ané), cols 363–93.

— (1963), 'Études géographiques II', *RdÉ*, 15, 106–14.

— (1971), 'Notes et Documents pour servir à l'histoire de Tanis', *Kêmi*, 21, 35–45.

— (1983), 'L' Amon de Naukratis', *RdÉ*, 34, 129–36.

— (1989), 'Le nom égyptien du "ministre de l'économie" – de Saïs a Méroé', *CRAIBL*, 73–90.

— (2006), 'An extraordinary pair of twins: the steles of the Pharaoh Nectanebo I', in F. Goddio and D. Fabre (ed.), *Egypt's Sunken Treasures* (Munich: Prestel), 313–23.

— (2012), *Les principautés du Delta au temps de l'anarchie libyenne* (Deuxième édition revue et augmentée edn; Cairo: IFAO).

Yurco, F. J. (1980), 'Sennacherib's third campaign and the coregency of Shabaka and Shebitku', *Serapis* 6, 221–40.

Zamazalová, S. (2011), 'Before the Assyrian Conquest in 671 B.C.E.: Relations between Egypt, Kush and Assyria', in J. Mynářová (ed.), *Egypt and the Near East – the Crossroads: Proceedings of an International Conference on the Relations of Egypt and the Near East in the Bronze Age, Prague, September 1–3, 2010* (Prague: Charles University in Prague, Czech Institute of Archaeology), 297–328.

Zauzich, K.-Th. (1992), 'Ein Zug nach Nubien unter Amasis', in J. H. Johnson (ed.), *Life in a Multi-Cultural Society: Egypt from Cambyses to Constantine and Beyond* (SAOC 51, Chicago: Oriental Institute of the University of Chicago), 361–64.

Zawadzki, S. (1988), *The Fall of Assyria and Median-Babylonia Relations in Light of the Nabopolassar Chronicle* (Delft: Adam Mickiewicz University Press).

— (1995), 'Hostages in Assyrian royal inscriptions', in K. Van Lerberghe and A. Schoors (ed.), *Immigration and Emigration within the Ancient Near East: Festschrift E. Lipinski* (Leuven: Peeters), 449–58.

Zivie-Coche, C. (ed.) (2008), 'Late Period temples', in W. Wendrich (ed.), *UCLA Encyclopedia of Egyptology*, Los Angeles, <http://digital2.library.ucla.edu/viewItem.do?ark=21198/zz0025h6fh>, accessed 13 January 2017.

Index

Note: italic numerals indicate an illustration caption

CPSIA information can be obtained
at www.ICGtesting.com
Printed in the USA
LVHW080230310321
683044LV00009B/102

9 781526 155788